# Ecology

*For*

BA, B.Com., and B.Sc.

***Useful For***

Delhi University (DU), IGNOU, Berhampur University (Odisha), University of Kashmir, Sambalpur University (Odisha), University of Kalyani (West Bengal), Gurukula Kangri Vishwavidyalaya (Uttarakhand), Himachal Pradesh University, Cooch Behar Panchanan Barma University (West Bengal), Ranchi University, University of Culcutta, Pune University, University of Mumbai, Andhra University, School of Open Learning (DU), Gondwana University (Maharashra), Babasaheb Bhimrao Ambedkar University (Lucknow), Dr. Babasaheb Ambedkar Marathwada University (Aurangabad), University of Madras, Netaji Subhas Open University (Kolkata), Odisha State Open University, all other Indian Universities.

**GULLYBABA PUBLISHING HOUSE (P) LTD.**

ISO 9001 & ISO 14001 CERTIFIED CO.

Published by:

**GullyBaba Publishing House Pvt. Ltd.**

**Regd. Office:**
2525/193, 1st Floor, Onkar Nagar-A,
Tri Nagar, Delhi-110035
(From Kanhaiya Nagar Metro Station Towards Old Bus Stand)
Ph. 011-27387998, 27384836, 27385249

**Branch Office:**
1A/2A, 20, Hari Sadan,
Ansari Road, Daryaganj,
New Delhi-110002
Ph. 011-23289034
011-45794768

E-mail: hello@gullybaba.com, Website: GullyBaba.com

**New Edition**

**Author:** GullyBaba.Com Panel

**ISBN:** 978-93-82688-16-7

# Preface

Ecology is the study of organisms and their environment and the interrelationship between the two. The term has in fact taken on a variety of other meanings in addition. Most commonly, it has come to be used, in lower case, to denote the way of life of a particular organism: a convenient term for the relationship itself between organism and environment.

Ecology is a rapidly developing subject: new information is being gathered all the time on variety of key questions; new approaches and techniques open up completely new areas of research and establish new principles. Keeping all these points, we are providing the book **"Ecology (LSE-02)".** In this book, we have tried to create a text that will review all the major principles and tenets within the whole field of Ecology, presenting the generally accepted theories and fundamentals and reviewing carefully the evidence on which such principles have been founded.

This book is written in question & answer format to help students in preparing for examination. In this book, we have tried to solve all possible questions from the exams' point of view. The book is enriched with useful and to-the-point matter. Previous years question papers have also been included to help students to understand the unique examination structure.

We wish you a successful and rewarding career. Feedback in this regard is solicited. **(feedback@gullybaba.com)**

**-GPH Panel of Experts**

# Acknowledgement

Our compliments go to the **GullyBaba Publishing House (P) Ltd.**, and its meticulous team who have been enthusiastically working towards the perfection of the book.

Their teamwork, initiative and research have been very encouraging. Had it not been for their unflagging support, this work wouldn't have been possible. The creative freedom provided by them along with their aim of presenting the best to the reader has been a major source of inspiration in this work. Hope that this book would be successful.

**– GPH Panel of Expert**


# Publisher's Note

The present book 'LSE-02' is common in elective course of 'Life science' of Bachelor degree [BA, B.Com., and B.Sc.]. This book is targeted for examination purpose as well as enrichment. With the advent of technology and the Internet, there has been no dearth of information available to all; however, finding the relevant and qualitative information, which is focused, is an uphill task.

We at **GullyBaba Publishing House (P) Ltd.**, have taken this step to provide quality material which can accentuate in-depth knowledge about the subject. GPH books are a pioneer in the effort of providing unique and quality material to its readers. With our books, you are sure to attain success by making use of this powerful study material. Provided book is just a reference book based on the syllabus of particular University/Board. For a profound information, see the textbooks recommended by the University/Board.

Our site **gullybaba.com** is a vital resource for your examination. The publisher wishes to acknowledge the significant contribution of the Team Members and our experts in bringing out this publication and highly thankful to Almighty God, without His blessings, this endeavor wouldn't have been successful.

**– Publisher**

# Topics Covered

# Contents



# Question Papers

# Environment and It's Components

## An Overview

Nature and its environment is not only mutually reactive, but is also interdependent and interrelated. Ecology deals with various principles that govern and tries to find out the relationship between such organisms and their environment. The man since times immemorial has been interested in understanding the basic components in his surroundings.

Each living organism constantly interacts with its surroundings and adapts to it. These surroundings are our environment. The physical environment, which consists of soil, air, water, sunlight among others, provided favourable conditions for the existence and growth of different life forms. Living beings constitutes the biological environment.

Both the physical and the biological environments closely interact with each other to form a stable self-perpetuating system. Everything that influences an organism and its living processes from outside is collectively known as environment. The living component of the environment is known as the biotic component and the non-living component (things) as the abiotic component. Hence, the term 'environment' can be defined as the sum total of living and non-living components, their influences and events surrounding an organism.

**Q1. What do you understand by ecology? Discuss the relationship between ecology and biology.**

**Ans.** The term "eco" is derived from the Greek word 'oikos', which mean "home". Because logia mean "study of" in Latin, ecology is the study of home.

In other words, ecology is a science, which studies the relation between the organisms and their milieu, as well as the relation between the organisms. The organisms within a habitat can be categorised under the following three classes:

- Primary producers - plants containing chlorophyll.
- Consumers -herbivorous and carnivorous animals and parasites.
- Decomposers - fungi and bacteria.

In the words of Wells, Huxley and Wells 'ecology is really an extension of economics to the whole world of life'. Economics and society might be thought of as the 'ecology of man' in a broad sense.

**Relationship between ecology and biology**

Ecology is one of the several basic divisions of biology that is concerned with principles, that the fundamentals common to all life. Physiology, genetics, embryology and evolution are examples of other basic divisions. We traditionally cut the biology 'layer cake into small pieces in two distinct ways as shown in fig. 1.1.

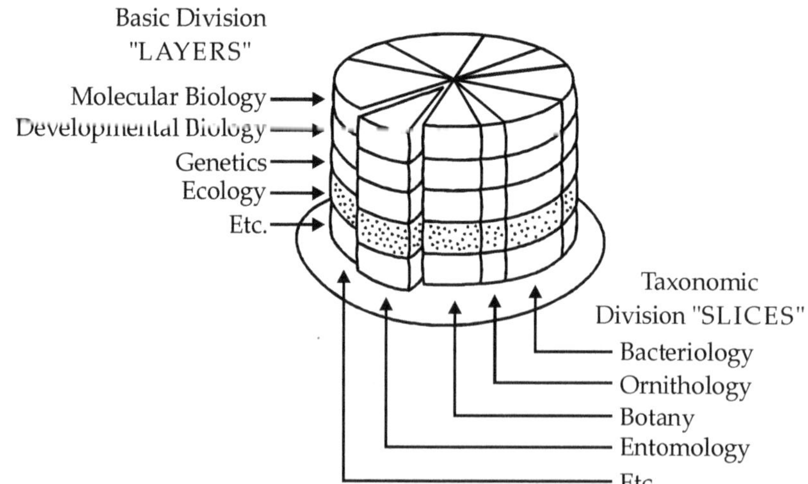


**Fig. 1.1: The layered biological cake showing the relationship of ecology with other biological disciplines**

We may cut it horizontally into what are usually called 'basic divisions' because they are concerned with the fundamentals common to all life. We may also cut the cake vertically into what may be called 'taxonomic divisions', which deal with the study of specific kinds of organisms. Thus, ecology is a basic division of biology.

**Q2. Trace the history of Ecology.**

**Ans.** History of ecology is a powerful perspective for understanding the complex past relationship between human beings and the biosphere. Humanity in its historic paths across earth has interceded in material and measurable ways in a biotic world that evolved previously by natural selection and other evolutionary forces, and that the changes thus imposed on nature have in turn been reflected in human cultures, societies, and languages through time. In effect, history of ecology encompasses the view that wherever humans have trodden, the natural environment is somehow different, sometimes in barely perceptible ways, sometimes in dramatic ways.

Ecology want comes from the same root as our word 'economics', the subject that we now call ecology was not given a name until a century later. Man being egocentric, began this type of study in his immediate surroundings. Not until long afterward did he realise that the man's economics is but a special case of the broader subject.

Though the word 'ecology' was coined only during the last century, the ecological ideas were deep rooted into human history. Man has been aware of the organism - environment relationships ever since he took keen interest in his surroundings. Scriptures of all old civilisations have reference to ecological concepts in a crude manner.

Ecology as an organised science dates back its origin at the end of the 19th century, when geographers began probing into the details of merely the distribution of flora and fauna. During the same period the relation between structure, function and distribution were also being studied, and this laid the basis of modern ecology. Simultaneously, soil science grew from the concept of Dokuchayev in the year 1889. Soil was conceived, for the first time, to be independent and unique entity, resulting from the combination of climate, living matter, parent materials, relief and time.

After 1996, ecological research greatly expanded by the establishment of ecological societies and publication of ecological journals. The European ecologists concerned themselves largely with the static approach of classifying vegetation on floristic basis, while their counterparts in America developed the dynamic system of vegetation analysis, which emphasises temporal changes in the community. In fact, Chements (1996) leader of the dynamic viewpoint went as far ahead to compare a unit of vegetation with the animals to a living organism which he called 'complex organism' or 'biome' in order to express the idea that the unit of vegetation is born, grows to adolescence, matures and finally dies even as a living organism does.

The relationship of climate and vegetation to the soil formation was an essential part of Coffey's (1912) classification in Britain Robinson had written 'soils, their origin and classification' in which he fully realised that neither climate nor geology alone could be a sufficient basis for a classification of soils or an explanation for their genesis.

During the beginning of the present century the population concept came into being, when statistical studies and sampling techniques were employed for solving the community problems. Cowles (1911) in his discussion on vegetation cycles, realised the three fold importance of climate, physiography and biota in ecology. Tansley and Ramkin (1911) for the first time used the successional concept in describing vegetation. By 1996 and 1920 Clements was able to produce two works, 'Plant succession' and 'plant indicators' which contain enormous information and still stimulate the reader.

By 1930s started the era of ecosystem approach to ecology. Tansley (1935) coined the term 'ecosystem' in order to combine plants, animals and environmental complex. The ecosystem forms the structural and functional unit of biosphere.

Growing population pressure and the need for decisions concerning the management and conservation of natural resources have been the greatest driving forces in the introduction of system analysis to ecology.

**History of Ecology in India**

The history of ecology in India is not very different from that of any other country. In Indian writings of Vedic, Epic, and Pauranic etc, we find many references to ecological thought. Chakra described the importance of Vayu (gases and air), jala (water), desha (topography) and time in regulation of life. Similarly, the concept of Panchatattva (five elements) -Earth (nutrients), water, fore (energy), sky (space) and air (gases) reflect the idea of circulation of materials, Indians have always regarded and respected plants and animals. In this country cutting of a green tree has been considered as a crime and planing of a tree as a charity.

We had always recognised the world as one family, which could be equated to the existence of an ecological balance on this planet, as is clear from our age old concept of:

वसुधैव कुटुंबकम

We have our age old unbroken links with nature and with life. We must again learn to invoke the energy of growing things and to recognise, as did our ancients in India centuries ago, that one can take from the earth and the atmosphere only so much as one can put back into them, as is clear from the following hymn from Atharva Veda:

यत ते भूमे विंखनामि क्षिप्र तदपि रोहात्।
मा ते मर्म विमृग्वरि मा ते हृदय मर्पिपम्।।

We have recognised the importance of vegetation, which supports diverse forms of life in this world, as expressed in the following Sanskrit couplet:

यस्या वृक्षा वानस्पत्या ध्रवास्तिष्ठांति विश्वहां।
पृथ्वी विश्वा धायसं घृतामच्छा वंदामसि।।

We have also recognised that one organism is the living of another organism throughout this world, and that they eat each other. The following couplet from Mahabharata mentions the importance of the food chain and interdependence of organisms:

बहुभि चमत बमदज मुर्तै चमत बमदज किंजातै चमत बमदज पुत्रधर्मार्थवर्जितै चमत बमदज।
वरमेक चमत बमदज पथि तरूर्यत विश्रश्रमते जन चमत बमदज।।

In India, the earliest contributions to modern ecology were made by British ecologist to the forest and grasslands. Our early ecological studies have been influenced by European thought mainly due to the fact that most of the workers were either European or were trained in Europe.

**Q3. Briefly outline the various parts of ecology with the help of suitable diagram.**

**Ans.** On the basis of nature of study, ecology can be subdivided into three category:

- Autecology
- Synecology
- Habitat ecology

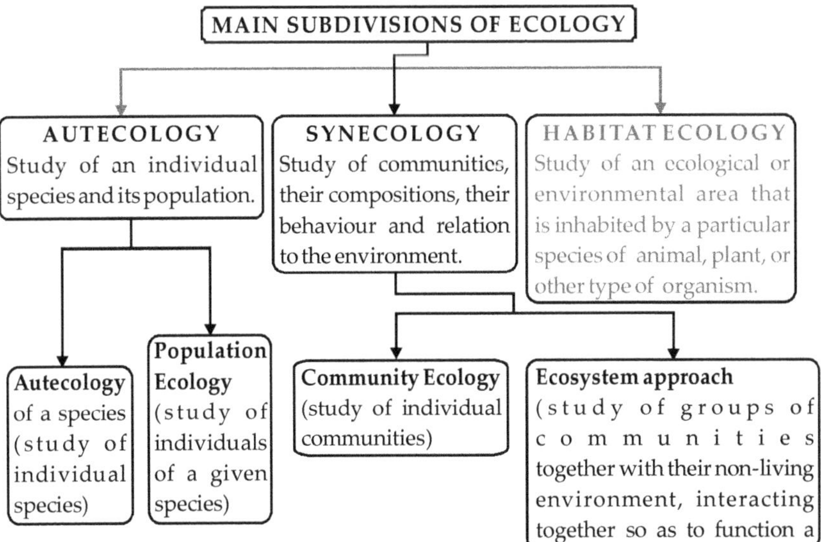


**Fig. 1.2: Subdivisions of Ecology**

### Autecology

Ecological study of individual species is called 'autecology' so it is also called "species ecology". Ecological study includes environmental inter - relationships of a species in a population of set of populations at all stages of life cycle.

In autecological studies, an assessment of potential and aggressiveness and susceptibility of a species under varying environmental conditions are studied. Studies on the life-histories greatly contribute to the understanding of the distribution, environmental responses, adaptation and speciation. It also helps in explaining the structure and dynamics of the communities. The essential purpose of such studies is to uncover the responses of various forms of stimuli and compulsions of the environment on life. These studies are used to arrive at inferences with respect to mode and magnitude of growth and dispersal in relation to the physical and the chemical environments.

### Synecology

Synecology is called "Ecology of communities". It is the study of groups of organisms, i.e. community. It is descriptive but also can be experimental with the aid of tools such as computer and radioactive tracers. It is subdivided into aquatic and terrestrial; Terrestrial includes Desert, Grassland, Forest and Aquatic includes Freshwater, Brackish and Marine water.

The difference between autecology and synecology could be explained by the following example.

If a neem tree (or several neem trees) or a crow (or several crows) are studied in relation to the environment then this would be an autecological study. However, if the study deals with a forest community as a whole in which many different birds, trees and animals share the same area, then it would be called a synecological approach.

### Habitat ecology

Habitat can be defined as regions in environmental space that are composed of multiple dimensions, each representing a biotic or abiotic environmental variable, that is, any component or characteristic of the environment related directly (forage biomass) and quality or indirectly (elevation) to the use of a location by the animal, e.g. Aquatic or terrestrial environment.

**Q4. Define Environment. Discuss its role also.**

**Ans.** 'Environment' is a term derived from the French word 'Environner' that means 'to surround'. There was a time when environment just meant surroundings. It was used to describe the physical world surrounding us including soil, rocks, water and air. Gradually it was realised that the enormous variety of plants, animals and micro-organisms on this earth, including human beings are an integral part of the environment. Hence, to make a sensible definition of environment, it was necessary to include the interactions and inter-relationships of all living organisms with the physical surroundings.

As per Environment (Protection) Act, 1986, environment includes all the physical and biological surroundings of an organism along with their interactions. Environment is thus, defined as "the sum total of water, air and land and the inter-relationships that exist among them and with the human beings, other living organisms and materials". The concept of environment can be clearly understood from Fig. 1.3.

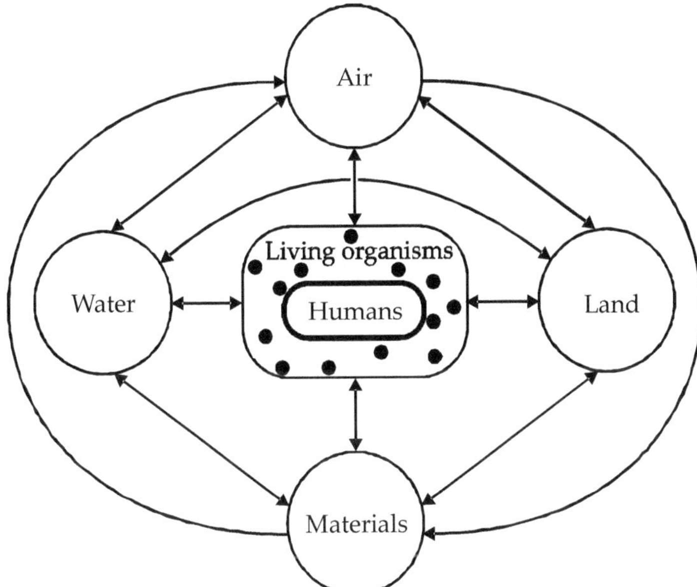


**Fig. 1.3: Concept of Environment: Air, Water, Land, living organisms and Material surroundings**

## Role of Environment

### *(a) Unique Importance of Environment*

Environmental studies is very important since it deals with the most mundane problems of life where each individual matters, like dealing with safe and clean drinking water, hygienic living conditions, clean and fresh air, fertile land, healthy food and sustainable development. If we want to live in a clean, healthy, aesthetically beautiful, safe and secure environment for a long time and wish to hand over a clean and safe earth to our children, grandchildren and great grandchildren, it is most essential to understand the basics of environment.

### *(b) Global and Local Importance of Environment*

Environment is one subject that is actually global as well as local in nature. Issues like global warming, depletion of ozone layer, dwindling forests and energy resources, loss of global biodiversity, etc. which are going to affect the mankind as a whole are global in nature and for that we have to think and plan globally.

However, there are some environmental problems, which are of localised importance. For dealing with local environmental issues, e.g. impact of mining or hydroelectric project in an area, problems of disposal and management of solid waste, river or lake pollution, soil erosion, water logging and salinisation of soil, fluorosis problem in local population, arsenic pollution of groundwater, etc., we have to think and act locally.

**Q5. Differentiate the following:**

**(i) External vs. Internal Environment**

**Ans.** Environment outside of the organism, which pertains to the physical, chemical, biological and social conditions surrounding the organism that called external environment. The external environment is used in contrast to the internal environment of organism.

External Environment consists abiotic and biotic components of environment. Light, temperature, water that are dissolved in nutrients, oxygen, organic matter and other gases are all, abiotic components of external environment. Biotic components include, microscopic plankton as well as higher plants and animals and decomposers. The plants are in different kinds such as phytoplankton, partly submerged plants and trees growing around the edge of the pond. The animals consist of zooplankton, insects, worms, mollusks, tadpoles, frogs, birds and various kinds of fishes.

The internal environment refers to the internal milieu of a multicellular organism. Every cell of a multicellular organism must regulate its surroundings to help keep a relatively stable internal environment.

The internal environment is relatively stable as compared to the external environment. However, it is not absolutely constant that injury, illness or excessive stress upsets the internal environment.

**(ii) Natural vs. Man-made environment**

***Or***

**Describe the differences between natural and artificial environment with appropriate examples.** **[Dec-2011, Q.No.-10]**

**Ans.** All living and non-living things that are naturally on Earth, e.g. water, soil, air, rivers, etc. are called Natural environment.

In a narrow sense, it is an environment that is not influenced by human. The environment that is influenced by humans can be called "the built environment" or cultural landscape.

The concept of the *natural environment* can be distinguished by components:

- Complete ecological units that function as natural systems without massive human intervention, including all vegetation, micro organisms, soil, rocks, atmosphere, and natural phenomena that occur within their boundaries.

- Universal natural resources and physical phenomena that lack clear-cut boundaries, such as air, water, and climate, as well as energy, radiation, electric charge, and magnetism, not originating from human activity.

The natural environment is contrasted with the built environment, which comprises the areas and components that are strongly influenced by humans. A geographical area is regarded as a natural environment.

Man has greatly altered the natural conditions and created new situations known as artificial or man-made environments. Examples of artificial environment are cultivated fields or cities.

The city environment is a product of man's own design. The atmosphere of the city is generally polluted due to the emission of various gases from factories, motor vehicles and electric power plants. Water is obtained not from streams directly but after it has been filtered and disinfected in a water treatment plant. The metabolic wastes and garbage are not disposed of locally but have to be carried through sewer lines for treatment or for dumping in a remote place far away from the city. No food is grown in the city but is imported from rural areas for the city dwellers.

In a city people live in buildings made of bricks, stones and cement. Houses and offices of well off people are air-conditioned creating an atmosphere which remains free from the influence of outside environment. Furthermore, to make life comfortable modern amenities like fans, fridge, radio, television, etc. are installed, requiring electricity which is generated by man artificially.

The man-made city environment consumes excessive amounts of energy and materials and needs constant care, supervision and management to keep it habitable.

**Q6. What do you understand by population? Enumerate the basic numerical and structural attributes of population.**

*Or*

**Draw the S - and J - shaped growth curves and explain them in terms of population ecology. [June-2011, Q.No.-4(a)]**

**Ans.** In a technical sense, 'population' is defined as a group of freely interbreeding individuals of the same species present in a specific area at a given time. For example, when we say that the population of a city is 2,00,000 we mean that there are 2,00,000 individuals of Homo sapiens in that town. Other living organisms, for example cats and dogs present in the city are not included as they are populations of two different species.

In nature, population of a species is subdivided into a number of local breeding populations called deme. Demes are geographically separated populations of the same species. For example, the garden lizards of Qutub Minar, Delhi, form a separate deme from the garden lizard of Lodi Gardens, Delhi or the garden lizards of Swaraj Bhawan Allahabad.

A population exhibits certain characteristics, which can only be expressed at the population level and not shared by the individuals of the population. For example, individual organisms are born, grow and die but characteristics such as birth rate, death rate density are only meaningful at the population level.

The attributes of a population are of two basic types: (a) Numerical attributes such as density, natality (birth rate), mortality (death rate), dispersal and (b) structural attributes like age distribution, dispersion and growth form. The attributes of population are briefly described below.

**(a) Numerical attributes**

- **Density:** number of individuals per unit area.
- **Natality (Birth rate):** the rate at which new individuals are added to a population through reproduction.
- **Mortality (Death rate):** the rate at which individuals are lost from a population by death.
- **Dispersal:** the rate at which individuals of a population emigrate from an area.

**(b) Structural attributes**

- **Population growth form:** It refers to the pattern of population growth. There are two basic patterns of population growth represented by "J" and "S" shaped growth curves, below figure shown two type of population.

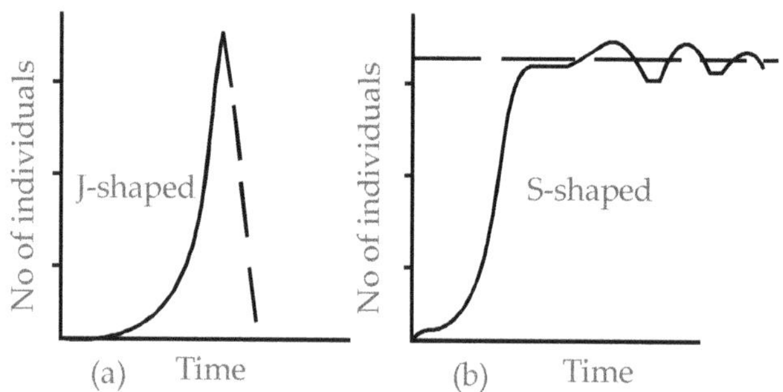


**Fig. 1.4: Two types of population (S-shaped and J-shaped) growth curves.**

- **Dispersion:** the pattern of distribution of individuals in space,
- **Age distribution:** the proportion of individuals of different age groups in a population.

**Q7. Define the term biological community. Also explain its Structure and type.**

***Or***

**What are guilds? Give one example of a guild.**

**[Dec-2011, Q.No.-8(b)]**

**Ans.** The term biological community refers to all the living components in an ecosystem. A slightly different concept is encompassed in the word biota, which refers to all flora and fauna, or plant and animal life, in a particular region.

Communities or guilds in most instances are named after the dominant plant form species. A grassland, for example, is dominated by grasses, though it may contain herbs, shrubs, and trees, alongwith associated animals of different species.

**Structure of Community**

A community may have one or several species. The environmental factors determine the characteristic of the community as well as the pattern of organisation of the members in the community, the characteristic pattern of the community is termed structure, which is reflected in the roles played by various populations, their range, the type of area they inhabit, the diversity of species in the community and the spectrum of interactions between them. As a result, the structure of community is as follows:

(1) **Dominance:** In each community, a few over topping species are present in greater bulk. By their greater number or biomass the dominate species modify the habitat characteristics and influence the growth of other species in the community. In such case, the community is named after the dominant species, as for example spruce forest community.

(2) **Species diversity:** An important attribute of a community is its species diversity. The diversity is calculated both by the number of species (richness) and the relative abundance of each species (evenness). The greater the number of species and more even their distribution the greater is the species diversity. Diversity is related to the stability of the community. A stable community is one, which is able to return to its original condition after being disturbed in some way. Communities with high species diversity are comparatively more stable because many alternative pathways exist in such communities to enable the individuals to obtain the required energy and nutrients. Stability is more dependent on the number of well adapted species than on the total number of species present.

(3) **Mutual interrelationship among individuals of community:** Mutual interrelationship includes all the indirect effects that organisms have upon each other. The three relationships which we shall discuss are (a) competition, (b) stratification, and (c) dependence.

(a) ***Competition:*** Demand for a common resource by different organisms results in competition. Competition between individuals of different species is called interspecific; when it occurs between individuals of the same species it is called intraspecific.

(b) ***Stratification:*** Different organisms in a community develop a characteristic pattern of stratification to minimise competition and conflict among the members of the community. Plants and animals of each layer differ in size, behaviour and adaptation from those of other layers.

(c) ***Dependence:*** In a community there are some species which are wholly dependent on the dominant member for survival. Bryophytes, thallophytes and a few vascular small plants are examples of such organisms. These dependent organisms require special conditions such as shade and moisture provided by the dominant species. The dependent species will die if the dominant species are eliminated.

(4) **Trophic structure:** Organisms in a community are closely interrelated with each other though feeding relationships. Another aspect which is quite obvious in a community is that in areas of extreme climate conditions both species diversity or the number of species are greatly reduced. This is because only a few species are able to adapt to the difficult environment.

Communities, which extend over a considerable area generally have also locally diverse conditions of soil or topography. Thus in a community local habitats may be supporting markedly different species which are very different from the general community composition.

**Types of community**

On the basis of size and degree of relative independence communities may be divided into two types:

- **Major community:** These are large sized, well organised and relatively independent. They depend only on the sun's energy from outside and are independent of the inputs and outputs from adjacent communities. A tropical ever green forest in the North-East of India is a good example of a major community.
- **Minor Communities:** These are dependent on neighbouring communities and are often called societies. They are secondary aggregations within a major community and are not therefore completely independent units as far as energy and nutrient dynamics are concerned. A cow dung pad would be a good example of such a community.

**Q8. What is an ecosystem? Explain its structural components.**

**Ans.** Ecosystem is a self sustaining structural and functional unit of biosphere. It is a segment of nature consisting of a community of living being and the physical environment, both interacting and exchanging materials between them. It is an open system and depends upon solar energy from outside as its energy source.

An ecosystem may be as small as a drop of pond water or may be as large as ocean. An ecosystem is not an isolated unit. There is frequent exchange of material and energy between adjoining ecosystems. Thus, all the ecosystems of the world are interrelated and exchange material and energy among themselves.

It is a unit or a system, which is composed of a number of sub-units, that are all directly or indirectly linked with each other. They may be freely exchanging energy and matter from outside—an *open ecosystem* or may be isolated from outside in term of exchange of matter—a *closed ecosystem.*

**Components of ecosystem**

They are broadly grouped into:

- Abiotic and
- Biotic components

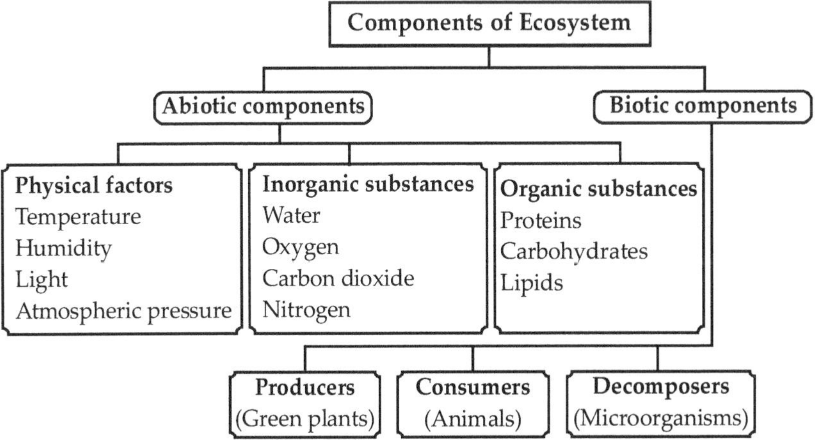


**Fig. 1.5: Components of Ecosystem**

*Abiotic Components*

- **Energy:** Basically from the sun is essential for maintenance of life. In the case of plants, the sun directly supplies the necessary energy. Since animals cannot use solar energy directly they obtain it indirectly by eating plants or animals or both. Energy determines the distribution of organisms in the environment.

- **Materials:** (a) organic compounds—proteins, carbohydrates, lipids, humic substances which are formed from inorganic substance and reconverted into them on decomposition. (b) inorganic compounds-oxygen, nitrogen, carbon, carbon dioxide, water, sulphur, nitrates, phosphates, and various metals are essential for organisms to survive.
- **Climate factors:** light, heat, temperature, wind, humidity, rainfall, snowfall, etc.
- **Edaphic factors (structure and composition of soil along with its physical and chemical characteristics):** also exert significant influence on the organisms.

***Biotic Components***

Different living organisms constitute the biotic component of an ecosystem and belong to the following categories:

- **Producers:** These are mainly producing food themselves, *e.g.*, Green plants produce food by photosynthesis in the presence of sunlight from raw materials like water and carbon dioxide. They are known as *photo-autotrophs* (auto = self, photo = light, troph = food).
- **Consumers:** These organisms get their food by feeding on other organisms. They are of the following types:
  (a) Herbivores: which feed on plants, *e.g.* rabbit, insect.
  (b) Carnivores: which feed on herbivores as secondary carnivores (*e.g.*, frog, small fish) or tertiary carnivores (*e.g.*, snake, big fish), which feed on other consumers.
  (c) Omnivores: which feed on both plants and animals, *e.g.*, humans, rats, many birds.
  (d) Detritivores: which feed on dead organisms, *e.g.*, earth worm, crab, ants.
- **Decomposers:** These are micro-organisms which break down organic matter into inorganic compounds and in this process they derive their nutrition. They play a very important role in converting the essential nutrients from unavailable organic form to free inorganic form that is available for use by plants, *e.g.*, bacteria, fungi.

**Q9. Taking a pond as an ecosystem, choose five of its biotic components and classify them as producers, consumers and decomposers.**

*Or*

**Describe the pond ecosystem with the help of a labelled diagram.**

**Ans.** An ecosystem is often defined as "a community of organisms living in a particular environment and the physical elements in that environment with which they interact". The elements of an ecosystem interact with each other in some way, and so depend on each other either directly or indirectly.

The living or biotic components of a pond ecosystem are different types of birds, frogs, insects, turtles, fungi, algae , etc. are considered as consumers. The plants clean the water, known as producers prohibit algae growth and help protect fish, biofalls naturally oxygenate water, skimmer filter removes leaves and other debris, plant pockets remove the need for bulky plant container, rocks provide a natural biomas and add flair to the pond and aquatic bacteria break down waste and keep water clean whereas different organisms such as fish, frogs, turtles, birds, etc. are considered as consumers because they depend on other organisms.

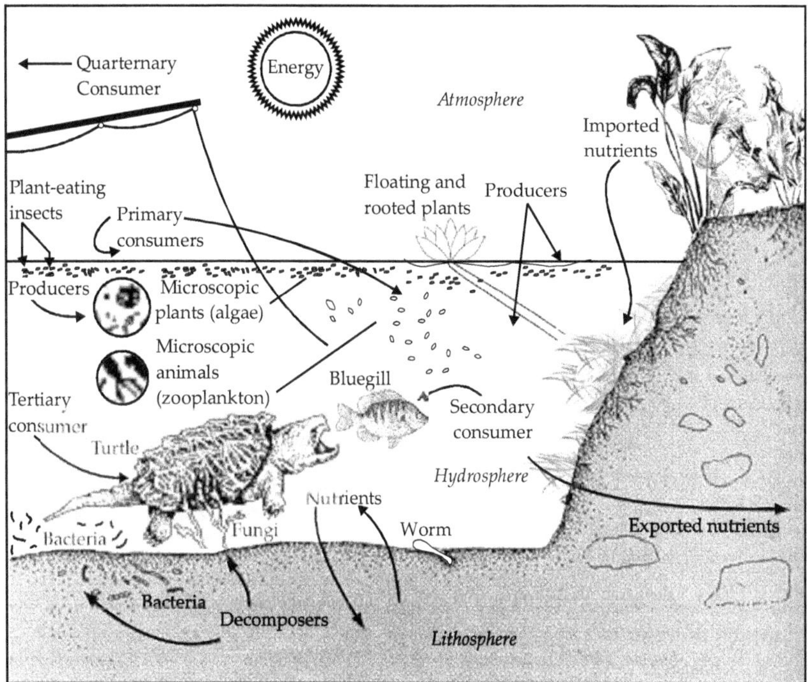


**Fig. 1.6: Pond Ecosystem**

## Q10. Define Biosphere with the help of a biospherical diagram.

**[June-2011, Q.No.-4(a)]**

**Ans.** The **biosphere** is the biological component of earth systems, which also include the lithosphere, hydrosphere, atmosphere and other "spheres". The biosphere includes all living organisms on earth, together with the dead organic matter produced by them.

It is that of the earth where life can exist. It is a narrow layer around the surface of the earth. If you visualise the earth to be the size of an apple the biosphere would be as thick as its skin.

In the hierarchy of ecological systems, the biosphere is the most

important and includes all other ecosystems as its components parts.

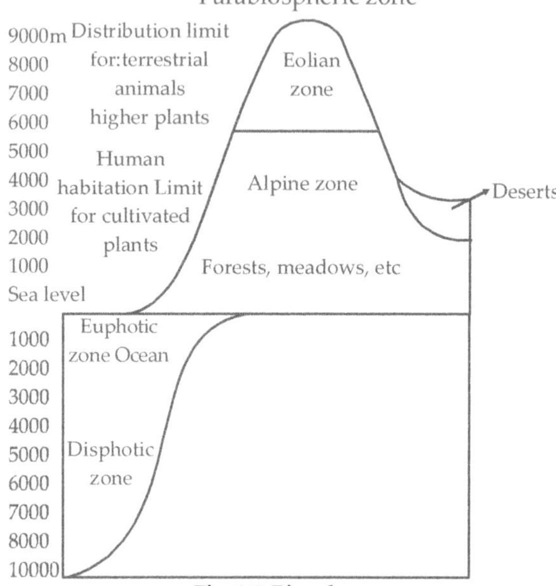


**Fig. 1.7: Biosphere**

This figure shows vertical extension of the biosphere. As the Earth's shell, biosphere is of somewhat irregular shape, being surrounded by an indeterminate "parabiospheric" region in which life exists only in a dormant state as fungal spores and bacteria. The euphotic, or illuminated, zone of water bodies cab span from several upper centimeters (in a very rapid river) to 100 m and more.

**Table 1.1: Major quantitative parameters of parameters of present-day Earth's biosphere**

| Parameter | Value |
|---|---|
| Biosphere area ($km^2$) | $509\times10^6$ |
| including land | $148\times10^6$ |
| including world ocean | $361\times10^6$ |
| Mass of living material (t) | $1840\times10^9$ |
| including plants (%) | 99 |
| including animals with microorganisms (%) | 1 |
| Ocean inhabitants | 0.1 |
| Land inhabitants | 99.9 |
| Elemental composition of biosphere (% by mass) | |
| Oxygen | 75 |
| Hydrogen | 10 |
| Carbon | 3 |
| Nitrogen | 0.3 |

*contd.*

| Parameter | Value |
|---|---|
| Nitrogen | 0.3 |
| Mass of living material (%) | <1 |
| Mass of bio-inert material (%) | >99 |
| Average amount of solar energy incident upon Earth (kcal $cm^2$ $year^{-1}$) | 167.00 |
| Solar radiation use efficiency for biosphere (%) | 0.13 |
| Bio-inert mass in soil humus (t) | $2400\times10^{16}$ |
| Net primary production (kcal/year) | $67\times10^{16}$ |
| Land (t) | $40\times10^{9}C$ |
| Ocean (t) | $30\times10^{9}C$ |

***Main quantitative parameters of the biosphere***

In space it extends down to 11 km, the maximal depths of the ocean, and to about the same distance up into the atmosphere (Figure1.7). The Earth's surface is almost everywhere, except maybe for some central parts of the Antarctic Continent, covered in relatively thin layer where life exists in the form of discrete organisms. The highest live biomass concentration and biological productivity can be found at phase interfaces: land-atmosphere and land-water. The major quantitative characteristics of the modern biosphere are listed in Table1.1.

**Q11. What is Light? Discuss the properties of a solar radiation.**

***Or***

**Write a short notes on Electromagnetic spectrum.**

**[Dec-2010, Q.No.-6(a)]**

**Ans.** Light plays a variety of roles in the living world. It is essential for photosynthesis, the process by which light is converted into usable chemical energy. It is involved in the transmission of information, it helps plants and animals to programme their life cycles, coordinates the opening of buds and flowers, dropping of leaves and a variety of other physiological processes. Variation in the amount of light generally effects the local distribution of plants. In animals, light regulates reproduction, hibernation and migration and of course makes vision possible. All these biological phenomena are readily influenced by variation in the intensity, and by seasonal or diurnal variations of light.

The properties of solar radiations are:

**(1) Electromagnetic Spectrum**

The electromagnetic spectrum extends from gamma rays, x-rays, ultra-violet, visible, infrared to radiowaves. The spectral distribution and the intensity of solar radiation incident on the earth surface is known. Electromagnetic radiation has a dual nature of wave and particle. Among the photobiological phenomena caused due to light, many are best explained in terms of wave nature of light and many others by the particle nature.

Electromagnetic radiation is a form of energy. It propagates in the form of discrete packets of energy called photons. The photons of each wavelength have different quanta of energy. The amount of energy of a particular wave depends upon its wavelength or frequency and can be expressed as:

$E \alpha \upsilon$ E = energy of wave (joule/sec)

$E h \upsilon$ $\upsilon$ = frequency of wave (Hertz cycles/sec)

h = Planck's proportionality constant. It has a value of ~1.6 × $10^{-34}$

cal/sec. = 6.6 × $10^{-34}$ joule/sec.

Frequency is inversely proportional to wavelength and can be expressed as:

$$\upsilon = \frac{C}{\lambda}$$

C = velocity of light (3.0 × $10^{10}$ cm/sec or 3.0 × $10^{8}$ m/sec)

$\lambda$ = wavelength (in cm or m)

**(2) Solar Energy Input**

Enormous amount of energy that is radiated by the sun $\left(5.6 \times 10^{27} \text{ cal/min}\right)$, only about one-half of 1 billionth of that amount is intercepted by the earth. Not all the solar radiation can penetrate the earth's atmosphere; however, the amount of solar energy received at the top of atmosphere is constant. This energy is refined to as solar constant. It is defined as the rate at which solar radiation falls on a unit area is a plane surface, which is oriented perpendicular to the solar beam, when the earth is at its mean distance from the sun. On an average the value of solar constant is 2 $\text{cal/cm}^2\text{/min}$. As the solar radiation travels through the atmosphere it interacts with it and gets diminished in three different ways: by reflection, scattering and absorption. About 30 per cent of the total incoming solar radiation is reflected by clouds and a portion of it is back-scattered and lost in space. About 19 per cent of it is directly absorbed by oxygen, ozone, water, ice crystals and suspended particles. This absorbed radiation is converted into heat energy and the air is warmed to some extent. The remaining 5 1 per cent is absorbed or reflected by earth's surface that is converted to heat. Thus, a total of 70 per cent (19 per cent by atmosphere aid 5 1 per cent by earth) of the radiation absorbed by earth and atmosphere is involved in the functioning of our biosphere.

The earth has a variety of surfaces - rough, smooth, ice-covered, or water-covered and areas with different types of vegetation. The amount of radiation absorbed or reflected depends upon the nature of surface features, i.e. topography of the area. The percentage of reflectivity of the incident radiation in meteorology is called albedo, which is

$$\text{Albedo} = \frac{\text{Reflected radiation}}{\text{Incident radiation}} \text{x } 100$$

Albedo of snow covered landscapes is higher than vegetated landscape or water column. Freshly fallen snow typically has an albedo between 75 to 95 per cent.

**(3) Radiation Instruments**

The instruments used for measuring solar energy, light intensity and duration of light are define as follows:

***Pyrenometer***

Many instruments have been designed to measure the energy of solar radiations of all wavelengths as well as of a particular range of wavelengths. Pyrenometer measures energy of sunlight of short wavelengths, indirect sunlight and scattered skylight radiation. The receiver of radiation A has alternate black and white strips. These act as hot and cold thermocouple junctions respectively. This arrangement is enclosed in a spherical glass bulb which shields the receiving surface from disturbances by wind. But the glass container limits the wavelength response of 280 nm to 3,000 nm.

***Radiometer***

Radiometer measures the flux of energy of all wavelengths received on a single surface of the receiver. There are also instruments that can measure the difference between the downward incident solar radiation and upward streams of reflected re-radiation and gives us the net value of radiation. This is called net radiometer. It has two exposed surfaces one upward facing (x) and another downward facing (y). The principle of this instrument is similar to that of the pyrenometer. The receiver A is a long thin blackened metal strip which is painted white on either side. The white and blackened parts of this strip are connected to a thermocouple.

***Measurement of Light Intensity***

Light spreads out uniformly in all directions from a source. The amount of light shining on a unit area decrease with increasing distance. This decrease is equal to the square of the distance away from the source. Fig 1.8 shows how the intensity of light decreases with distance from the source.

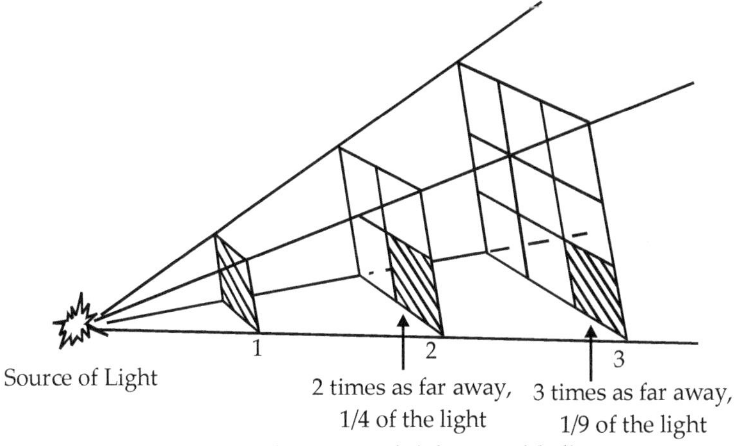


**Fig. 1.8: Decrease in apparent brightness with distance**

Light intensity is measured in lux (metre candle). A lux is the amount of illumination shed on a square metre of curved surface, one metre from a standard candle. Previously, the unit foot candle (ft-c) was used. A foot candle is the amount of illumination shed on a square foot of curved surface, one foot from a standard candle. To get an idea of the magnitude of foot-candle, please read the accompanying margin remark.

### *Photometer*

Photometer measures the intensity of light. The metallic plate A is a photocell which emits electrons from its surface when light of sufficient frequency impinges upon it. The emission of electrons emerging from the irradiated surface constitute the current. This current is measured by a sensitive ammeter which is calibrated to give the amount of current generated as the value of light intensity in metre candle.

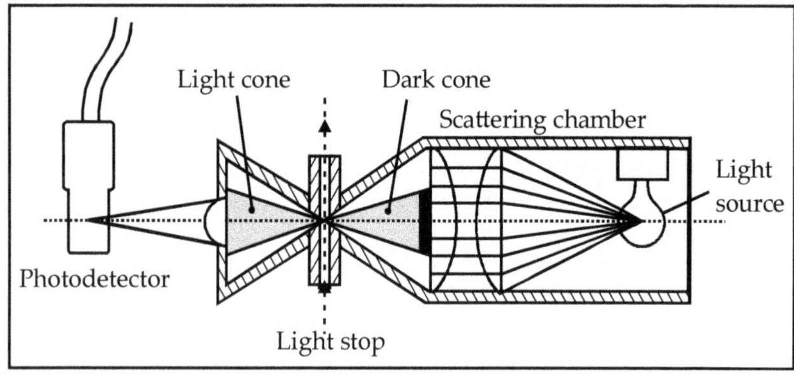


**Fig. 1.9: Photometer**

### *Duration of Light*

Sunshine recorder measures the duration of sunshine. The recorder consists essentially of a glass sphere of about 10 cm in diameter mounted concentrically in a spherical metallic bowl (B) which itself is mounted on a marble base. The inner surface of the bow is flanged to take 3 sets of special cards for use at different periods of the year. A semi-circular brass bar supports the bowl and sphere and has degrees of latitudes engraved on it can be moved and set to any latitude in its range. The rays of the sun when focussed sharply on the card, burn a trace on the card gradually. The length of the burn indicates the duration of sunshine, which is read off the hour marks printed on the cards.

### (4) Periodic Variations in Light

Rotation of the earth on its axis accounts for day-to-night variations in the amount of radiations falling at a given place and seasonal variations occur due to the orbiting of the earth around the sun. Since the earth's equatorial plane is inclined to its orbit at an angel of 27', the rays of the sun do not fall vertically on all parts of the earth. From March 22$^{nd}$ to September 22$^{nd}$

(Autumnal equinox), the northpole is inclined towards the sun. So the most intense solar beam is focussed on the northern hemisphere. We in the northern hemisphere, have summer season and on the sun shines for 24 hours of the day. While on South pole it is dark for six months and the southern hemisphere has winter season. The opposite situation exists on the poles from September 24 to March 20 (spring equinox) when the northern hemisphere has winter season and southern hemisphere has summer season.

**(5) Light and Distribution**

Light plays a great role in species composition and development of vegetation. In a thick forest the light interception by the multistoreyed vegetation is very efficient. Due to selective absorption, spectral light quality changes as it passes through the tree canopies. The intensity of light at which energy harnessed in photosynthesis is just-sufficient to meet the energy requirement of respiration is called **light compensation point**. In deep shade, under trees the amount of light is not enough to carry on photosynthesis to satisfy the immediate need of the plants. Amount of photosynthesis is directly related to the intensity of light and thus the light compensation point in water reaches at a certain depth which is called **compensation depth**. The zones above and below this depth are called photic zone and aphotic zones respectively.

**(6) Photoperiodism**

Activity like breeding and migration in animals; flowering, seed germination in plants are regulated by the length of daily period of light and darkness. The behavioural phenomenon is known as photoperiodism. For example, plants such as radish, potatoes and spinach bloom when the light duration is more than 12 hours/day. Such plants are called **long day plants**. Cereal, tobacco, dahelia and many other plants bloom when light duration is less than 12 hrs/day. These are called **short day plants**. Such responses show that plants have built-in mechanisms for measuring the duration of illumination and darkness and hence flower in a specific seasons. Similar photoperiodic responses are observed in animals. There may be diurnal, lunar or annual. Reproduction and migration in birds are such annual photoperiodic responses. From such responses it seems that distribution of some plants and animals may be restricted because the necessary photoperiodic stimulus is available only at certain latitudes.

**Q12. What is temperature? Describe how the altitude and latitude variations in temperature influence the formation of biomes?**

*Or*

**Explain the reason for decrease in temperature with increasing altitude in Troposphere.** **[Dec-2010, Q.No.-3 (a)]**

**Ans.** Temperature is a measure of heat. It of the surface soil fluctuates daily and seasonally. The temperature of the surface soil may be 30°C higher in the sunlight than in the shade and upto 17°C higher during the day than during the night. On the desert this spread may be as high as 40°C. The Thar Desert of Rajasthan show a diurnal change of 20-30°C for all seasons. The lowest temperature recorded for any land mass is-70°C (Siberia in 1947). Higher temperature may likewise go often 85°C as in certain desert at noon.

Atmospheric temperature varies from to night, from latitude to latitude, from altitude to altitude, and the season. A daily maximum of atmospheric temperature usually comes in the mid-afternoon, and minimum just before the sun rise. Since, the total insolation decreases with distance from the equator, obviously, the temperature values are maximum at equator, decreasing gradually towards the poles. Besides latitude and altitude, colour and composition of surface, plant cover, water content of soil, physiographic factors such as steepness of stope, exposure of slope and direction of mountain chains greatly affect the temperature conditions. In nature, valleys and low lands are some times much cooler due to sinking in of the heavier cold air.

**Temperature variation at different altitudes and latitudes**

***Altitude variation***

It is clear that when altitude is increase, temperature is decrease. This is mainly due to convection currents in the troposphere — the lowermost (and most dense) region of the earth's atmosphere. The surface of the earth gets heated up on account of solar radiation and it also heats the air which is in immediate contact with the surface. This gives rise to convection currents which continuously transport air from lower region to higher ones and vice versa. When the air from sea level rises to the upper atmosphere of lower pressure it expands, i.e. the volume increases. While expanding, the molecules push aside the neighbouring molecules. In doing so the molecules lose their kinetic energy and it is his energy loss which is reflected in a decrease in temperature. The same amount of energy is gained by the gas molecules when they are compressed while descending and thus the temperature increases. Such a change in temperature where no addition or subtraction of heat takes place between the system and the surrounding is called adiabatic changer.

***Latitude variation***

The amount of direct sunlight that reaches different parts of the Earth varies because the Earth is round. For example, if you were to hold a basketball up in front of a flashlight, the portion of the basketball that is closer to the light will be brighter than the top and bottom because those parts only get indirect light from the flashlight. If you were to hold up a sheet of paper, the light would be more evenly spread out. When the light comes from the sun, there is also solar radiation, which increases the temperature on the Earth so that regions around the Equator are warmer than the North and South Poles.

The Tropic of Cancer, at the latitude of 23.5 degrees north, and the Tropic of Capricorn, at the latitude of 23.5 degrees south, mark the region where the sun appears directly overhead for at least a fraction of the year. This is significant because that means the area experiences direct sunlight, which increases temperatures more than indirect sunlight. If you live north of the Tropic of Cancer or south of the Tropic of Capricorn, you do not receive direct sunlight at any point during the year.

**Q13. What are the adaptations of organisms against climatic conditions?**

*Or*

**Differentiate between Exotherms and Endotherms.**

**[Dec-2010, Q.No.-2(a)]**

**Ans.** The special characteristics that enable plants and animals to be successful in a particular environment are called adaptations.

Camouflage, as in a toad's ability to blend in with its surroundings, is a common example of an adaptation. The combination of bright orange and black on a monarch butterfly is an adaptation to warn potential predators that the butterfly is poisonous and prevent it from being eaten. These special features have evolved over long periods of time, through the process of natural selection. Adaptations afford the organism a better chance to survive in its surroundings.

Every organism can live and reproduce within a certain range of climatic conditions. Organisms that live in hot or cold environments have behavioural and physiological features that enable them to survive extremes of temperature. For example, plants cope up with high temperatures in the desert by developing a thick layer of cuticle, succulence, i.e., water storage tissue in the leaves and stems. In many cacti the stem is green and carry out the functions of leaf and makes food by photosynthesis. These plants also have physiological adaptation. The stomata remain closed during the day to prevent the loss of water due to transpiration. $CO_2$ diffusion cannot occur in stomatal closure in the day. To carry on photosynthesis these plants have evolved special physiological adaptation. During night when their stomata open they trap $CO_2$ and store it in the form of four carbonic acid. The $CO_2$ trapped in the leaf at night is subsequently released during the day and used in photosynthesis. This type of metabolism is called crussulacean acid metabolism (CAM).

Plants are adjusted to natural rhythmic diurnal cycle temperature changes. The regulation of plant responses to periodic thermal changes is called thermoperiodism.

Animals have advantage over plants as they can move from one place to another. They cope with temperature stress by regulating their internal and external environment by physiological and behavioural means. Probably we know that birds and mammals are capable of maintaining constant body temperature. They do so by using the energy of metabolism released during cellular respiration. They are called homeotherms or endotherms because they control constant body temperature by internal means. The body fat, feather, fur or hair, etc. help to retain this heat. Some animals use a number of behavioural mechanisms to regulate their body temperature. This type of regulation is termed as behavioural thermoregulation. The desert animals such as snakes, lizards, scorpions and rats are mostly nocturnal, i.e. they remain hiding during the day to avoid the scorching sun and roam in search of food at night or early in the morning when temperature is generally low. Reptiles like lizard and snake are considered cold blooded because they cannot control their body temperature. However, experiments on these animals have revealed that they can also control their body temperature effectively by behavioural means. Reptiles move in and out of burrow in such a way that their body temperature remains fairly constant. It has been found that in spite of great temperature fluctuation of environment, desert lizard can maintain its body temperature between 31°C to 39°C. These animals are called **poikilotherms** or **exotherms** because they control body temperature to a considerable range by behavioural means. Animals also regulate their body temperature by losing excess heat by sweating and evaporation.

In colder climates, animals have adaptation to gather heat. Birds warm up their body by increasing the muscular activity in their wings by shivering. The chameleons change their colour to black, thus increasing their heat absorbing capacity, the ectotherms bask in the sun. The animals also manipulate by exposing a certain portion of their body so as to acquire desirable heat.

Birds of northern or colder regions migrate to warmer southern regions during the winter season. Fishes also swim long distances until they reach water masses which have suitable temperature for their survival.

Some animals such as bats, hedgehogs, ground-squirrels, lizards reduce their metabolic activity and thus enter into hibernation to minimise their energy needs during winter. To overcome high temperature during summer insects, lungfish, amphibians, etc. also suspend their activities and lead dormant life. This state is called aestivation.

**Q14. What do you mean by composition of atmosphere? Write down the present day composition of atmosphere.**

**Ans.** The atmospheric composition is a layer of gases surrounding the planet Earth that is retained by Earth's gravity. The atmosphere protects life on Earth by absorbing ultraviolet solar radiation, warming the surface through heat retention (greenhouse effect), and reducing temperature extremes between day and night (the diurnal temperature variation).

If a piece of the atmosphere, measuring one cubic inch, containing one million parts, the gases which comprise the atmosphere would be represented by a part of that cubic inch, or a percentage of those one million parts.

**Present Day Composition of different gases**

**Nitrogen-78 per cent:** Dilutes oxygen and prevents rapid burning at the earth's surface. Living things need it to make proteins. Nitrogen cannot be used directly from the air. The Nitrogen Cycle is nature's way of supplying the needed nitrogen for living things.

**Oxygen-21 per cent:** Used by all living things. Essential for respiration. It is necessary for combustion or burning.

**Argon-0.9 per cent:** Used in light bulbs.

**Carbon Dioxide-0.03 per cent:** Plants use it to make oxygen. Acts as a blanket and prevents the escape of heat into outer space. Scientists are afraid that the burning of fossil fuels such as coal and oil are adding more carbon dioxide to the atmosphere.

**Water Vapour-0.0 to 4.0 per cent:** Essential for life processes. Also prevents heat loss from the earth.

**Trace gases:** Gases found only in very small amounts. They include neon, helium, krypton, and xenon.

**Q15. What is atmospheric stratification? Explain with the help of diagram. [June-2011, Q.No.-3(a)]**

**Ans.** Planetary atmospheres are sometimes composed of a number of layers. These atmospheres are said to be stratified. Atmospheric pressure decreases with altitude, but temperature will increase or decrease with altitude depending upon the layer and the atmospheric conditions. On the basis of the variation in air temperature the atmosphere has been divided into five concentric layers:

- Troposphere
- Stratosphere
- Mesosphere
- Thermosphere
- Exosphere

The earth's atmosphere from the surface upto about 20 km (8 km on poles) is called troposphere. The troposphere concerns us most because it is the only part that supports plants and animals. The important weather events, such as cloud formation, lightening, thundering etc take place in the troposphere. Air temperature in the zone gradually decreases with height at the rate of about $6.5^{\circ}$ c per km. Towards the upper layers of the troposphere, the temperature might decrease upto - $60^{\circ}$ c. The water vapour in the atmosphere, and most of the air, is confined to the troposphere.

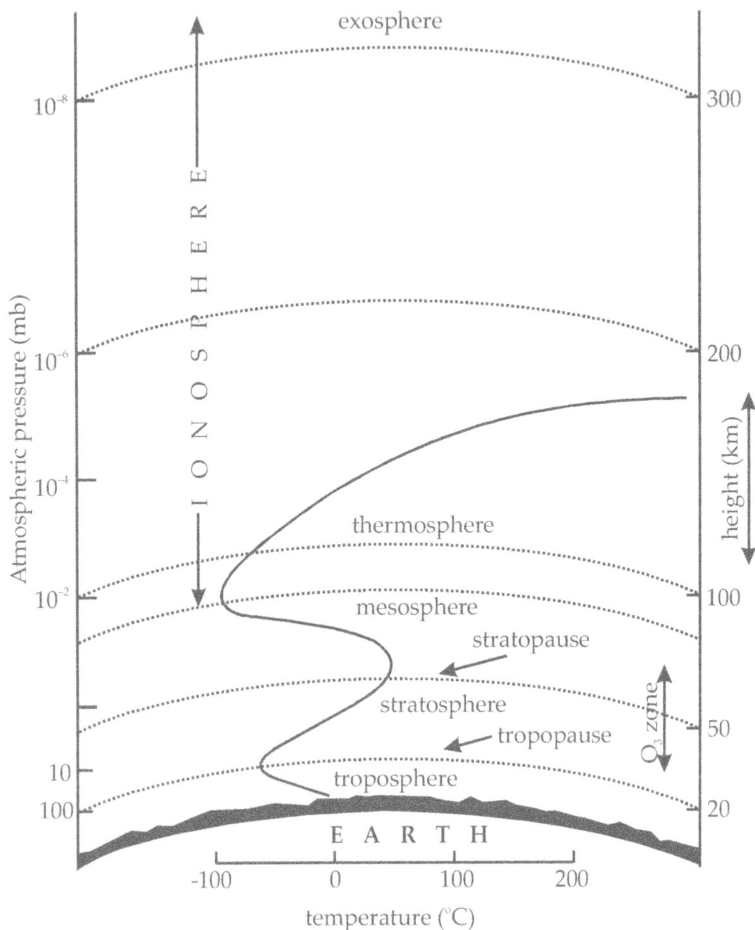


**Fig1.11. Principal zones of atmosphere along with variations in temperature**

Stratosphere is the second zone of about 30 km where temperature are about 90° c. In this zone the temperature shows an increase from a minimum of about - 60° c to a maximum of about 5° c. the increase in temperature is due to ozone formation under the influence of ultraviolet rays of solar radiation. Ozone is formed from oxygen by a photochemical reaction, in which solar energy splits the oxygen molecules to form atomic oxygen which then combines with oxygen molecules to form ozone. Stratosphere is the region of horizontal motion with no up-and-down wind motions. In the lower layers of the stratosphere, the horizontal winds reach the highest speeds of any wind in the entire atmosphere. The high speed winds are known as jet-streams. The stratosphere is above clouds, violent storms and precipitation. The upper layers of the stratosphere form the stratopause.

Mesosphere is the third layer of the atmosphere, about 40 km in height. In this zone, temperature shows a decrease upto $-80°$ c. The upper limit of the mesosphere in termed as mesopause.

The region of atmosphere above the mesosphere is the thermosphere, which extends upto 500 km above the earth's surface, and is characterised by steady increase in temperature with height. In this region ultraviolet radiation and cosmic radiation cause ionisation of oxygen and nitric oxide. Hence, this region is also called as ionosphere.

Exosphere is the region above the thermosphere. It lacks atoms except that of hydrogen and helium and extends upto 32190 km from the earth. The earth's magnetic field becomes more important than gravity in the distribution of atomic particles in the exosphere. Exosphere has a very high temperature due to solar radiation.

All these layers of the atmosphere are of interest to the ecologists since together they form the total blanket of air which moderates the solar energy reaching the biosphere, and also serve as a blanket and regulates the earth's radiation escaping into the space.

**Q16. What are the properties of water?**

**Ans.** Most of the physical properties of water relevant to the living systems are due to its hydrogen bonding and lattice structure.

### Water the Universal Solvent

Scientists often call water the "universal solvent" because water can dissolve more substances than any other liquid. Some substances, like common table salt (sodium chloride, NaCl), dissolve in water very easily. When placed in water, sodium chloride molecules fall apart. Thc positively charged sodium ion ($Na+$) binds to oxygen, while the negatively charged chloride ion ($Cl^-$) attaches to hydrogen. This makes a very stable "salty" water molecule. This property of water allows for the transport of nutrients vital to life in animals and plants.

### Surface Tension

Water molecules at the surface (next to air) hold closely together, forming an invisible film. Water's surface tension can hold weight that would normally sink. You can carefully float a paper clip on top of the water. Some aquatic insects such as the water strider or pond skater rely on surface tension to walk on water. Surface tension is essential for the transfer of energy from wind to water to create waves. Waves are necessary for rapid oxygen diffusion in lakes and seas. Next to mercury, water has the highest surface tension of all commonly occurring liquids.

### Water is Sticky

- *Cohesion:* Water molecules stick to each other. This is due to the hydrogen bonds among the molecules. Water molecules at the surface have a much greater attraction for each other than for molecules in the air. This cohesiveness creates a high surface tension at the surface of the water. The water molecules at the surface crowd together, producing a strong layer as they are pulled downward by the attraction of other water molecules beneath them.

- ***Adhesion:*** Water molecules stick to other substances. You can see this property when water creeps up the inside of a drinking glass. Think of a sponge or a paper towel used to "soak up" spilled water. This is how water makes things wet. Water also clings to living things. Most plants have adapted to take advantage of water's adhesion that helps move water from the roots to the leaves. This is called capillary action. This can also be seen as blood moves through our capillaries, carrying nutrients to each cell within our body.

**Thermal Properties**

Water absorbs or releases more heat than many substances for each degree of temperature increase or decrease. Because of this, it is widely used for cooling and for transferring heat in thermal and chemical processes. Differences in between lakes and river's temperature and the surrounding air may have a variety of effects. For example, local fog or mist is likely to occur if a lake cools in the surrounding air enough to cause saturation—small water droplets are suspended in the air. Large bodies of water, such as the oceans or the Great Lakes, have a profound influence on climate. They are the world's great heat reservoirs and heat exchangers and the source of much of the moisture that falls as rain and snow over adjacent landmasses. When water is colder than the air, precipitation is curbed, winds are reduced, and fog banks are formed. These properties of water are crucial in stabilising temperatures on earth.

**Specific Heat**

Water has a high specific heat. The amount of energy required to raise the temperature of water by one degree Celsius is quite large. Because so much heat loss or heat input is required to lower or raise the temperature of water, the oceans and other large bodies of water have relatively constant temperatures. Thus, many organisms living in the oceans are provided with a relatively constant environmental temperature. The high water content of plants and animals living on land helps them to maintain a relatively constant internal temperature.

**Heat of Vaporisation**

Water has a high heat of vaporisation. Water absorbs heat as it changes from a liquid to a gas; the human body can dissipate excess heat by the evaporation of its sweat. A leaf can keep cool in the bright sunlight by evaporating water from its surface. Water's high heat conductivity makes possible the even distribution of heat throughout the body.

**Boiling and Freezing**

Pure water at sea level boils at $100°C$ and freezes at $0°C$ but extra energy is needed to push water molecules into the air. This is called latent heat—the heat required to change water from one phase to another. At higher elevations (lower atmospheric pressure) water's boiling temperature decreases. This is why it takes longer to boil and egg at higher altitudes. The temperature does not get high enough to cook the egg properly. If a substance is dissolved in water, then the freezing point is lowered. That is why we spread salt on streets in winter to prevent ice formation. Energy is lost when water freezes. A great deal of heat is released into the environment when liquid water changes to ice. It is lost when the high energy phase of liquid water moves to the low energy phase of ice. Nights when ice freezes often feel warmer than nights when ice melts

**Water density**

Water is most dense at $4^{\circ}$ and then begins to expand again (becoming less dense) as the temperature decreases further. This expansion occurs because its hydrogen bonds become more rigid and ordered. As a result, frozen water (ice floats) upon the denser cold water. The expansion of water takes place even before it actually freezes. This explains why a pond freezes from the surface down, rather than from the bottom up. As water temperature drops, the colder water $(0-4)^{\circ}$ C where it is less dense—rises to the pond surface. It freezes to form a lid of ice. This ice insulates the water below from the wintry chill so that it is less likely to freeze. Organisms that inhabit the pond are able to survive the frigid winter below the icy surface.

**Q17. What are the major sources of water?**

**Ans.** The major sources of water include: rainwater, surface water (stored in lakes, streams, and ponds), and groundwater. The distribution of water, however, is quite varied; many locations have plenty of it while others have very little. Water exists on earth in three forms solid (ice), liquid or gas (water vapour). Oceans, rivers, clouds, and rain, all of which contain water, are in a frequent state of change (surface water evaporates, cloud water precipitates, rainfall infiltrates the ground, etc.). However, the total amount of the earth's water does not change. Owing to glaciers, rivers and groundwater flow.

Water is essential to life. Without it, the biosphere that exists on the surface of the earth would not be possible. The earth is called as the 'water' planet, water's molecular arrangement of water is very simple, two hydrogen atoms to each oxygen atom. One special characteristic of water is its ability to change state very easily under earth conditions. It can be found readily on the planet in all of its three forms, solid, liquid, and gas.

**Q18. Discuss the structure of water.**

**Ans.** To understand the nature of water in soil and plants, we need a mental picture of the water molecule. The water molecule figure below is composed of two hydrogen atoms and one oxygen atom. The water molecule is positively charged on one side and negatively charged on the other and is, thus, a dipole. Two hydrogen atoms each share a pair of electrons with a single oxygen atom. The two hydrogen atoms of the water molecule are separated at an angle of 103 to 106 degrees, measured with the oxygen atom as the apex of the angle and with the two hydrogen protons as points on the angle sides. The electron pairs shared between the oxygen nucleus and the two hydrogen protons only partially screen (neutralise) the positive charge of the protons. The result is that the proton side of the molecule becomes the positive side of the water molecule.

There are two concentrations of negative electricity, one concentration above and one concentration below a plane defined by the two hydrogen protons and the oxygen atom. They are called the lone-pair electrons. One pair is above the plane and one pair is below. These two lone pairs of electrons do not take part directly in bond formation, as do the electrons shared between the hydrogen and oxygen atoms of the water molecule. The electric charge structure of the water molecule resembles a tetrahedron with the oxygen near the center, two of its corners positively charged due to the partially screened protons of the hydrogen, and the remaining two corners

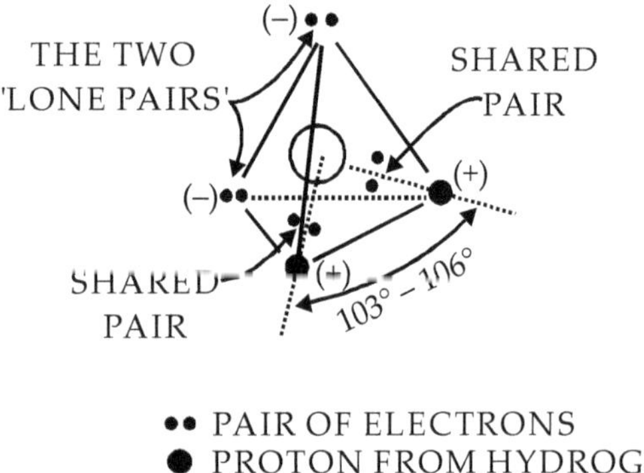


**Fig. 3.1: Tetrahedral charge structure of a water molecule.**

of the tetrahedron negatively charged due to the two pairs of lone-pair electrons. (The word tetrahedron comes from the Late Greek tetraedros, which means four-sided, and is a solid figure with four triangular surfaces.) This arrangement makes the water molecule a dipole, that is, one end of the molecule tends to be positive and the other end tends to be negative. Dipole is a term used in physics and physical chemistry and is anything having two equal but opposite electric charges or magnetic poles, as in a hydrogen atom with its positive nucleus and negative electron.

**Q19. Explain the components of Hydrological Cycle with the help of diagram. Also evaluate the significance of Hydrological Cycle.**

**Ans.** The movement of water on the earth' surface and through the atmosphere is known as the hydrologic cycle. The water cycle is also known as the hydrologic cycle it is the circulation of water within the earth's hydrosphere, involving changes in the physical state of water between liquid, solid, and gas phases. The hydrologic cycle refers to the continuous exchange of water between atmosphere, land, surface and subsurface waters, and organisms.

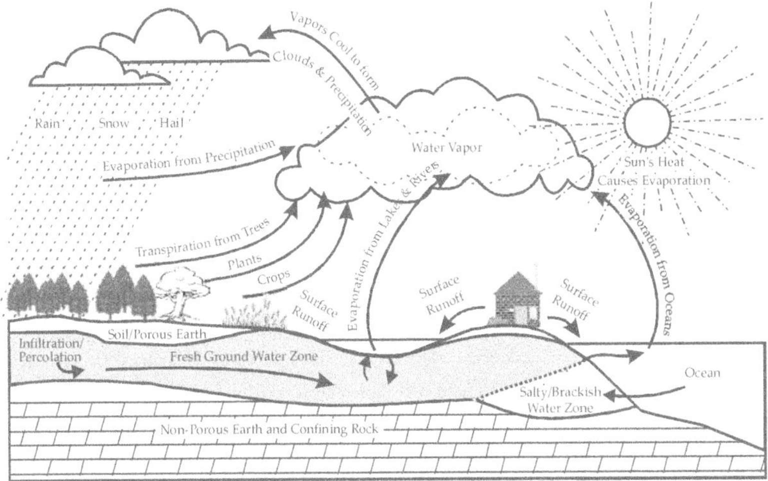


**Fig. 1.12: Hydrological Cycle**

**Evaporation:** It occurs when radiant energy from the sun heats water, causing the water molecules to become so active that some of them rise into the atmosphere as vapour. It is the transfer of water from bodies of surface water into the atmosphere. This transfer entails a change in the physical nature of water from liquid to gaseous phases. Along with evaporation can be counted transpiration from plants. Thus, this transfer is sometimes referred to as evapotranspiration. Evapotranspiration is water *evaporating* from the ground and *transpiration* by plants. Evapotranspiration is also the way water vapour re-enters the atmosphere.

**Precipitation:** In cold air way up in the sky, rain clouds will often form. Rising warm air carries water vapor high into the sky where it cools, forming water droplets around tiny bits of dust in the air. Some vapor freezes into tiny ice crystals, which attract cooled water drops. The drops freeze to the ice crystals, forming larger crystals we call snowflakes. When the snowflakes become heavy, they fall. When the snowflakes meet warmer air on the way down, they melt into raindrops. In tropical climates, cloud droplets combine together around dust or sea salt particles. They bang together and grow in size until they're heavy enough to fall.

**Infiltration:** Infiltration into the ground is the transition from surface water to groundwater. The infiltration rate will depend upon soil or rock permeability as well as other factors. Infiltrating water may reach another compartment known as groundwater (i.e., an aquifer). Groundwater tend to move slowly, so the water may return as surface water after storage within an aquifer for a period of time that can amount to thousands of years in some cases. Water returns to the land surface at lower elevation than where it infiltrated, under the force of gravity or gravity induced pressures.

**Runoff:** Precipitation that reaches the surface of the Earth but does not infiltrate the soil is called runoff. Runoff can also come from melted snow and ice. Also it includes the variety of ways by which land surface water moves down slope to the oceans. Water flowing in streams and rivers may be delayed for a time in lakes. Not all precipitated water returns to the sea as runoff; much of it evaporates before reaching the ocean or reaching an aquifer.

The amount of water that infiltrates the soil varies with the degree of land slope, the amount and type of vegetation, soil type and rock type, and whether the soil is already saturated by water. The more openings in the surface (cracks, pores, joints), the more infiltration occurs. Water that doesn't infiltrate the soil flows on the surface as runoff.

Hence, we can say that the hydrologic cycle is used to model the storage and movement of water between the biosphere, atmosphere, lithosphere and hydrosphere. Water is stored in the following reservoirs: atmosphere, oceans, lakes, rivers, glaciers, soils, snowfields, and groundwater. It moves from one reservoir to another by processes like: evaporation, condensation, precipitation, deposition, runoff, infiltration, sublimation, transpiration, and groundwater flow.

**Q20. Signify adaptation of water in different types of plants and animals.**

**Ans.** Rooted plants with floating leaves: These plants grow on margins and in shallow water bodies. Roots of these hydrophytes are fixed in mud, but leaves have long petioles which keep them floating on the water surface. The remaining parts of the plant except leaves, remain in water. Some of the rooted hydrophytes are Nymphaea, Nelumbo, Trapa, and Marsilea.

- **Submerged floating plants:** These plants remain in contact with only water, being completely submerged in water and are not rooted in the mud. Their stems are long and leaves generally small. Some of the examples are Ceratophyllum and Utricularia.
- **Rooted submerged plants:** These hydrophytes are found completely submerged in water but remain rooted in soil. Hydrilla is one of the examples which is a slender weed with fibrous roots.
- **Rooted emerged plants:** These are plants of shallow waters. These hydrophytes requite excess water but their shoots remain

partly or completely to air. The root system remains completely submerged in water, fixed in soil.

- **Mesophytes:** These plants grow in moist habitats and well-aerated soils. They prefer soil and air of moderate humidity but fail to survive in areas with water-logged soils or over-abundance of salts. In some respects they stand in between the hydrophytes and xerophytes.
- **Xerophytes:** Xerophytes are sometimes loosely defined as 'plants of dry habitats'. But others have defined xerophytes as 'plants which grow on the substratum that usually becomes depleted of water to a depth of at least 2 decimetres during a normal season'. Thus, in arid zones, all plants not confined to the margins of streams of lakes have been considered as xerophytes.

**Adaptation of water in Animals**

Adaptation of water in Animals on osmotic pressure between body fluids of aquatic organisms and their surrounding fluids aquatic organisms have developed osmoregulatory mechanisms to deal with this problem. The salt content to body fluids in freshwater animals is relatively high as compared to the surrounding water medium. Hence, the water tends to diffuse continuously into the body. Extra water from the body needs to be removed frequently. most aquatic animals (e.g. protozoans and fishes) excrete the extra amount of water from the body by osmoregulation. Protozoa employ contractile vacuoles and other multicellular invertebrates and chordates use excretory organs such as nephridia and kidney. In marine animals the situation is just the opposite. The concentration of salts in the body fluids is low as compared to the surrounding medium, (i.e. hypotonic). Under these conditions the body tends to lose water. But through metabolic osmoregulation water is retained in the body and salt is excreted. Animals vary widely in their salinity tolerance. Organisms which have a narrow tolerance and cannot withstand salinity fluctuation are called stenohaline. Organisms which can survive under a wider range of salinity conditions are termed euryhaline. Usually animals inhabiting cooler fresh water and marine environments tend to have large body size except in a few cases such as diatoms and sea urchins which have relatively larger sizes in warmer waters.

Some examples of these adaptations are as follows:

- Streamlined body reduces friction when the animal moves through the water.
- Smooth, almost furless body helps aquatic mammals move through the water with little friction.
- Dense fur helps streamline the bodies of some aquatic mammals and keeps them warm.

- Dense waterproof feathers keep cold water away from bird's skin and prevent wetting of the feathers.
- Webbed feet, formed from thin skin between the toes, work like paddles.
- Long legs and necks keep the bodies of wading birds out of the water and are thin, light, and easy to move, and the long neck helps the birds to reach the water, or below it, for food.
- Strainers in the mouth filter food particles from the water.
- Flippers provide a large surface for pushing against water and act like paddles.
- Eyes positioned on top of the head allow animals to hide almost fully submerged in water and still detect predators or prey above the water.
- Nostrils positioned near the top of the head allow animals to come to the surface to breathe while only a small part of the body can be seen.
- Nostrils close when the animal goes under the water.
- Blubber, a thick layer of fat or oil stored between the skin and muscles of the body, provides insulation.
- Transparent eyelids cover the eyes of animals swimming underwater.
- Flattened tails serve as paddles.

**Q21. Describe the history and development of soil.**

**Ans.** From the time immemorial, the soil or the earth has been recognised as the mother of us all-plants, animals and man. Soil receives at last there discarded forms. It is imperishable store house of eternity. Dokuchayev a Russian worker writes, 'by soil one should mean the day or externals horizons of rocks (whatever rocks) modified naturally by the combined influence of water, air and various kinds of organisms, living and dead.

Today, almost all areas of the earth's land surface are covered with a thin mantle of soil that varies in thickness from a few centimeters to several meters. But this condition was not always so. At one time in the history of the earth, there was no soil. To gain a better appreciation of soil and its importance to the terrestrial environment it would be worthwhile to discuss here the process through which soil was formed and is still being formed. How soil first appeared we must go back in time a few billion years-to that point in the development of the earth when most volcanic activity has ceased and there was a gradual cooling of the surface. During this period the surface of the earth was a consolidated mass of volcanic rock. This rock took various forms such as lava, basalt and granite.

Through millions upon millions of years the exposed rock surfaces were acted upon by various weathering agents. The action of water and wind upon the rock caused it slowly to disintegrate. Chemical reactions occurred to form acids and alkalies. These agents began to eat away the surface of the rocks. Millions of years later, after the earth had cooled and the weathering process had proceeded, small fissures and crannies appeared in the surface of the rocks that held small amounts of water. The tiny openings provided footholds for the earliest and most primitive of plants-bacteria, algae, fungi and lichens. This early plant life aided in the breakdown of the original rock material through further chemical action that disintegrate the rock and released chemical nutrients which were, in turn, required by the plants. Secondly, dead plants material combined with the fragmented rocks to form the first primitive soil.

During this period another process was taking place in the vast seas that covered most of the earth's surface. Aquatic plants, especially algae, were extracting calcium compounds from water. Over millions of years the insoluble calcium, precipitated by plant processes, settled slowly to the bottom of the seas, layer upon layer, until the weight of the upper layer so compacted the lower layer that beds of lime-stone were formed. While all this was going on, the earth's surface was buckling and heaving, and portions once below the seas rose above them to form dry lands. The combination of physical, chemical and biological activity though the years served to disintegrate the surface of the original rock material and produce the beginning of that thin unconsolidated mass of material the we know as soil.

As soil layers developed and became deeper, they formed a base for more advanced kinds of plants life. Early relatives of such plants as the ferns and mosses formed a suitable environment in which to develop. These plants continued the process of biological weathering, as their fibrous roots penetrated into the surface of the soil and into the many porous openings into the rocks. Expansion and contraction water within the fissures developed down of rock surfaces. As the plants went though their yearly and life cycle of growth, death and decay, organic material was added to the primitive soil and thus paved the way for the coming of the higher plants-grasses, herbs, shrubs and trees-the forms dominant in our landscape today.

All these processes that have proceeded for such a long time in the history of the earth are still going on. Visitors to the high peaks in the Chambla Command Area, and other igneous rocks can observe lichens clinging tenaciously to exposed rock surfaces. These simple plants today are duplicating the activities which took place hundreds of millions of years ago in forming soil.

Once the higher plants became established on the land, soil formation became more rapid. The larger plants are very productive, producing countless tons or organic matter that added to the soil, has built up what we recognise as top soil.

**Q22. Write down the process of soil formation.**

**Ans.** Soil formation could be regarded as two major steps:

- The accumulation of the parent material
- The differentiation of the horizons within the soil profile by soil-forming processes, which can be categorised as:

**(1) Additions**

- Dissolved ions and dust via precipitation ($H_2O$)
- Organic residues from above and below ground
- Nitrogen fixation
- Solar energy

**(2) Removals or Losses**

- Volatilisation of nitrogen and Carbon
- Leaching of dissolved ions, nitrates
- Surface erosion of SOM and colloidal materials

**(3) Transfers or translocations of materials**

- Internal movement of dissolved ions, salts, organic matter, carbon, clays and calcium carbonates

**(4) Transformations**

- Organic matter into organic colloids (humus), primary minerals into secondary ones and release of nutrients compounds and salts, buffering capacity.
- Transformation process includes:
  (a) Hydrolysis
  (b) Hydration
  (c) Oxidation/reduction
  (d) Carbonation
  (e) Dissolution
  (f) Complexation (chelation)

All processes are active to some degree in all soils. The balance between the combination of processes determines the ultimate nature of the soil profile.

**Q23. What are the factors that affect soil formation?**

**Ans.** There are various factors that affect formation of soil may briefly be understood by consideration of each one of them:

The effect of various factors which operate in the formation of soil may briefly be understood by consideration of each one of them:

**(1) Parent material**

The nature of the parent material generally affects the rate of soil profile development as well as the texture and nutrient content. The parent material is the product of the bed-rock and if it consists of a mixture of clay, silt and gravel, and the soil type that develops from such a parent material will be fine textured and fertile loam. If the parent material consists of quartz and sand the soil type will be coarce textured infertile sand. The parent material influences broadly physical and chemical properties of the soil.

**(2) Climate**

Soil are the residual products of the action of meteorological agencies upon rocks, and so there should exist an intimate relation between the soil of a region and the climatic conditions that prevail. The effect of climate on soil formation are direct because the climate effects the weathering of rocks, and also indirect because the climate effects plant and animal life. The moisture relations of the soil are partly a function of the climate, for example, soil developed in humid climates are subjected to intense leaching and will have profiles different from those developed in arid zones. The influences of temperature upon soil formation are primarily on the rate of weathering of rocks and soil minerals.

**(3) Living Organisms**

The effect of living organisms of on soil formation is remarkable. The plant alter the micro-climate, their residue are incorporated into the mineral body. They transfer the elements from the lower to the upper horizons. The vegetation favours soil development by diminishing erosion. Different types of vegetation effect soil development differently. In the view of differences in their size or life-form, depth of rooting and physiological behaviour, they contribute the organic remains of the soil, for example, the roots of annuals which remain in the soil, or the organic matter supplied by the forest trees in the form of falling leaf on the surface of the soil. Deep rooted species contribute more to the soil development while the shallow rooted ones less because the deep roots help in weathering of the parent material in the lower layers and absorb nutrient elements which are subsequently retained to the soil surface in leaf fall. The micro-organisms also help in rock weathering and in the decomposition of organic matter. Many of the chemical processes in the soil are directly or indirectly due to the activity of fungi and bacteria.

**(4) Topography**

The effect of topography on soil development is mainly through its effect on water relation, erosion, temperature relations and vegetation cover. The rainfall on the soil always tends to rung along the slopes and collect in depressions, as a result soil on steep slopes receive more water than those in the flat areas. The soil that are developed from the slopes are therefore characterised by reduced amount of water entering the soil. The process or erosion is also maximum on the slopes and therefore the soil remains in the youthful state of development.

**(5) Time**

The length of time required for soil development depends upon the different factors which contributes to the soil formation.

**Q24. Write down the physical and chemical properties of soil.**

*Or*

**Differentiate between Residual and Transported soils.**

**[Dec-2010, Q.No.-2(d)]**

*Or*

**What are the types of soil water? Describe each in one or two lines.**

**[Dec-2011, Q.No.-6(a)]**

*Or*

**Describe the physical properties of soil. [Dec-2012, Q.No.-6(b)]**

**Ans.** The proper use of soil is determined by its physical and chemical properties, which determine the flow, storage, type of chemical compound and exhibits of water, the movement of air and the ability of the soil to supply nutrients to plants.

**Physical Properties of Soil**

The common physical properties of the soil are profile, skeleton, porosity, colour, permeability, moisture holding capacity, surface drainage, erosion, etc.

- ***Soil profile:*** A vertical section through soil body usually shows a number of layers of horizons of varying thickness. These horizons in natural sequence are collectively called as 'soil profile'. Unfortunately, there is no universally accepted system of horizon designation. The upper part of the profile may be designated as 'A' horizon' the middle part 'B' horizon, and the consolidated material that has been affected very little by the plant root as 'C' horizon. Subscript such as 0,1,2,3,4 are use to denote the sub-divisions of A, B, and C horizons.
- ***Soil skeleton:*** The soil horizons are heterogeneous systems, made up of materials in three different states-solid, liquid and gases. Proper proportions of these constituents are necessary for the soil to be a good medium for plant growth. The solid part of the soil consisting of both organic and inorganic matter forms the skeleton. The air and water fill the intervening spaces. The inorganic part of the soil is made up of particles ranging in size from that soil is made up of particles ranging in size from that of fine clay to large rocks.
- ***Soil Texture:*** Texture has been fieldman's term for how a soil feels or how it behaves under cultivation. Soil texture relate to the relative proportion of sand, silt and clay that are present in the soil. A large amount of sand in the soil make it coarse and light. If silt is present in large amount, the soil is medium textured. While a large amount of clay in the soil makes it sticky when wet and hard when dry, such a soil is heavy.
- ***Soil Classification:*** There are several systems of soil classification. On the basis of the mode of their formation,

particularly the nature of the origin of mineral matter soils are sometimes classified as (i) Residual soils, and (ii) Transported soils.

- **Residual soils** are those in which the whole process of soil formation, that is, weathering and pedogenesis occurs at the same place. These are also called sedentary soils.

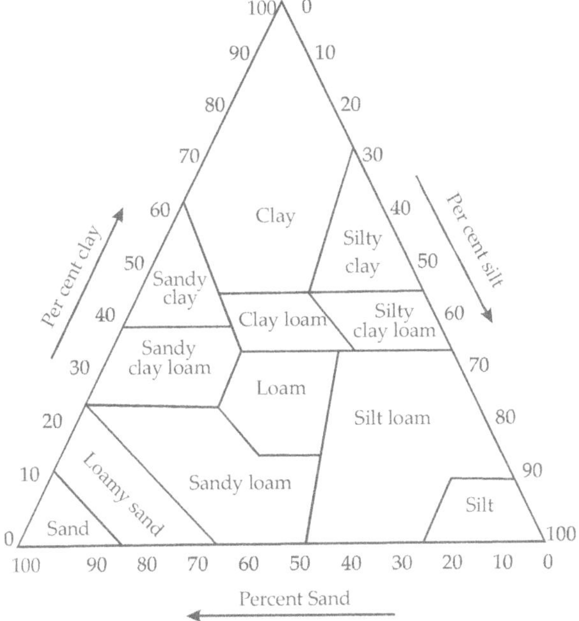


**Fig. 1.13: Classification of Soil Texture**

- **Transported soils** are those where the weathered material is taken away at other places. This is at these different places, where, through pedogenesis, soil formation in completed. The weathered matter may be taken away to other places by several agents. Depending upon the nature of these transporting agents, the transported soils mat be:
  - Celluvial (by gravity)
  - Alluvual (by running waters)
  - Glacial (by glaciers)
  - Eolin (by wind)
- ***Porosity:*** The total porosity or pore space, of a soil is dependent upon both its size distribution and structure. In terms of total porosity clay soil are more porous than sandy soil. The pores are, however, so small that in the absence of structural development or aggregation, there is essentially no movement of water or air into or through the soil. If the soil is too porous

water moves through too freely. On the other hand, heavy clay soils may hold much water that is not available for plant growth.

- *Colour:* Soil colour is mainly due to the presence of iron and manganese compounds and the organic matter in soil. Organic matter makes soil black, brown on grey. Iron and manganese oxides impart red, brown and yellow colours to soil depending on the oxidation status and extent of hydration of these compounds. Red, yellow or reddish brown colours are produced by well oxidised salts of the above metals. Sometimes the colour is used as an indication of soil drainage. Well and moderately well drained soils have generally a uniform brown colour when moist but in some cases it may be various shades of red or yellow. A pale or grey soil denotes poor drainage for long periods. A black soil usually indicates that the land is either rich in organic matter has remained wet for long periods. A preponderance of quartz particles makes soil grey of whitish. Mica particles produce glittering appearance.
- *Permeability:* Permeability refers to the ease of movement of water and air through soil. Sandy or gravelly soils have rapid permeability, loam soils have moderate permeability and the clay soils are slowly permeable.
- *Moisture Holding Capacity or soil water:* This refers to the amount of water that can be stored by a soil for use by plants. Water, the earth's most abundant compound is a vital constituent in all living matter. It is highly mobile liquid and can exist in three physical states-solid, liquid and gas. Hence, it may be considered as the life blood of the earth. There are three main types of soil gravitational water, capillary water, and hygroscopic water.

  When water reaches a soil profile, it percolates down to the bed rock as gravitational water. Some water is retained by the soil particles due to adhesion -**hygroscopic water**. Hygroscopic water content has been defined as the moisture that an initially dry soil will adsorb when brought into equilibrium with an atmosphere of 50 per cent relative humidity at 20°C. Some amount of water is retained by the soil particles due to cohesive forces - **capillary water**. Capillary water is an important source of water for plants. This water is held by a force of 1/3 atmosphere. Water retaining capacity of soil at 1/3 atmosphere is known as the field capacity of soil. In general the coarser the soil, the lower is the moisture holding capacity. Black soils in India have higher moisture holding capacity than the red soils.
- *Surface Drainage:* Surface drainage is the relative rate of removal of water which is in excess of the amount that can be absorbed by the soil. If water is removed so slowly that the soil remains

wet for a long time, the surface drainage is poor. It is fair if water is removed at such a rate that soils do not remain wet for a long period.

**Chemical Properties of Soils**

Soils is a mixture of various inorganic and organic chemical compounds and exhibits certain significant chemical properties:

- ***Inorganic Components of Soil:*** The chief inorganic components of soil are the compounds of Aluminium, Silica, Calcium, Magnesium, Iron, Potassium and Sodium. Soil also contains smaller amounts of compounds of Boron, Manganese, Copper, Zink, Molybdenum, Cobalt, Iodine, etc. Most of these inorganic salts exists in soil in the form of weak solution. Soil solution may contain complex mixtures of minerals as carbohydrates, sulphates, nitrates, chlorodes and also organic salts. The chemical nature of the nutrients solution depends upon the nature of the parent matter though which water has percolated and climatic conditions of the region. For example, temperate soils with high rainfall has hydrogen ions in abundance, due to which leaching of basic nutrients like calcium, Magnesium, and Potassium occurs and fertility of soil is greatly reduced. The fertility of a soil depends upon the amount of plant nutrients that it possesses and their availability to the plant.

  Phosphorus is the vehicle of life. It is derived from rocks, leaf and other organic deposits. If deficient, it effects germination, but when in excess it hastens maturity.

  Potassium is found combined with silicates, chlorides, nitrates, etc. It prolongs the growing season of the plant and stimulates starch formation in crops like potato.

  Calcium is normally found in the form of calcium carbonate and as oxide and hydroxide. It neutralises the soil and makes plant food readily available to the plant. It also helps in building up the structure of the soil.

  Copper, zink, molybdenum, etc. are present in the soils in micro quantities, and are known as trace elements. In the absence of them, plants suffer from deficiency diseases. Application of even very small dose of these micronutrients cures the disease and promotes a healthy plant growth.

- ***Organic Components of Soil:*** The chief organic component of soil is humus, which chemically contains amino acids, proteins, purines, pyrimidines, aromatic compounds, hexose sugars, sugar alcohols, methyl sugars, fats, oils, waxes, resins, tannins, lignins and some pigments. Further humus is a dark coloured, odourless, homogeneous complex substance.

**Q25. How does soil biota help in maintaining the soil fertility?**

**[Dec-2010, Q.No.-4(b)]**

**Ans.** Soil biota constantly adds organic matter in various forms to the soil. Different kinds of soil organisms carry out sequential reactions to breakdown the organic matter into its component simpler forms, so that they can be reused by plants and other organisms. Many soil organisms produce growth promoting substances that influence the growth of several other microorganisms in their activity, which in turn through their activities improve the soil. Numerous kinds of bacteria and blue green algae in soil fix atmospheric nitrogen by converting it into organic nitrogen. Due to the burrowing activities of various animals, the soils are constantly upturned and mixed, this increases their aeration and drainage. Organisms like bacteria, blue green algae, etc. also improve the aggregate structure of the soil. Death and decay of soil organisms is a source of organic matter in soil.

**Q26. Briefly explain the following terms:**

**(i) Aeolian Soil**

**Ans.** Aeolian type of soil that is transported from one place to another by the wind. It deposited materials that consist primarily of sand or silt-sized particles. These materials tend to be extremely well sorted and free of coarse fragments. Some rounding and frosting of mineral grains is detectable. Loess and dunes are examples of aeolian soils.

Loess is a material finer than sand. It can be transported and deposited by wind to great distances. Loess soils have neutral pH, well-balanced content of clay and organic matter, and are rich in plant nutrients. They possess a high nutrient storage capacity and are, therefore, productive.

Loess soils, which are mostly silt, have unique properties. For instance, they (a) are open and porous, (b) have vertical cuts more stable than the slopes, and (c) can have problems (like the formation of sinkholes, cavities and subsurface channel cutting) when used for earthen dams. There are large areas of loess in countries like Argentina, China, Germany and the United States.

**(ii) Alluvial Soil**

**Ans.** Alluvial soil is formed by accumulated sediments transferred by the rivers and rapids, thus, it is amongst the most fertile soils. It is a fine-grained fertile soil deposited in river beds or by water flowing over flood plains. They generally lack humus and nitrogen. Alluvial soil is composed of alluvium deposits by the rivers, when they slowly lose their carrying capacity due to decrease in velocity. While slowing down, a river loses its potential to hold the large soil particles in a suspended state and these particles thus settle down on the riverbed. Further slowing down in the speed of the river enables smaller particles in the water to settle.

Two types of alluvium are generally found throughout the Indo-Gangetic plain, namely Khadar, consistent in texture and rather fertile, and Bhangar, which consists of alkaline.

Alluvial soil is found mostly in the plains, like Assam, Gujarat, Madhya Pradesh, Punjab, Orissa and Tamil Nadu. Alluvial soil is predominant in the valleys of Narmada, along Mahanadi, Tapti, Cauvery and Godawari, etc.

**(iii) Brackish Water**

**Ans.** Brackish water is a mixture of salt and fresh water mixed together. It is saltier than fresh water, but not as salty as seawater. It may result from mixing of seawater with fresh water, as in estuaries, or it may occur in brackish fossil aquifers. The word comes from the Middle Dutch root "brak," meaning "salten" or "salty". Certain human activities can produce brackish water, in particular certain civil engineering projects such as dikes and the flooding of coastal marshland to produce brackish water pools for freshwater prawn farming. Brackish water is also the primary waste product of the salinity gradient power process. Because brackish water is hostile to the growth of most terrestrial plant species, without appropriate management it is damaging to the environment.

Technically, brackish water contains between 0.5 and 30 grams of salt per litre—more often expressed as 0.5 to 30 parts per thousand (ppt or ‰). Thus, brackish covers a range of salinity regimes and is not considered a precisely defined condition. It is characteristic of many brackish surface waters that their salinity can vary considerably over space and/or time.

**(iv) Colluvial Soil**

**Ans.** Colluvial soils are considered to be the direct result of accelerated soil erosion, resulting in accumulation of humus-rich soil material in terrain depressions and base parts of slopes. The organic carbon concentration in these soils and their depth make them an important organic carbon storage. Mapping the Colluvial soils, therefore, represents an important contribution in total carbon stock estimation. A method of delineating Colluvial soils is proposed by applying a combination of high resolution digital elevation model analysis and detailed field survey. Two models based on fuzzy classification of soil units were created using different topographic derivatives as the only input parameters to predict the Colluvial soil area on a morphologically diverse study site in the Southern Moravia, Czech Republic. The model that considers only the derivatives with a strong relationship to Colluvial soil occurrence reached 71 per cent accuracy in Colluvial area delineation, while the model combining six commonly used derivatives showed less favourable results. The main advantage of the method lies in a low demand of input soil data and its relatively high accuracy.

**(v) Glacial Soil**

**Ans.** Glacial are the soils, which are formed by grinding action of ice snow. Moving, heavy ice-masses and glaciers push before them gather within themselves large amounts of unconsolidated surface material. They also scoop up rock fragments, which further scrape the surface.

Sharp corners and edges of the even the hardest rock fragments are ground smooth by this abrasive action. Glacial soils are found in Dehradun region and parts of Kashmir.

This soil was encountered beneath the granular fill at the landside portions of the alignment on Staten Island and Brooklyn. Glacial soil typically consists of dense to very dense, fine to coarse and fine to medium SAND with variable amounts of silt and gravel. Occasional layers of stiff to hard, fine-grained soils consisting primarily of SILT with little to some sand and variable amount of gravel were also encountered in the glacial soils.

**(vi) Drought**

**Ans.** Droughts are the resultant of acute water shortage due to lack of rains over extended periods of time affecting various human activities and lead to problems like widespread crop failure, unreplenished ground water resources, depletion in lakes/reservoirs, shortage of drinking water and, reduced fodder availability, etc. Often a region adopts itself to a certain level of water shortage based on the long-term climatic conditions experienced by it. Any negative departure from these levels creates conditions of drought, depending on the intensity and duration of this deficit. Thus drought conditions differ from region to region. Also the impact of drought over a region varies depending on which economic activity is impaired. Because drought affects many economic and social sectors, scores of definitions have been developed by a variety of disciplines and the approaches taken to define it also reflect regional and ideological variations.

**(vii) Fresh Water**

**Ans.** Freshwater is defined as having a low salt concentration — usually less than 1 per cent. Approximately 97 per cent of the water found on Earth is saltwater leaving around 3 per cent of Earth's water as freshwater. Of this, 70 per cent is in the form of ice in glaciers, ice caps and as permanent snow. The remaining useable freshwater is in the form of lakes, ponds, rivers, streams, and general wet "boggy" areas. Lakes, ponds and bogs are generally stationary (lentic) bodies of water, although bogs can be a source of rivers and streams, which are moving (lotic) bodies of water. Pollution and waste due to industrial exploitation and overpopulation are a serious threat to our freshwater resources. Residential, commercial and industrial premises are often concentrated near waterways, lakes and rivers.

**(viii) Ground Water**

**Ans.** Groundwater is water that is found underground in the cracks and spaces in soil, sand and rock. Groundwater is stored in--and moves slowly through--layers of soil, sand and rocks called aquifers. Aquifers typically consist of gravel, sand, sandstone, or fractured rock, like limestone. These materials are permeable because they have large connected spaces that allow water to flow through. The speed at which groundwater flows depends on the size of the spaces in the soil or rock and how well the spaces are connected.

The area where water fills the aquifer is called the saturated zone (or saturation zone). The top of this zone is called the water table. The water table may be located only a foot below the ground's surface or it can sit hundreds of feet down.

Groundwater can be found almost everywhere. The water table may be deep or shallow; and may rise or fall depending on many factors. Heavy rains or melting snow may cause the water table to rise, or heavy pumping of groundwater supplies may cause the water table to fall.

Water in aquifers is brought to the surface naturally through a spring or can be discharged into lakes and streams. Groundwater can also be extracted through a well drilled into the aquifer. A well is a pipe in the ground that fills with groundwater. This water can be brought to the surface by a pump. Shallow wells may go dry if the water table falls below the bottom of the well. Some wells, called artesian wells, do not need a pump because of natural pressures that force the water up and out of the well.

Groundwater supplies are replenished, or recharged, by rain and snow melt.

In some areas of the world, people face serious water shortages because groundwater is used faster than it is naturally replenished. In other areas groundwater is polluted by human activities.

In areas where material above the aquifer is permeable, pollutants can readily sink into groundwater supplies. Groundwater can be polluted by landfills, septic tanks, leaky underground gas tanks, and from overuse of fertilisers and pesticides. If groundwater becomes polluted, it will no longer be safe to drink.

**(ix) Marine Water**

**Ans.** The term "marine" is most frequently associated with seas and oceans. It may thus reflect water that contains high salt concentration like as in seas and oceans. Marine portrays a deeper sense; much deeper than sea or ocean. A mere sea is a large stretch of salty water, but marine environment comprises the sea water fishes and other organisms that thrive in the depths of the water, totally lacking the warm touch of the sun.

Marine waters cover two-thirds of the surface of the Earth. Such places are considered ecosystems because the plant life supports the animal life and vice-versa.

**(x) Monsoon**

**Ans.** A monsoon is a seasonal shift in the prevailing wind direction that usually brings with it a different kind of weather. It almost always refers to the Asian monsoon, a large region extending from India to Southeast Asia where monsoon conditions prevail.

During the winter monsoon, a persistent and large high pressure zone over Asia drives cool, dry air outward towards the tropics. This provides the monsoon region with its dry season.

Then during May and June of each year, the summer monsoon arrives with persistent southerly wind flow driven by a warm air mass with low pressure at the surface that forms over southern Asia as it is warmed by the sun. Air from the relatively higher pressure air mass over the Indian and tropical western Pacific Ocean flows northward towards the low pressure over land, bring with it torrential rains. A late arrival of the monsoon can be bad for agriculture, as the monsoon rains are necessary for summer crops.

In India, for example, the dry northerly wind flow over India changes direction, and warm humid air from the Indian Ocean flows from the south, gradually overspreading the Indian subcontinent. Widespread torrential rains, and even severe thunderstorms, large hail and tornadoes can accompany the onset (arrival) of the summer monsoon.

The Indian Ocean version of the hurricane, which is traditionally called a "cyclone" in the Indian Ocean, can also form and move ashore in association with the onset of the monsoon. These cyclones have at times killed many thousands of poor people who live in the low-lying areas along the eastern coast of India and Bangladesh.

**(xi) Water Logging**

**Ans.** Water logging occurs whenever the soil is so wet that there is insufficient oxygen in the pore space for plant roots to be able to adequately respire. Other gases detrimental to root growth, such as carbon dioxide and ethylene, also accumulate in the root zone and affect the plants.

Plants differ in their demand for oxygen. There is no universal level of soil oxygen that can identify waterlogged conditions for all plants. In addition, a plant's demand for oxygen in its root zone will vary with its stage of growth.

✍✍✍

# Ecosystem: Functioning, Types

## An Overview

A biotic community lives in an environment, which provides material, energy requirement and other living conditions to it. The biotic community together with the physical environment forms an interacting system called ecosystem. The term ecosystem was introduced by Sir Arthur Transely (1935).

An ecosystem can be defined 'as a structural and functional unit of biosphere or segment of nature consisting of community of living beings and the physical environment both interacting and exchanging materials between them'. In an ecosystem, the biotic communities and abiotic environment influence each other. This relationship is called holocoenosis.

An ecosystem may be natural (e.g. lake, forest, grassland, etc.) or man-made (e.g. an aquaria, crop field, etc.), temporary (e.g. grassland, forest, etc.). The aquatic ecosystems can be either fresh water (e.g. ponds, lakes, streams), or salt-water (e.g. marine, estuaries) type. An ecosystem may be small as drop of pond water. Such a small ecosystem is called micro ecosystem. It may be as large as as an ocean. Ecosystems are so varied in form and structure, that whatever has a distinct community of its own, can be called an ecosystem, e.g. a crop field, part, laboratory culture, grassland, etc.

Human activities may modify or convert natural ecosystem into man-made or anthropogenic ecosystems. Cutting forests and the conversion of land for tree plantations or agricultural systems, construction of dam often resulting into submergence of forests and formation of water reservoirs are some examples of conversion of natural ecosystem into man-made ecosystem. Spacecrafts and aquariums may also be considered as manmade ecosystem.

**Q1. Why consider ecosystem as a unit of nature?**

**Ans.** The concept of ecosystem was put forth by A.G. Tansley (1935). Transley viewed the ecosystem as a "unit of nature", but not one with boundaries. Like a solar system, a planet, an individual organic molecule, or an atom, it was a system isolated mentally by scientists for the purpose of study. In reality, ecosystem overlapped, interlocked, and interacted with one another. Transley denounced the drawing of a line between so called natural biotic communities and areas under the influence of human activity.

An ecosystem can be visualised as a functional unit of nature representing complex interactions between living and non-living components. The study of any ecosystem involves systematic description of the components and understanding of the close relationship between the biotic and the abiotic components. If one wishes to study the various aspects of relationships of living and non-living components of the environment. It would be easy to understand and interpret these relationships in a smaller component of the biosphere, that is the ecosystem.

Ecosystems are conceptual models and these models can be applied at any scale, from a bowl of water to the whole earth. Ecosystems represent enormous contrast in size and complexity. For the purpose of study, an ecosystem can be delineated in almost any way convenient to the interest of the investigator. In the case of some ecosystems such a lake, river or pond, distinct boundaries can be recognised but in the case of other ecosystems, such as a grassland, forest, village or town, boundaries are not so sharp however, they can be delineated according to the object of study or any other practical consideration.

**Q2. What is the limiting factor in most terrestrial ecosystems?**

**Ans.** An aquatic community has several unique characteristics. The aquatic community operated under the same ecologic principles as terrestrial ecosystems, but the physical structure of the community is more isolated and exhibits limiting factors that are very different from the limiting factors of a terrestrial ecosystem.

Certain materials and conditions are necessary for the growth and reproduction of organisms. If, for instance, a farmer plants wheat in a field containing too little nitrogen, it will stop growing when it has used up the available nitrogen, even if the wheat's requirements for oxygen, water, potassium, and other nutrients are met. In this particular case, nitrogen, is said to be the limiting factor.

A limiting factor is a condition or a substance (the resourced in shortest supply) that limits the presence and success of an organism or a group of organisms in an area.

The limiting factor in most of the terrestrial ecosystem is water, which governs the growth, establishment and ability of the ecosystem.

The common physical limiting factors in freshwater ecology include the following:

- Temperature
- Light
- Turbidity
- Dissolved atmospheric gases, especially oxygen
- Biogenic salts in macro and micronutrient forms
    - Macronutrients, such as nitrogen, phosphorus, potassium, calcium, and sulfur
    - Micronutrients such as iron, copper, zinc, chlorine, and sodium
- Water movement-stream currents, especially rapids

**Q3. Describe the concept of trophic level.**

**Ans.** In order analyse the intricate co-actions involved in the food web and balance of nature, it is desirable to simplify the relationship into nutritional or trophic levels. The lowest level is composed of photosynthetic plants that are able to use solar energy for manufacturer of food. They are producers. The herbivores or primary consumers form the second level; the smaller carnivores, or secondary consumers are at the third level; and the large carnivores or tertiary consumers at the fourth level. Occasionally, there may be quaternary consumers. The terms 'producers' for plants and 'consumers' for animals are used and the essential relationship is understood.

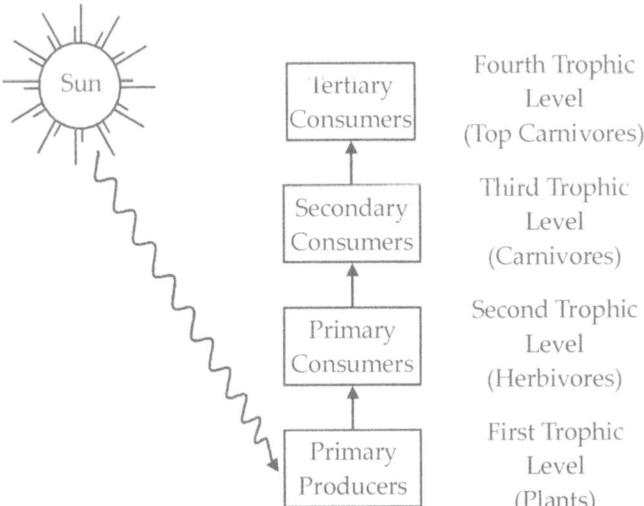


**Fig. 2.1: Diagrammatic presentation of trophic levels in an ecosystem**

The study of trophic level gives us an idea about the energy transformation in an ecosystem. It provides a useful conceptual basis to include all organisms that share the same general mode of feeding into one group and they together are said to belong to the same trophic level. This feeding level concept implies that organisms obtain food through the same number of steps from the producer.

**Q4. What do you understand by ecological pyramids? Discuss the several types of ecological pyramid.**

*Or*

**Differentiate between Pyramid of numbers and biomass.**
**[Dec-2010, Q.No-2(a)]**

*Or*

**Why does pyramid of biomass in some aquatic ecosystems acquire on inverted shape? [June-2012, Q.No.-10(a)]**

**Ans.** An ecological pyramid is a graphical representation designed to show the number of organisms, energy relationships, and biomass of an ecosystem. They are also called Eltonian pyramids after Charles Elton, who developed the concept of ecological pyramids. Producer organisms (usually green plants) form the base of the pyramid, with succeeding levels above representing the different trophic levels (respective position of the organisms within ecological food chains). Succeeding levels in the pyramid represent the dependence of the organisms at a given level on the organisms at lower level.

There are three types of pyramids:

**(1) Pyramid of Biomass**

Biomass is renewable organic (living) material. A pyramid of biomass is a representation of the amount of energy contained in biomass, at different trophic levels for a particular time. It is measured in grams per metre square. This demonstrates the amount of matter lost between trophic levels. Each level is dependent on its lower level for energy, hence the lower level determines how much energy will be available to the upper level. Also, energy is lost in transfer so the amount of energy is less higher up the pyramid.

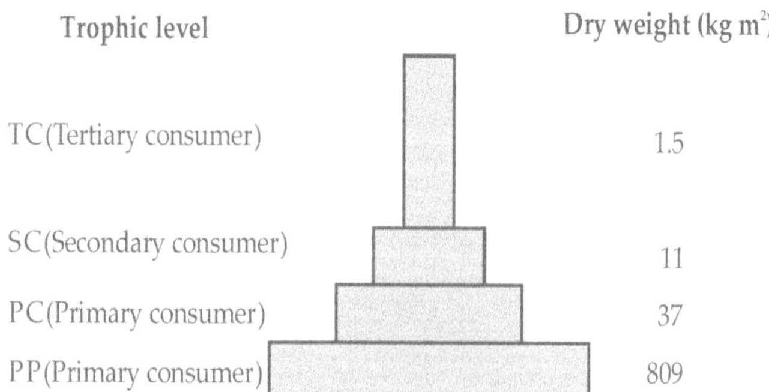


**Fig. 2.2: Pyramid of biomass shows a sharp decrease in biomass at higher trophic levels**

There are two types of biomass pyramids: upright and inverted. An upright pyramid is one where the combined weight of producers is larger than the combined weight of consumers. An example is a forest ecosystem. An inverted pyramid is one where the combined weight of producers is smaller than the combined weight of consumers. An example is an aquatic ecosystem.

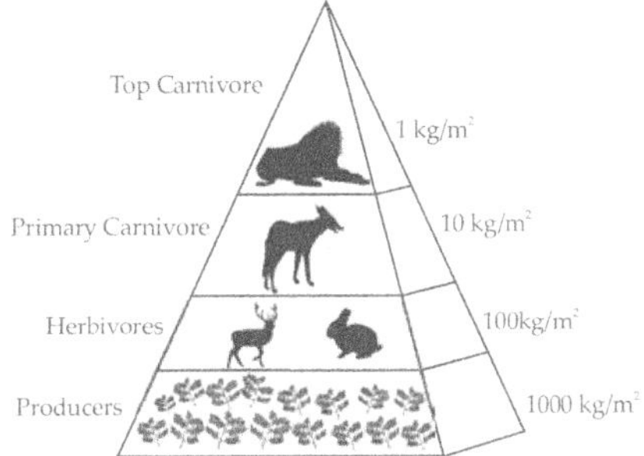


**Fig. 2.3: Upright Pyramid of biomass in a Terrestrial Ecosystem**

Pyramid of biomass in some aquatic ecosystems acquire on inverted shape. In lakes and oceans, the producers are the aquatic plants and algae which are short lived and less in number. The higher trophic levels are occupied by big fishes which are larger than number and also live long. There, the pyramid of biomass is inverted for aquatic ecosystem.

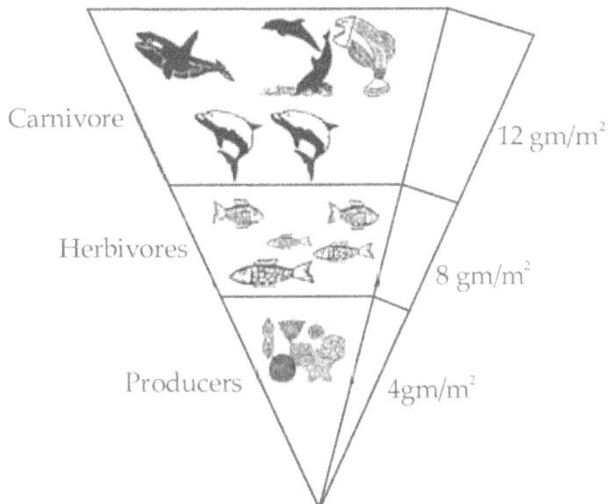


**Fig. 2.4: Inverted Pyramid in an Aquatic Ecosystem**

## (2) Pyramid of Numbers

The pyramid of numbers represents the number of organisms in each trophic level. This pyramid consists of a plot of relationships between the number herbivores (primary consumers), first level carnivore (secondary consumers), second level carnivore (tertiary consumers) and so forth. This shape varies from ecosystem to ecosystem because the number of organisms at each level is variable.

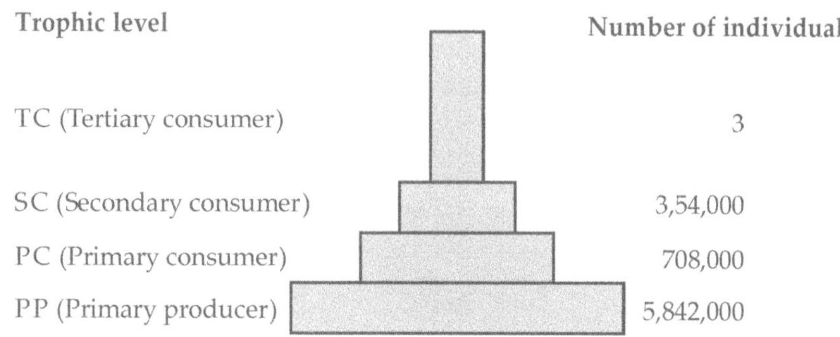


**Fig. 2.5: Pyramid of Numbers in a grassland ecosystem**

Upright, partly upright and inverted are the three types of pyramids of numbers. An aquatic ecosystem is an example of upright pyramid where the number of organisms becomes fewer and fewer higher up in the pyramid. A forest ecosystem is an example of a partially upright pyramid, as fewer producers support more primary consumers, but there are less secondary and tertiary consumers. An inverted pyramid of numbers is one where the number of organisms depending on the lower levels grows closer towards the apex. A parasitic food chain is an example.

**(3) Pyramid of Energy**

The pyramid of energy represents the total amount of energy consumed by each trophic level. An energy pyramid is always upright as the total amount of energy available for utilisation in the layers above is less than the energy available in the lower levels. This happens because during energy transfer from lower to higher levels, some energy is always lost. Pyramid of energy is always upright, can never be inverted, because when energy flows from a particular trophic level to the next, some energy is always lost as heat at each step.

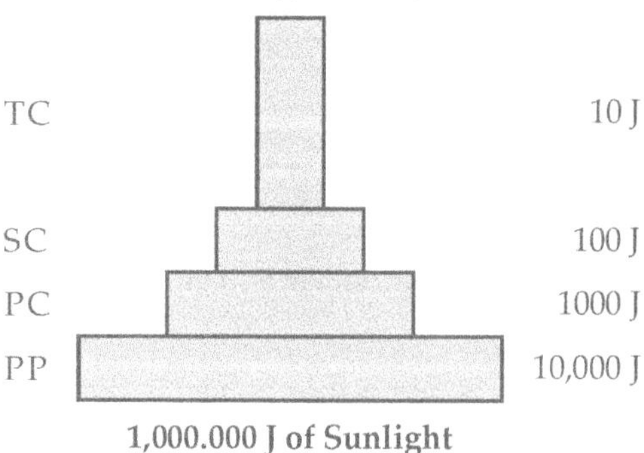


**Fig. 2.6: An ideal pyramid of energy**

**Q5. What are the limitations of ecological pyramids?**

**[June-2012, Q.No.-10(b)]**

**Ans.** The pyramid of energy is a significant improvement over the other two types of ecological pyramids, yet all of them overlook one or another important aspect. Some of these limitations are discussed below:

- Some species practice more than one mode of nutrition or belong to two or more trophic levels. This is particularly true in the case of consumers of higher trophic levels. Man is an example. He gets his food from primary producers as well as from higher trophic levels. Such organisms which feed at more than one trophic level are extremely difficult to depict in ecological pyramids.
- Saprophytes play a vital role in ecosystem but they are not represented in ecological pyramids.
- Detritus such as litter and humus is an important source of energy and exerts considerable influence on ecosystem function, yet it is not depicted in ecological pyramids.
- Ecological pyramids do not provide any clue to seasonal and diurnal variations.
- The rate of transfer from one trophic level to another is not reflected in the ecological pyramids.

**Q6. Give an account of energy flow from different trophic levels in an ecosystem.**

*Or*

**Explain why the sun is considered as the ultimate source of energy in the Ecosystem?**

*Or*

**Define Standing Crop. [June-2012, Q.No.-4(a)]**

**Ans.** Energy flow is unidirectional. First, plants capture solar energy and then, food is transferred from the producers to decomposers. Organisms of different trophic levels in nature are connected to each other for food or energy relationship forming a food chain. The storage and movement of nutrient elements through the various components of the ecosystem is called nutrient cycling; nutrients are repeatedly use through this process. Nutrient cycling is of two types-gaseous and sedimentary. Atmosphere o hydrosphere is the reservoir for the gaseous type of cycle (carbon), whereas Earth's crust is the reservoir for sedimentary type (phosphorus). Products of ecosystem processes are named as ecosystem services, e.g., purification of air and water by forests.

All living things need food for energy. **The ultimate source of all this food and all ecosystems on earth starts with the Sun**.

Of the incident solar radiation less than 50 per cent of it is photosynthetically active radiation (PAR). We know that plants and photosynthetic and chemosynthetic bacteria (autotrophs), fix suns' radiant energy to make food from simple inorganic materials. Plants capture only 2-10 per cent of the PAR and this small amount of energy sustains the entire living world. So, it is very important to know how the solar energy captured by plants flows though different organisms of an ecosystem. All organisms are dependent for their food on producers, either directly or indirectly.

The green plant in the ecosystem-terminology are called **producers**. In a terrestrial ecosystem, major producers are herbaceous and woody plants. Likewise, primary producers in an aquatic ecosystem are various species like phytoplankton, algae and higher plants.

Starting from the plants (or producers) food chains or rather webs are formed such that an animal feeds on a plant or on another animal and in turn is food for another. The chain or web is formed because of this interdependency. No energy that is trapped into an organism remains in it forever. The energy trapped by the producer, hence, is either passed on to a consumer or the organism dies. Death of organism is the beginning of the detritus food chain/web.

All animals depend on plants (directly or indirectly) for their food needs.

They are hence called **consumers** and also heterotrophs. If they feed on the producers, the plants, they are called primary consumers, and if the animals eat other animals, which in turn eat the plants (or their produce) they are called secondary consumers. Likewise, you could have tertiary consumers too. Obviously the primary consumers will be **herbivores**. Some common herbivores are insects, birds and mammals in terrestrial ecosystem and molluscs in aquatic ecosystem.

The amount of energy decreases at successive trophic levels. When any organism dies it is converted to detritus or dead biomass that serves as an energy source for decomposers. Organisms at each trophic level depend on those at the lower trophic level for their energy demands.

Each trophic level has a certain mass of living material at a particular time called as the **standing crop**. The standing crop is measured as the mass of living organisms (**biomass)** or the number in a unit area. The biomass of a species is expressed in terms of fresh or dry weight. Measurement of biomass in terms of dry weight is more accurate.

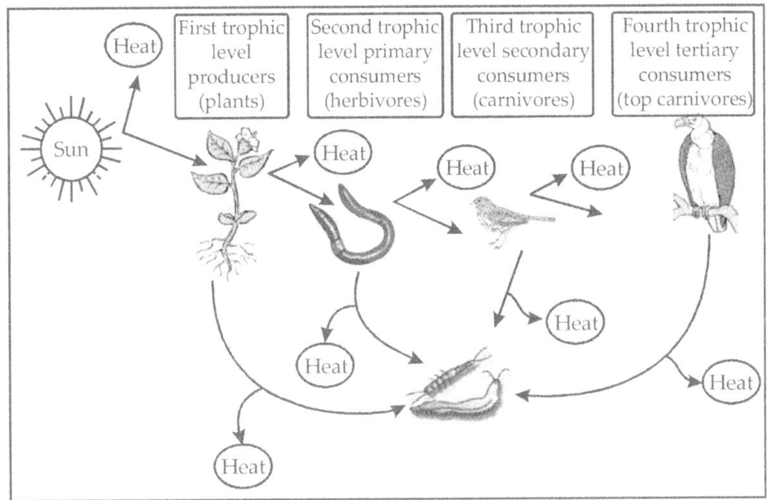


Fig.2.7

The number of trophic levels in the grazing food chain is restricted as the transfer of energy follows 10 per cent law – only 10 per cent of the energy is transferred to each trophic level from the lower trophic level. In nature, it is possible to have so many levels – producer, herbivore, primary carnivore, secondary carnivore in the grazing food chain.

**Q7. What do you understand by primary productivity? Give brief description of factors that affect primary productivity.**

***Or***

**Define Net primary production. [Dec-2010, Q.No.-1(ii)]**

**Ans.** Primary production is defined as the amount of biomass or organic matter produced per unit area over a time period by plants during photosynthesis. It is expressed in terms of weight ($g^{-2}$) or energy (kcal $m^{-2}$). The rate of biomass production is called productivity. It is expressed in terms of $g^{-2}$ $yr^{-1}$ or (kcal $m^{-2}$) $yr^{-1}$ to compare the productivity of different ecosystems. It can be divided into gross primary productivity (GPP) and net primary productivity (NPP). Gross primary productivity of an ecosystem is the rate of production of organic matter during photosynthesis. A considerable amount of GPP is utilised by plants in respiration. Gross primary productivity minus respiration losses (R), is the net primary productivity (NPP).

GPP – R = NPP

**Net primary productivity** is the available biomass for the consumption to heterotrophs.

Primary productivity depends on the plant species inhabiting a particular area. It also depends on a variety of environmental factors, availability of nutrients and photosynthetic capacity of plants. Therefore, it varies in different types of ecosystems. The annual net primary productivity of the whole biosphere is approximately 170 billion tons (dry weight) of organic matter. Of this, despite occupying about 70 per cent of the surface, the productivity of the oceans are only 55 billion tons.

**Q8. Define secondary production. How it is different from primary production?**

**Ans.** An understanding of the food chain and trophic relationship concepts are fundamental to the study of secondary production. The following energy flow diagram illustrates the concept of secondary production.

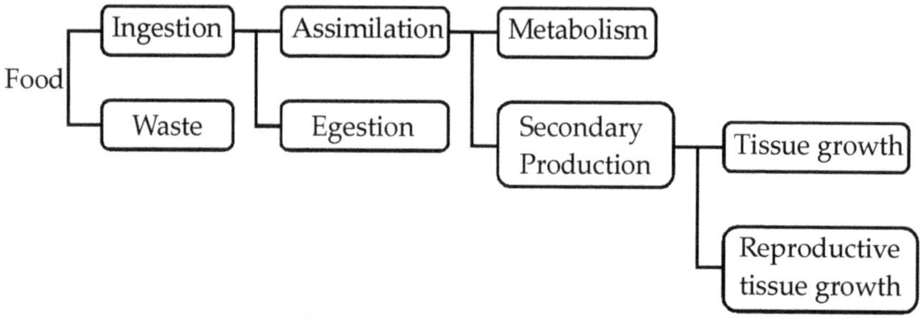


**Fig.2.8: Secondary Production**

Thus secondary productivity refers to the net quantity of energy transferred and stored in the somatic and reproductive tissues of heterotrophs over a period of time. Some heterotrophs (consumers and decomposers) feed on net primary production and some on other heterotrophic organisms. Thus, productivity by organisms in the ecosystem is called secondary productivity. Secondary production is one of the interrelated processes in the energy flow mechanism. For energy flow and secondary productivity studies, two kinds of information, (a) a census of the members of a species population over a period of the, and (b) an estimate of the separate energy components for each population, are required. Secondary productivity is of great importance, since it serves as an index of significance of the population in terms of food resources available to the heterotrophic populations, including man, in the food chain. It involves the production of herbivores, carnivores and decomposer organisms.

The secondary producers may be poikilothermic animals such as annelids, arthropods fish, amphibia and reptiles, homeothermic animal like birds and mammals including man, or saprophytic organisms. But in general, secondary production is a function of the amount of primary production in the ecosystem, the size and metabolism of heterotrophic organisms and the number of links in the food chains in an ecosystem.

**Q9. Write a detailed note on Ecosystem control/ecological balance.**

*Or*

**Define Homeostasis.** **[Dec-2012, Q.No-1(iv)]**

**Ans.** Ecological balance has been defined as "a state of dynamic equilibrium within a community of organisms in which genetic, species and ecosystem diversity remain relatively stable, subject to gradual changes through natural succession." and "A stable balance in the numbers of each species in an ecosystem."

The most important point being that the natural balance in an ecosystem is maintained. This balance may be disturbed due to the introduction of new species, the sudden death of some species, natural hazards or man-made causes. This capacity of an ecosystem to self-regulate or self-maintain is called homeostasis.

Consider an example, Grassland, when there is a drought, plants do not grow well. The mice that eat the grass become malnourished. When this happens, their birth rate decreases. And also the hungry mice retreat to their burrows and sleep. By doing so, they need less food and are less exposed to predators, so their death rates decrease. Their behaviour protects their own population balance as well as that of the grasses, which are not being consumed while the mice hibernate. Such a mechanism is known as feedback regulation and is very important to maintain the ecological balance. It is the prime regulatory mechanism for the ecosystem as a whole. A feedback loop may be defined as relationship in which a change in some original rate alters the rate of direction of further change.

Now we take up, another parameter of ecosystem balances. One factor that affects the stability or persistence of some ecosystems under small or moderate environmental stress is species diversity, the number of species and their relative abundance in a given ecosystem. High species diversity tends to increase long-term persistence of the ecosystem. It is because with so many different species and the linkages between them, risk is spread more widely. An ecosystem having a good variety of species has more ways available to respond to most environmental stresses. For example, the loss or drastic reduction of one species in an ecosystem, with complex food web usually does not threaten the existence of others, because most consumers have several alternative food suppliers. In contrast highly specialised agricultural ecosystem, planted with only one type of crop such as wheat or rice is highly vulnerable to destruction from a single plant diseases or insects. Therefore, the essence of the whole discussion contains many different species.

**Q10. What is the role of decomposition in the terrestrial ecosystem? Explain it with the help of diagram.**

**Ans.** The earthworm being referred to as the farmer's 'friend'. This is so because they help in the breakdown of complex organic matter as well as in loosening of the soil. Similarly, decomposers break down complex organic matter into inorganic substances like carbon animals, including faecal matter, constitute detritus, which is the raw dioxide, water and nutrients and the process is called decomposition. Dead plant remains such as leaves, bark, flowers and dead remains of material for decomposition. The important steps in the process of decomposition are fragmentation, leaching, catabolism, humification and mineralisation.

**Detritivores** (e.g. earthworm) break down detritus into smaller particles. This process is called **fragmentation.** By the process of **leaching,** watersoluble inorganic nutrients go down into the soil horizon and get precipitated as unavailable salts. Bacterial and fungal enzymes degrade detritus into simpler inorganic substances. This process is called as **catabolism**.

It is important to note that all the above steps in decomposition operate simultaneously on the detritus (Fig. 2.9). Humification and mineralisation occur during decomposition in the soil. **Humification** leads to accumulation of dark coloured amorphous substance called **humus** that is highly resistant to microbial action and undergoes decomposition at an extremely slow rate. Being colloidal in nature, it serves as a reservoir of nutrients. The humus is further degraded by some microbes and release of inorganic nutrients occur by the process known as **mineralisation**.

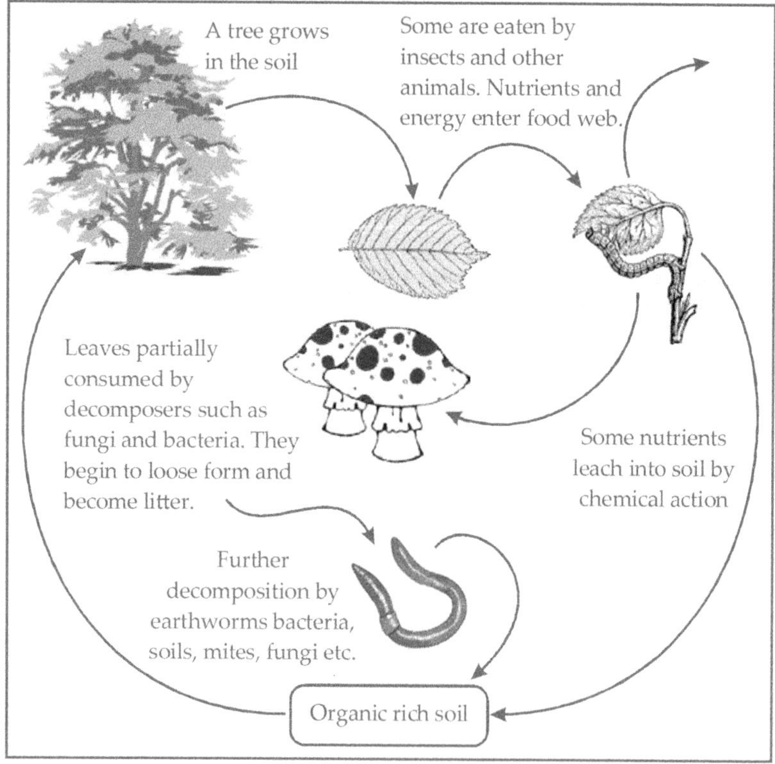


**Fig. 2.9: Decomposition cycle in a terrestrial ecosystem**

Decomposition is largely an oxygen-requiring process. The rate of decomposition is controlled by chemical composition of detritus and climatic factors. In a particular climatic condition, decomposition rate is slower if detritus is rich in lignin and chitin, and quicker, if detritus is rich in nitrogen and water-soluble substances like sugars.

**Q11. Define the term food chain. Explain various kinds of food chains.**

*Or*

**Define Detritus food Chain.** **[June-2012 Q.No.-4(c)]**

**Ans.** A ***food chain*** is a simplified way of showing the food relationships between plants and animals. For example, [Grass ⟶ Cow ⟶ Human] is a food chain. When drawing a food chain, the arrows point in the direction the food energy is moving. Usually, food chains show the living elements. However, some food chains can also show the non-living elements like sun, air, water and soil, since they are used by plants to make their own food.

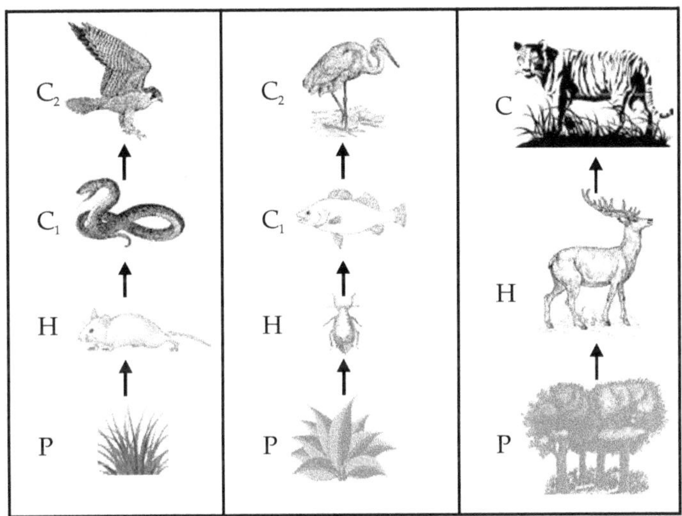


**P = Producer, H = Herbivore, C = Carnivore, $C_1$ = First level carnivore, $C_2$ = Top Carnivore**

**Fig. 2.10: Some examples of food chain**

**Kinds of food Chain:**

**(1) Grazing food chain:** The grazing food chain starts from green plants passes on to herbivorous primary consumers and ends with carnivorous animals. Thus the nutrition produced by plants utilising energy of solar radiation are used in the following three ways:

(i) Used for respiratory activity of the plant

(ii) Get decayed

(iii) May be consumed by herbivores

In a grazing food chain there are basically four trophic levies - Auto trophic, primary consumers, secondary consumers and tertiary consumers. Grazing food chain is the most important food chain in nature.

(2) **Detritous food chain:** Detritous or decomposing food chain begins with dead organic matter goes to micro organisms and then passes on to organisms that feed on detrivores (organisms that - eat detritus) and their predators. Ecosystems of this type are less dependent on direct solar energy. On the other hand they depend on the supply of organic matter produced by another ecosystem.

Detritus food chains are seen in those areas where there is plenty of organic matter in the soil as in temperate forests. In a detritus food chain organic matter to start the chain comes from outside. The main source of organic matter is the leaf fall from the trees producing lot of litter. The fallen leaf fragments are acted upon by saprophytic fungi and bacteria and are eaten by a small group of animals.

These animals include crabs, copepods, insect larvae, grass shrimps, nematodes, etc. All these animals are called detritus consumers or detritivores. These animals are in-turn eaten by small fish. These small fish form food for large fish, fish eating birds constituting the large carnivores.

(3) **Parasitic food chain:** In this type of food chain, either the producer or the consumer is parasitised and therefore the food passes to the smaller organism. The energy transfer through this kind of food chain is not significant.

Producer → Herbivores → Parasite → Hyperparasites

Trees → Fruit eating birds → Lice and bugs → Bacteria and fungi

**Q12. Define food web. How the complexity of food web is decided?**

**Ans.** A **food web** is a more realistic way of looking at the relationships of plants and animals in an environment. A food web illustrates the interrelationships between several food chains or pyramids. It is created when several food chains are linked together. It shows how all the living things in a community get their energy.

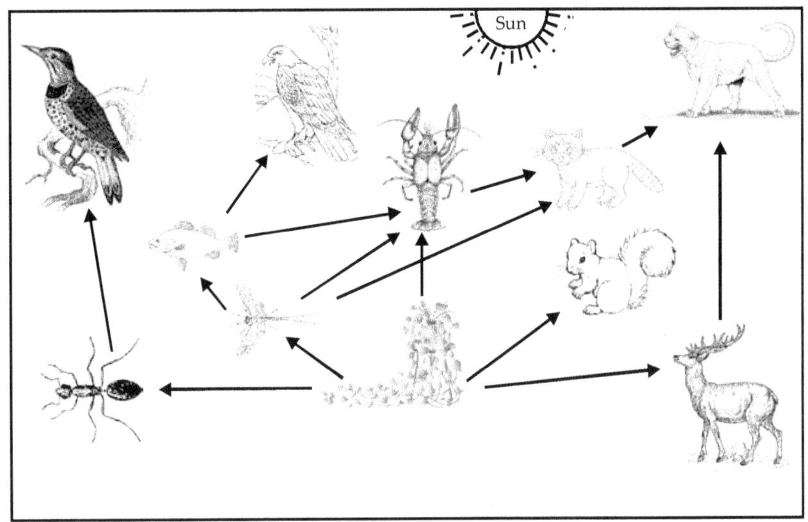


**Fig.2.11: Food Web**

The complexity of any food web depends upon the diversity of organism in the system. It would accordingly depend upon two main points:

- Length of the Food Chain: More diverse the organisms in the food chain, more is the length of the food chain.
- Alternatives at different points of consumers in the chain: As more the alternatives, more would be the interlocking pattern. So in deep oceans, seas, etc. where variety of organisms are present, the food webs are more complex.

**Q13. List the various steps of carbon cycling in an ecosystem.**

**Ans.** The source of all carbon is carbon dioxide present in the atmosphere. It is highly soluble in water; therefore, oceans also contain large quantities of dissolved carbon dioxide. The global carbon cycle consists of following steps:

**Photosynthesis**

Green plants in the presence of sunlight utilise $CO_2$ in the process of photosynthesis and convert the inorganic carbon into organic matter (food) and release oxygen. A part of the food made through photosynthesis is used by plants for their own metabolism and the rest is stored as their biomass which is available to various herbivores, heterotrophs, including human beings and microorganisms as food. Annually 4-9 $\times 10^{13}$ kg of $CO_2$ is fixed by green plants of the entire biosphere. Forests acts as reservoirs of $CO_2$ as carbon fixed by the trees remain stored in them for long due to their long life cycles. A very large amount of $CO_2$ is released through forest fires.

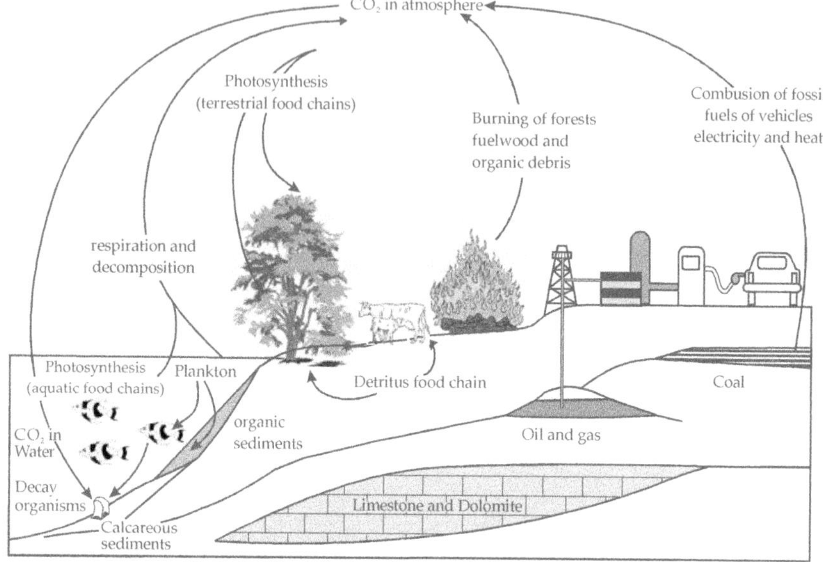


**Fig.2.12 Model of carbon cycle in the biosphere**

### Respiration

Respiration is carried out by all living organisms. It is a metabolic process where food is oxidised to liberate energy, $CO_2$ and water. The energy released from respiration is used for carrying out life processes by living organism (plants, animals, decomposers, etc.).

Thus $CO_2$ is released into of the atmosphere through this process.

### Decomposition

All the food assimilated by animals or synthesised by plant is not metabolised by them completely. A major part is retained by them as their own biomass which becomes available to decomposers on their death. The dead organic matter is decomposed by microorganisms and $CO_2$ is released into the atmosphere by decomposers.

### Combustion

Burning of biomass releases carbon dioxide into the atmosphere.

### Impact of human activities

The global carbon cycle has been increasingly disturbed by human activities particularly since the beginning of industrial era. Large scale deforestation and ever growing consumption of fossil fuels by growing numbers of industries, power plants and automobiles are primarily responsible for increasing emission of carbon dioxide.

**Q14. Discuss the phosphorus Cycle with a suitable diagram and explain human impact on it.**

**Ans.** Phosphorus is a major constituent of biological membranes, nucleic acids and cellular energy transfer systems. Many animals also need large quantities of this element to make shells, bones and teeth. The natural reservoir of phosphorus is rock, which contains phosphorus in the form of phosphates. When rocks are weathered, minute amounts of these phosphates dissolve in soil solution and are absorbed by the roots of the plants (Fig. 2.13). Herbivores and other animals obtain this element from plants. The waste products and the dead organisms are decomposed by phosphate-solubilising bacteria releasing phosphorus. Unlike carbon cycle, there is no respiratory release of phosphorus into atmosphere. Atmospheric inputs of phosphorus through rainfall are much smaller. Gaseous exchanges of phosphorus between organism and environment are negligible.

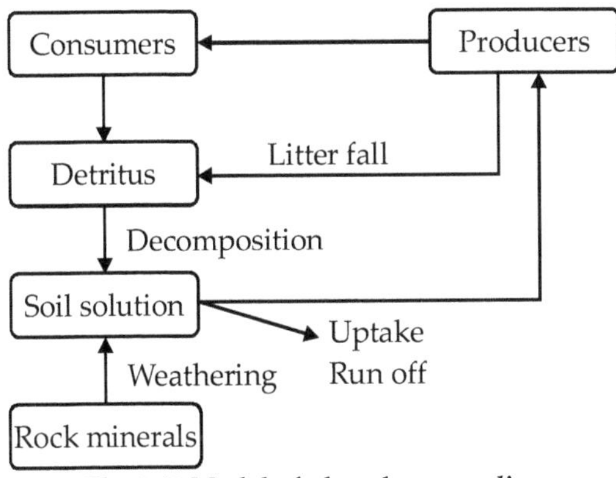


**Fig. 2.13 Model of phosphorus cycling**

## Human Impact on the Phosphorus Cycle

Human influences on the phosphate cycle come mainly from the introduction and use of commercial synthetic fertilisers. The phosphate is obtained through mining of certain deposits of calcium phosphate called apatite. Huge quantities of sulphuric acid are used in the conversion of the phosphate rock into a fertiliser product called "super phosphate".

Plants may not be able to utilise all of the phosphate fertiliser applied, as a consequence, much of it is lost form the land through the water run-off. The phosphate in the water is eventually precipitated as sediments at the bottom of the body of water. In certain lakes and ponds this may be redissolved and recycled as a problem nutrient.

Animal wastes or manure may also be applied to the land as fertiliser. If misapplied on frozen ground during the winter, much of it may lost as run-off during the spring thaw. In certain area very large feed lots of animals, may result in excessive run-off of phosphate and nitrate into streams.

Other human sources of phosphate are in the out flows from municipal sewage treatment plants. Without an expensive tertiary treatment, the phosphate in sewage is not removed during various treatment operations. Again an extra amount of phosphate enters the water.

**Q15. Explain sulphur cycle.**

**Ans.** The sulphur cycle corresponds to biochemical degradation or decomposition of sulphurous organic matter, and is also an endless chain connecting the processes of life and decay of both animal and plant worlds. This is illustrated in Fig. 2.14.

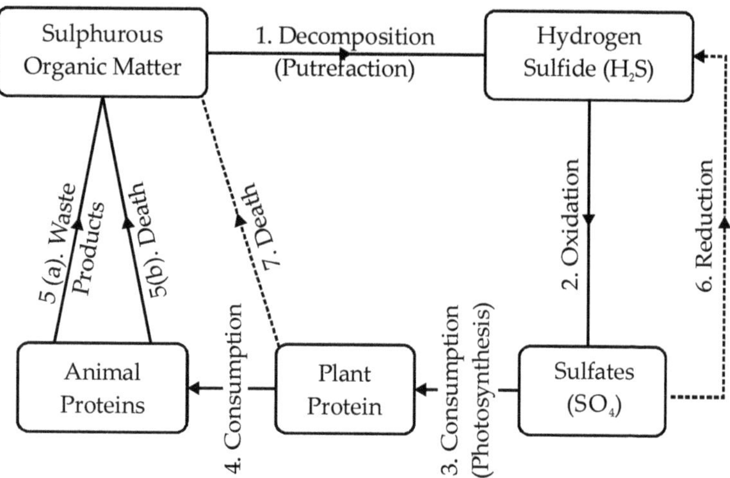


**Fig. 2.14: The Sulphur Cycle**

## Main steps

(1) The decomposition of sulphurous organic matter, through the action of anaerobic bacteria, in absence of oxygen, results in the formation of hydrogen sulphide ($H_2S$).

(2) By process of oxidation, $H_2S$ is first converted into sulphur and finally to sulphates.

(3) Sulphates, when consumed by plants, through photosynthesis, changes into plant proteins.

(4) Animals consume the plant proteins. This results in the formation of animal proteins.

(5) Wastes produced by animals and their dead bodies results in the formation of sulphurous organic matter.

The sulphur is thus completed. However, there may be some short circuits in the above cycle, as shown by dotted lines in Fig 2.142.

## Short circuit steps

(6) Sulphates, in the absence of oxygen, are converted into $H_2S$, by the process of reduction.

(7) Organic sulphurous matter may directly be produced by the death or decay of plants.

## Impact of human activities

Human impact on the sulphur cycle is primarily in the production of sulphur dioxide ($SO_2$) from industry (e.g. burning coal) and the internal combustion engine. Sulphur dioxide can precipitate onto surfaces where it can be oxidised to sulphate in the soil (it is also toxic to some plants), reduced to sulphide in the atmosphere, or oxidised to sulphate in the atmosphere as sulphuric acid, a principal component of acid rain. Without human impact sulphur would stay tied up in rocks for millions of years until it was uplifted through tectonic events and then released through erosion and weathering processes. Instead it is being drilled, pumped and burned at a steadily increasing rate. Over the most polluted areas there has been a 30-fold increase in sulphate deposition.

**Q16. Explain the nitrogen cycle with help of diagram.**

**Ans.** Nitrogen cycle is the most abundant element in the atmosphere and its global circulation (Figure 2.15) provides an inexhaustible reservoir for the organisms which supply almost all of the nitrogen utilised by plants. The quantity of nitrogen combined in living and dead organic matter is small in comparison to the total capacity of the atmospheric reservoir, a characteristic in which nitrogen differs from carbon cycling. Besides the gaseous reservoir of enormous magnitude nitrogen also occurs as a complex soil based reservoir which is localised and of small magnitude. Through the atmosphere contains 79 per cent nitrogen, yet most of the plants and animals cannot make use of this gaseous nitrogen. Plants can make use of nitrogen salts like nitrates and animals must have nitrogen in the form of amino acids.

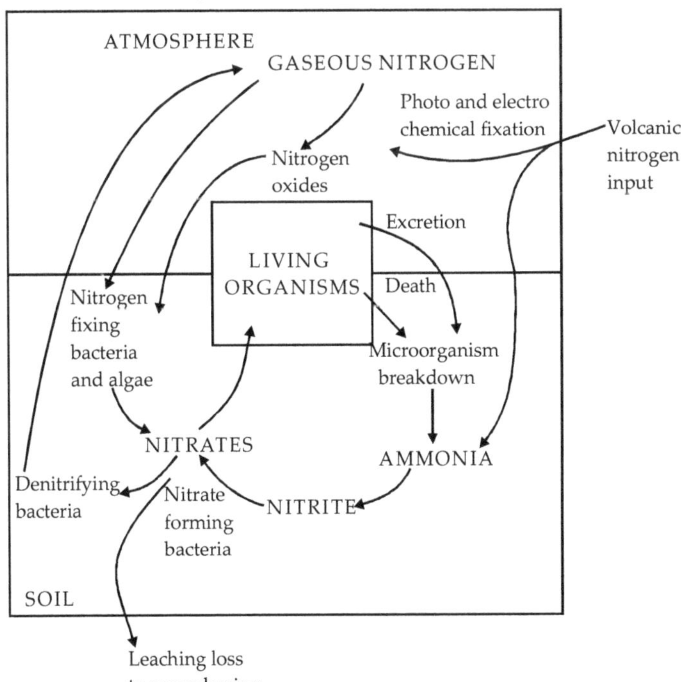


**Fig. 2.15: The Nitrogen Cycle**

The global emission rate of ammonia from soils and from plants and animals has been estimated at $75 \times 10^6$ tons/year (NRC<1979). Pollution sources primarily from ammonia production plants and from fertiliser applications account for $0.32 \times 10^6$ tons/years in the United States (Lamp, 1984). According to Hutchinson (1944) biologically 140-170 mg/ $m^2$ /year nitrogen is fixed whereas a small amount 35 mg/ $m^2$ /year is fixed by electrification and photochemically. But, according to Delwiche (1965, 1970) the amount of nitrogen fixed biochemically is 1 gm/ $m^2$ /year. The amount of nitrogen fixed in fertile areas may range up to 20 gm/ $m^2$ /year.

**Q17. What do you understand by biogeochemical cycle? Explain the types of biogeochemical cycle.**

*Or*

**Write a short note on Sedimentary cycle. [June-2011, Q.No.-6(e)]**

*Or*

**Write a short note on Biogeochemical cycle. [Dec-2012, Q.No.-5(c)]**

**Ans.** In a self-sufficient ecosystem, there occurs the flow of minerals $(N_2, H_2, O_2, P, C etc.,)$, and energy through the abiotic and biotic components of the system. Thus, these elements tend to circulate in a characteristic path from the environment to the organism and back to the environment. This cyclical path of the element from the abiotic system to the biotic system and back is called biogeochemical cycle. (Bio refers to living organisms, geo refers to soil, rock, etc., and chemical refers to the elements and their compounds). It is often argued that ecosystems can best be understood not from the path of energy through them but the biogeochemical cycles.

Chemical elements and compounds are not uniformly distributed in the ecosystem. They are found to be present in compartments or pools. The reservoir pool is normally large, slow-moving non-biological component. There is very slow exchange of materials with the organism. The cycling pool or exchange pool is rather small, more active portion. In cycling pool there is rapid exchange of chemical elements and compounds with the organisms.

**Types of biogeochemical cycles**

On the basis of location of these pools, the nutrient cycles are of two types.

**(1) Gaseous cycles:** The essential feature of these cycles is that the elements have main reservoir in gaseous phase. The cycles of hydrogen, carbon, nitrogen, oxygen, etc., are classified under the gaseous cycle. In nature, water occurs in three phases—solid (ice and snow), liquid (water) and gaseous (water vapour) phase. In liquid phase, it is essential for the existence of life on the earth. The gaseous phase is important for cycling although the main reservoir is not the gaseous phase. Thus, water cycle is considered separately as hydrological cycle.

**(2) Sedimentary cycle:** The elements undergoing this type of cycling do not have a gaseous phase. The elements are usually found in soil and sediments and cycle through soil, water and organism. The only exception to these cycle is sulphur cycle which has a gaseous phase as $H_2S$ and $SO_2$ . But sulphur remains in this phase for a very short period. The sulphur forms sediments. The plants usually take sulphur from soil as sulphate form. Bacteria can use elemental sulphur.

## Diagrammatic presentation of biogeochemical cycle

In following figure, a simplified biogeochemical cycle is shown. Abiotic pool is composed of atmosphere, hydrosphere and lithosphere. Biotic pool is composed of autotrophic, heterotrophic and carnivorous and saprophytic organisms.

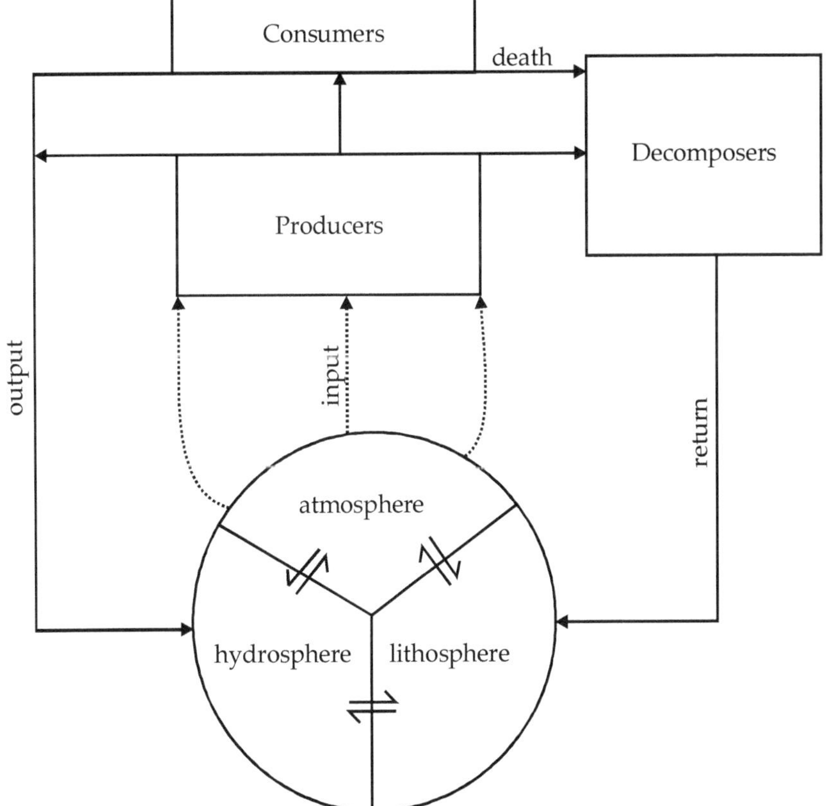


**Fig. 2.16: Model of the transport of a chemical element within the biosphere**

There exists varying degrees of exchange in every pool and among both the pools. An atom and the cycling pool is instantly available to the organism, while an atom in the reservoir pool may or may not be permanently unavailable to the organisms. Usually, there is a slow movement of atoms between the unavailable and the available pools.

**Q18. Differentiate between atmospheric nitrogen fixation and biological nitrogen fixation. [June-2011, Q.No.-5(b)]**

**Ans.** The process of converting free nitrogen of the atmosphere into nitrogen compounds is called nitrogen fixation. It takes place in two ways:

- Atmospheric nitrogen fixation
- Biological nitrogen fixation

**Atmospheric nitrogen fixation**

During lightning in the sky, when a high temperature and pressure is created in the air, the nitrogen gas present in the atmosphere reacts with oxygen to produce oxides of nitrogen. These oxides of nitrogen get dissolved in rainwater forming dilute nitric and nitrous acids, and fall on land alongwith rainwater. These nitric and nitrous acids react with the alkalis of the soil (like limestone) to turn into nitrates, which is used by various life forms.

$$N_2 + O_2 \rightarrow 2NO$$

$$2NO + O_2 \rightarrow 2NO_2$$

$$4NO_2 + 2H_2O + O_2 \rightarrow 4HNO_3$$

$$CaCO_3 + HNO_3 \rightarrow Ca(NO_3)_2 + H_2O + CO_2$$

**Biological nitrogen fixation**

It is the conversion of atmospheric nitrogen into nitrogen compounds by nitrogen-fixing bacteria. Nitrogen-fixing bacteria can be free-living like Azotobacter and Clostridium, or symbiotic like Rhizobium, which lives in the root nodules of dicot leguminous plants and can fix atmospheric nitrogen into nitrates. Certain blue-green algae like Anabaena and Nostoc and non-leguminous plants like ginkgo can also fix atmospheric nitrogen into nitrates.

**Q19. How biological adaptations in plants promote the cycling of nutrients?**

**Ans.** Recycling of nutrients is aided by number of nutrient conserving biological adaptations in plants. These are given as follows:

- Roots mats consisting of many fine feeder roots penetrate surface of the litter, etc. before they are reached away.
- Mycorrhizal fungi associated with root system act as nutrient traps and help in retention of nutrients.
- Evergreen leaves have waxy cuticle to prevent nutrient and water loss.

- Algae and lichen cover surface of many leaves and hence pick up nutrients from rainfall.
- Thick bark inhibits diffusion of nutrients out from the phloem and subsequent loss by stem flow.

**Q20. What is the difference between Tropical and temperate forest?**
**[June-2011, Q.No.-2(b)]**

**Ans.** In tropical forests a large portion of the nutrients are held in the biomass and not in the soil. This is due to the plant recycling of nutrients aided by various nutrients conserving biological adaptations. Therefore if tropical forests are cleared the soil's ability to hold nutrients is lost, making it unsuitable for long-term agriculture.

While temperate forests a large portion of the nutrients are in the soil rather than in plant biomass. So soil still retain nutrients and hence remains suitable for cultivation.

Soil of tropical forests are generally poor in nutrients they are able to maintain high productivity under natural conditions due to these nutrient-conserving mechanisms that almost bypass the soil by having a plant to plant cycling. When such forests are cut or cleared for agriculture these mechanisms are destroyed and productivity declines very rapidly. Forest removal takes away the land's ability to hold nutrients as well as to combat pests in the face of year round high temperatures. Crop production declines and in a few years the land is abandoned.

Soil in temperature forest have relatively large nutrient pools and when these forests are cleared, the soil retains nutrients and may be cultivated for many years by ploughing one or more times a year, planting short season annual plants and applying inorganic fertilisers. During winter, freezing temperatures help hold in nutrients and combat disease and pest.

**Q21. What is biome? Identify various biomes of the world.**

*Or*

**Describe the salient features of a desert. [Dec-2011, Q.No.-11(b)]**

**Ans.** Biome is a large community unit, which is characterised on the basis of types of plants and animals present in it. In other word, a biome is a community of living organism of a single ecological region. A biome is determined by climate and rainfall. It signifies the relationship of plants and animals forming a biotic unit.

**Various biomes in the world**

*Arctic Tundra*

The Arctic tundra is a cold, vast, treeless area of low, swampy plains in the far north around the Arctic Ocean. It includes the northern lands of Europe (Lapland and Scandinavia), Asia (Siberia), and North America (Alaska and Canada), as well as most of Greenland. Another type of tundra is the alpine tundra, which is a biome that exists at the tops of high mountains.

*Forests*

- **Coniferous Forest:** The coniferous forest biome is south of the Arctic tundra. It stretches from Alaska straight across North America to the Atlantic Ocean and across Eurasia. The largest stretch of coniferous forest in the world, circling the earth in the Northern Hemisphere, is called the "taiga." It supplies the bulk of the world's commercial softwood timber, which is used to make paper.
- **Deciduous Forest:** This biome is in the mild temperate zone of the Northern Hemisphere. Major regions are found in eastern North America, Europe, and eastern Asia.
- **Rainforests:** Rainforests are found in Asia, Africa, South America, Central America, and on many of the Pacific islands. They are often found along the equator. Almost half of the world's tropical rainforests are in the South American country Brazil.

*Desert*

A desert is an area where little or no life exists because of a lack of water. Scientists estimate that about one-fifth of the earth's land surface is desert. Deserts can be found on every continent except Europe.

- **Distribution:** Deserts are hot and low rain areas suffering from water shortage and high wind velocity. They show extremes of temperature. Globally deserts occupy about 1/7th of the earth's surface.
- **Flora and fauna:** *Cacti, Acacia, Euphorbia* and prickly pears are some of the common desert plants. Desert animals include shrew, fox, wood rats, rabbits, camels and goat are common mammals in desert. Other prominent desert animals are, reptiles, and burrowing rodents insects.
- **Adaptations:** Desert plants are hot and dry conditions.
  - (i) These plants conserve water by following methods:
    - (a) They are mostly shrubs.
    - (b) Leaves absent or reduced in size.
    - (c) Leaves and stem are succulent and water storing.
    - (d) In some plants even the stem contains chlorophyll for photosynthesis.
    - (e) Root system well developed spread over large area.
  - (ii) The animals are physiologically and behaviourally adapted to desert conditions.
    - (a) They are fast runners.
    - (b) They are nocturnal in habit to avoid the sun's heat during day time.

(c) They conserve water by excreting concentrated urine.

(d) Animals and birds usually have long legs to keep the body away from the hot ground.

(e) Lizards are mostly insectivorous and can live without drinking water for several days.

(f) Herbivorous animals get sufficient water from the seeds, which they eat.

Camel is known as the ship of the desert as it can travel long distances without drinking water for several days.

### *Mountains*

Mountains exist on all the continents of the earth. Many of the world's mountains lie in two great belts. The Circum-Pacific chain, often called the Ring of Fire, runs from the west coast of the Americas through New Zealand and Australia and up through the Philippines to Japan. The other major belt, called the Alpine-Himalayan, or Tethyan, system, stretches from the Pyrenees in Spain and France through the Alps and on to the Himalayas before ending in Indonesia.

**Q22. What are Grasslands? Write the Economic importance of Grasslands. Write the major types of grasslands.**

*Or*

**Write the economic importance of grassland biomes.**

**[Dec-2012, Q.No.-6(a)]**

**Ans.** Grasslands are places with hot, dry climates that are perfect for growing food. They are known throughout the world by different names. In the US they are called prairies and extend from the Midwest to the Rocky Mountains. In South Africa, grasslands are called the veld. Hot, tropical grasslands called savannas are found in South America and Africa. In Eurasia, temperate zone grasslands are called steppes; in South America, pampas.

### Economic importance of Grasslands

Grasslands herbaceous layer and non-ligneous organs of the woody shrubs and trees constitute the fodder. The young and green succulent shoots of grasses are forbs of the leguminosae family, constituting the ground cover or the lower stratum of grazing land, provide the best choice for grazing material.

India with just a fortieth of the total land area of the world supports more than half of its buffaloes, 15 per cent of its cattles, 15 per cent of its goats and 4 per cent its sheeps. The livestock wealth plays a crucial role in Indian life; it is a major source of fuel, draught power, nutrition and raw material for village industries. But this huge mass of livestock needs fodder for sustenance while there is not enough of it. Only about 13 million hectares in the country are classified as permanent grazing lands. On top of it, they exist in a highly degraded state. The animals scrounge, for whatever they can get on millions of hectares of fallow and uncultivated land and uncultivable wastelands, as well 36 million hectares of tropical forestlands. In all, almost all accessible vegetation in more than half the total land area of the country is grazed by livestock - which snap up almost everything except non-palatable weeds.

Grasslands biomes are important to maintain the crop of many domesticated and wild herbivores such as horse, mule, ass, cow, pig, sheep, goat, buffalo, camel, deer, zebra, etc. which provide food, milk, wool, hide or transportation to man.

Due to absence of humus cover, mineral soil surface is heavily trampled when wetness produces puddling of the surface layer, which is turn reduces the infiltration of water into the soil and accelerates its run off, producing drought. These changes contribute to the reduction of the rate of energy flow and the disruption of the stratification and periodicity of the primary producers results in a breakdown of the biogeochemical cycles of water, carbon and nitrogen. Water and wind erosion completely breakdown a very dry grassland microclimate. Further, intensive grazing results in increased areas of bare soil, which creates a new habitat for burrowing animals such as mice, jack-rabbits, gophers, prairie dogs, locusts, etc. which render large areas of forage lands sterile.

**Types of Grasslands**

- **The Sehima-dichanthium** type covers the whole of peninsular India (dry subhumid zone except Nilgiri). The thorny bushes of the savanska range land, are Acacia catechu, Mimosa rubicaulis, Zizyphus and sometimes fleshy Euphorbia, along with low trees of Anogeissus latifolia, Soymida febrifuga and other deciduous species. The floristic list includes 24 perennial grasses and 129 other herbaceous species of which 56 are legumes. Sehima is more prevalent on gravel and the cover may be 27 per cent. Dichanthium flourishes on level soils and may cover 80 per cent of the ground.
- **The Dichanthium-cenchrus-lasiurus** type (semi-arid zone) extends to the northern portion of Gujarat, Rajasthan (excluding Aravallis), western Uttar Pradesh, Delhi and Punjab. The topography is broken up by hill spurs and sand dunes. Eleven perennial grasses: 45 other herbaceous species (including 19 of the leguminosae) are listed. To this list may be added shrubby, growth of Acacia senegal, Calotropis gigantia, Cassia auriculata, Prosopis cineraria, Salvadora oloides and zizyphus Nummularia which make the savanna rangeland look like scrub.

- **The Phragmities-sacchrum-imperata** type (moist subhumid zone) covers the Ganga alluvial plain in Northern India. The topography is level, low lying and ill-drained. There are 19 principal grass species and 56 other herbaceous ones including 16 legumes. Bothriochloa pertusa, Cynodon dactylon and Dichanthium annulatum are found in transition zones. The common trees and shrubs are Acacia arabica, Anogeissus, latifolia, Butea monosperma, Phoenic sylvestris and Zizyphus nummularia. Some of these are replaced by Borassus sp in the palm savannas especially near Sunderbans.
- **The Themeda:** Arundinella grass cover extends to the humid mountain regions and moist sub-humid areas of Assam, Manipur, West Bengal, Uttar Pradesh, Punjab, Himachal Pradesh and Jammu and Kashmir. The savanna is derived from the humid forests. On account of shifting cultivation and sheep grazing.

**Q23. Define deforestation. Identify the various causes and effect of deforestation.**

*Or*

**Discuss why deforestation is one of the most important factors for wild life loss in India.**

*Or*

**Discuss the various causes and consequences of deforestation.**

**[June-2012, Q.No.-11(b)]**

**Ans.** Deforestation is defined as the destruction of forested land. It has proved to be a major problem all over world. However, the rates of destruction of forests are particularly high in the tropics.

**Fig. 2.17: Deforestation**

The most common reason for deforestation is cutting of wood for fuel, lumber and paper. Another important cause relates to the clearing of forest land for agriculture, including conversion to crop land and pasture (Fig. 2.17).

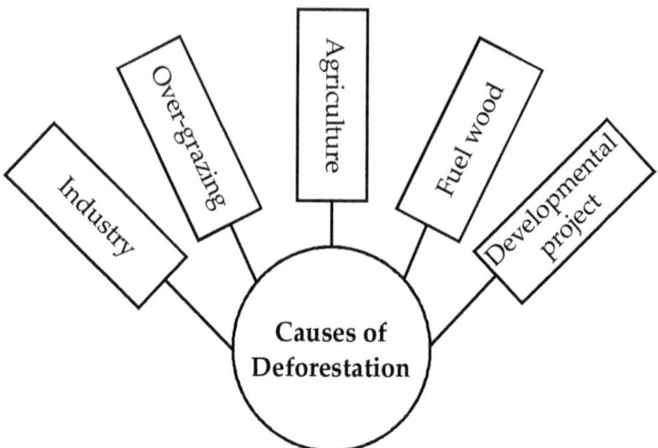


Fig.2.18: Causes of Deforestation

## Causes of Deforestation:

(1) **Agriculture:** The expanding agriculture is one of the most important causes of deforestation. Man has always modified the natural ecosystems in such a way that environment becomes more favourable for crop growth whether using traditional or modern methods of agriculture. As demands for agricultural products rises, more and more land is brought under cultivation and for that more forests are cleared, grasslands and even marshes, and lands under water are reclaimed. Thus, there is much more ecological destruction than gain in term of crop yield. The forest soil after clearing are unable to support farming for long periods due to exhaustion of nutrients. Once the soils become unfit for cultivation, the area suffers from to soil erosion and degradation.

(2) **Shifting cultivation:** Hunting and gathering has been the main form of sustenance practiced in the earlier periods of human history. Shifting cultivation or Jhoom farming is a 12000-year old practice and a step towards transition from food collection to food production. It is also known as slash-and-burn method of farming. Annually about 5 lakhs ha (hectares) of forest is cleared for this type of farming. In this type of cultivation there is a limited use of tools with not very high level of mechanisation. However, this method of cultivation causes extreme deforestation, as after 2-3 years of tilling, the land is left to the mercy of nature to recover. This type of cultivation was always meant to fulfil local needs or onsite demands to meet the requirements of the cultivating villagers. Even today, shifting cultivation is practiced in the states of Assam, Manipur, Meghalaya, Mizoram, Nagaland, Tripura and Andaman and Nicobar Islands.

(3) **Demand for firewood:** Firewood has been used as a source of energy for cooking, heating, etc. Almost 44 per cent of the total global wood produced fulfils the fuel requirements of the world. Close look at the pattern of utilisation of wood produced will show that the developed countries utilise 16 per cent of their share for fuel requirements. India consumes nearly 135-170 Mt (Million tonnes) of firewood annually and 10-15 ha of forest cover is being stripped off to meet the minimum fuel needs of urban and rural poor.

**Table 2.1: Use of wood**

| **Region** | **Total wood Consumption** | **Wood use (in billion m$^3$)** | | **Wood use (%)** | |
|---|---|---|---|---|---|
| | | **Industrial** | **Firewood** | **Industrial** | **Firewood** |
| Global | 3.2 | 1.5 | 1.7 | 46 | 54 |
| Developing countries | 1.8 (57%) | 0.324 | 1.476 | 18 | 82 |
| Developed countries | 1.4 (43%) | 1.176 | 0.224 | 84 | 16 |

(4) **Wood for industry and commercial use:** Wood, the versatile forest produce, is used for several industrial purposes, such as making crates, packing cases, furniture, match boxes, wooden boxes, paper and pulp, plywood, etc. 1.24 lakh ha of forest have been cut for various industrial uses. Unrestricted exploitation of timber as well as other wood products for commercial purposes is the main cause of forest degradation. The paper industry accounts for about 2 per cent of country's annual consumption of wood and 51 per cent this requirement is met by bamboo wood. This has led to the depletion of bamboo stocks in most of the peninsular India. For example the apple industry in the Himalayan region has led to the destruction of fir and other tree species, for making wooden boxes used for transporting apples. Similarly, plywood crates were used for packing particularly tea and other produce.

(5) **Urbanisation and developmental projects:** Often urbanisation and developmental activities lead to deforestation. The process of deforestation begins with building of infrastructure in the form of roads, railway lines, building of dams, townships, electric supply, etc. Thermal power plants, mining for coal, metal ores and minerals are also important causes of deforestation.

Nowadays you must have heard about the Tehri power project which is a 260.5m high earth and rock fill dam near the Tehri town in Garhwal Himalayas. The project site is situated a little downstream the junction of Bhagirathi and Bhilganga rivers. An estimated 4,600 ha of good forest land will be submerged under water. This has displaced an estimated 3,500 odd families.

**Effects of deforestation**

Deforestation affects both physical and biological components of the environment.

(1) **Soil erosion and flash flood:** A shrinking forest cover coupled with over exploitation of ground water has accelerated erosion along the slopes of the lower Himalayas and Aravali hills, making them prone to landslides. Destruction of the forests has altered rainfall pattern. In 1978 India suffered some of the worst flooding in its history. There was two days of heavy rainfall and 66,000 villages were inundated, 2,000 people drowned, and 40,000 cattle were swept away. In 2008 Bihar state suffered worst flood in the river kosi. Several lives were lost and a huge number of cattle were swept away. Lack of forest cover has resulted in water flowing off the ground, washing away the top soil which is finally deposited as silt in the river beds. Forests check soil-erosion, landslides and reduce intensity of flood and drought.

(2) **Climatic change:** Forests enhance local precipitation and improve water holding capacity of soil, regulate water cycle, maintain soil fertility by returning the nutrients to the soil through leaf fall and decomposition of litter. Forests check soil-erosion, landslides and reduce intensity of flood and droughts. Forests, being home of wildlife are important assets of aesthetic, touristic and cultural value to the society. Forests have profound effect on the climate. Forest absorbed carbon dioxide from the atmosphere and help in balancing carbon dioxide and oxygen in the atmosphere. The forests play a vital role in maintaining oxygen supply in the air, we breathe. They also play a vital role in the regulation of water (water cycle) in the environment and act as environmental buffers regulating climate and atmospheric humidity. Heat build-up in the atmosphere is one of the important problems of the century known as **green house effect** is the partly caused by the result from deforestation. The entire Himalayan ecosystem is threatened and is under severe imbalance as snow –line has thinned and perennial springs have dried up. Annual rainfall has declined by 3 to 4 per cent. Chronic droughts have begun even in areas like Tamilnadu and Himachal Pradesh where they were not known earlier.

(3) **Biodiversity:** "Biodiversity" include all variety of life forms. Biodiversity - (biological diversity) is a measure of variation, the number of different varieties, among living things. Biodiversity can be expressed in number of ways, which includes the number of genetic strains (differences) within species and the number of different ecosystem in an area. The most common expression of biodiversity is the number of different species,

within a particular area (local biodiversity), or in a specific habitat (habitat biodiversity) or in the world (global biodiversity). Biodiversity is not static. It changes over the time during evolution new species have come up while some species become extinct. Our knowledge is incomplete at the global level; nearly 1.4 million species have been identified. Different species inhabiting the earth have been estimated to vary between 10 and 100 million. There is lot of concern about preserving biodiversity. The one good reason for preserving biodiversity is that it provides wide variety of products for human use and welfare. It is a great potential resource for agriculture, medicine and industry. There are several **causes** for biodiversity loss:-

- hunting, poaching and commercial exploitation.
- elimination and disturbance of wildlife habitats.
- selective destruction of habitat/life forms.
- domestication.
- introduction of new alien species in new area which threaten the indigenous species.
- use of pesticides.
- pests, medical research and zoos.

All the above factors adversely affect biodiversity.

(4) **Loss of wildlife in India:** India has nearly 45,000 species of plants and 75,000 species of animals. This biological diversity ought to be preserved for maintaining stability of ecosystems. Deforestation coupled with desertification has destroyed the natural treasure of the earth to a large extent. The population of elephant, lion and tiger is fast diminishing. 'Cheetah' is already extinct.

Elephants once found all over India have now disappeared from Andhra Pradesh, Madhya Pradesh and Maharashtra. The Asiatic lion which was very common in Asia has practically vanished from Asia except for a few hundred sq km (square kilometer) of Gir forest in India.

In India four species of mammals and three species of birds have been extinct in the last 100 years. Another 40 species of mammals, 20 species of birds and 12 species of reptiles are considered highly endangered due to over exploitations, of forests.

**Q24. Define forest. What are its types?**

***Or***

**Differentiate between Tropical rain forest and temperate rain forest.**

**[Dec-2012, Q.No.-2(c)]**

**Ans.** Forests are ecological as well as a socio-economic resource. Forests have to be managed judiciously not only because they are source of various products and industrial raw materials but also for environmental protection and various services they provide.

In other words, forest is a complex ecosystem consisting mainly of trees that support a myriad form of life. The trees are the most important component that helps to create a unique environment, which, in turn, supports various kinds of animals and plants.

Approximately 1/3$^{rd}$ of the earth's total land area is covered by forests. The forests provide habitat for wildlife, resources such as timber, fire wood, drugs, etc. and aesthetic environment. Indirectly, the forests benefit people by protecting watersheds from soil erosion, keeping rivers and reservoirs free of silt, and facilitate the recharging of groundwater. Forest plays an important role in the cycling of carbon, water, nitrogen and other elements.

Forests may be subdivided into natural forests and plantations or man made forests. Natural forests are forests composed of mainly naturally grown indigenous (local) trees while plantations are forests established by growing trees by humans.

### Types of Forests

Forests are large areas supporting rich growth of trees. Depending on the climate and type of trees they are generally grouped into:

#### (1) Tropical rain forest

- **Distribution:** These are found in the high rain fall areas on either side of the equator. Such forests are found in the western coast of India, scattered in south east Asia, some parts of Africa and south America.
- **Flora and fauna:** Tropical rainforests occur in areas by having high temperature and high humidity and receives above 200 cm of rainfall per year. Soil is rich in humus. These forests have a very rich biodiversity, e.g. Brazilian tropical rain forests have more than 300 species of trees in an area of 200 square kilometer. Trees are tall growing upto 50 to 60 m. These forests also support epiphytes, like vines, creepers, woody creepers and orchid, etc. These forests are rich in tree dwelling animals such as monkeys, flying squirrels, snails, centipedes, millipedes, and many insect species are common on the forest floor.

#### (2) Temperate deciduous forests

- **Distribution:** They occur mostly in northwest, central and eastern Europe, eastern north America, north China, Korea, Japan, far eastern Russia and Australia. Trees of deciduous forests shed their leaves in autumn and a new foliage grows in spring.
- **Climate:** These forests occur in the areas of moderate climatic conditions such as temperature ranging but 10 to 20°C with a 6 month long winter and an annual rainfall **between 75 to 150 cm. They have its brown soils which are rich in nutrients.**

- **Flora and fauna:** Common trees are oak, beach, heath, chest nut, birch, pine. These forests also show stratification and have a under storey of saplings shrubs and tall herbs. Prominent grazers include deer, bison and rodents. Rodents play a very important role in these forests. They feed on seeds, fruits and tree leaves. Black bear, raccoons, wild cat, wolves, fox and skunks are the omnivores found in these forests. Hibernation or winter sleep during winter is a common feature of animals found in these forests. Invertebrate fauna comprises green flies, aphids, certain moths and butterflies.

**(3) Boreal or north coniferous forests:**

- **Distribution:** Coniferous forests are also known as 'Taiga'. They extend as a continuous belt across north America and north Eurasia below the arctic tundra. There is no counterpart of these forests in southern hemisphere as there is no land at this latitude. Climate is cold with long, harsh winter, with mean annual temperature below $0°C$. The soils are acidic and poor in nutrients.
- **Flora and fauna:** Coniferous forests are characterised by evergreen, drought resistant and woody. Conifers (gymnospreπms), e.g. spruce, fir and pine trees, which bear naked seeds in cones. The animals found in these forests, are red squirrel, deer, goat, mule, moose, etc. The carnivores which feed upon them are timber wolves, lynxes, and bear. Some common birds are crossbill, thrushes, warblers, flycatchers, robin and sparrow.

**Q25. Appreciate the importance of forest in an ecosystem. What are the functions of forests?**

**Ans.** Forests play an important role in environmental and economic sustainability. They provide numerous goods and services and maintain life-support systems essential for life on earth. Some of the major life-support systems of economic and environmental importance of forests are as follows:

**Biodiversity**

A wide variety of flora and fauna consisting of more than 5,150 species of plants, 16,214 species of insects, 44 mammals, 42 birds, 164 reptiles, 121 amphibians and 435 fish, is found in the Indian forests (NATCOM, 2003). However, in recent times, heavy biotic pressures have started to exert tremendous stress on natural resources and hence many of plant and animal species are under various degrees of threat. In order to conserve biodiversity of the country, about 14.8 Mha of forests comprising 80 National Parks and 441 Wildlife Sanctuaries have been converted into protected area.

**Biomass supply**

The forests meet nearly 40 per cent of the energy needs and 30 per cent of the fodder needs of India. Many tribals of India live in close proximity of forests and largely depend on them for their fuel requirement. It is estimated that approximately 270 Mt of fuelwood, 280 Mt of fodder, over 12 million $m^3$ of timber, and several non-timber forest products (such as fruits, nuts, edible flowers, medicinal herbs, rattan and bamboo, honey and gum) are annually harvested from forest.

**Livelihoods to forest dependent communities**

About 15,000 plant species are found in India; about 20 per cent of these species yield non-timber products. Millions of forest dwellers and agricultural communities depend on forests for a range of non-timber forest products. Moreover, all forest related activities are labour intensive and lead to rural employment generation.

**Gross Domestic Product**

The forest sector provides a range of goods and services whose value is pegged at `26,000 crores annually. Nearly half of it is from fuelweed.

Concerns have been raised about the impact of deforestation in Himalayas on floods in the Ganga basin. Results of some studies have shown that the deforestation of the Himalayas is not likely to have a significant effect on the extent of the floods in the plains and the delta below.

Forest carry out many important vital functions given in the following tables.

**Table 2.2: Main functions of the forests**

| Functions | Benefits |
|---|---|
| Productive functions | Production of various types of wood, fruits and a wide range of compounds such as resins, alkaloids, essential oil, latex and pharmaceutical substances. |
| Protective functions | Provides habitats for various organisms conservation of soil and water, prevention of drought, shelter against wind, cold, radiation, noise, sounds, smells and sights. |
| Regulative functions | Absorption, storage and release of gases (most importantly carbon dioxide and oxygen), water, minerals, elements and radiant energy. All such functions improve the atmospheric and temperature conditions and enhances the economic and environmental value of the land. Forests also effectively regulate floods and drought and all the biogeochemical cycles. |

**Q26. Give reasons how the tribal communities were able to live in forest without harming it.**

**Ans.** About 4 per cent the world's population lives in special territories. These indigenous or tribal people have claims on a particular place; they have cultural, spiritual and economic ties with the particular area and in most cases they have ability to manage the area and sustain it. In this way they protect the biodiversity of that particular area and the local culture, including knowledge and resource-management skills of the local community. For example, the tribal people knew the agricultural practices which were ecologically sound and these were passed from generation to generation for many centuries. They knew how to grow different kinds of food and fibre crops simultaneously on the same plots and keep the land productive for several years in a row, and then plots were left to recover for several years to grow back into forests, before clearing the area again to begin the cycle afresh.

**Q27. What do you mean by desertification? How desertification and human well-being are linked with each other?**

**Ans.** Desertification is the development of any property of the climate or land surface that is more characteristics of desert, whether the change is natural or anthropogenic. It can be defined as **"the diminution or destruction of the biological potential of the land which can ultimately lead to desert like conditions."**

The arid and semi-arid areas where climate is dry, restoration is very slow, mining and overgrazing, etc. adds to several other desertification pressures. Desertification is a systemic phenomenon resulting from excessive felling of trees, which manifests itself in the loss of soil fertility, high wind velocity, low precipitation, increasing aridity and extremes of temperatures in the affected area.

Desert supports very little of vegetation and animals which are especially adapted to extremely unfavourable conditions. Although desertification can develop from natural causes alone, in a majority of instances human intervention promoted arid conditions in an already dry areas. This can happen in any climatic zone or ecosystem, resulting from exploitative interaction of man with the natural ecosystem. Most of the deserts of recent origin have resulted from any one or more of the following human activities.

- Uncontrolled and overexploitation of grazing land, indiscriminate cutting of trees and forest resources leading to drought, soil erosion, deterioration of soil fertility which results in stunted plant growth.
- Excessive mining in arid and semi-arid regions for extraction of minerals, coal or limestone resulting in loss of trees, and green cover, and leading to total destruction of conditions conducive to vegetation growing.

- Uneconomic land use for agriculture by cultivation on marginal lands affecting adjacent fertile lands and causing soil erosion.
- Intensive and uneconomic exploitation of water resources leading to fall in water table, seepage and problems of excessive salinisation of soil.

**Q28. What are the major causes of desertification?**

**Ans.** In order to understand desertification processes in the Indian context, it is necessary to know the geomorphic processes under natural set-up and acceleration to the processes through human interventions.

**(1) Water Erosion**

Soil erosion through fluvial processes affect large areas in the Saurashtra and Kutch uplands, and along the eastern margin of the Thar Desert where the average annual rainfall varies from 350 to 500 mm, but has very few occurrences to the west of 250 mm isohyets in the Thar.

The manifestations can be deciphered the pattern of sheet, rill and gully erosion features. Increased ploughing and destruction of vegetation cover for fuelwood, overgrazing and other destructive uses, must have accelerated the erosion in recent decades, but in the absence of specific data, it is difficult to suggest how much of the gulling activity is due to human activities alone and how much due to the natural processes. In Kutch region, a part of the problem is related to a slow natural uplift of the terrain over the centuries, which leads to a change in base level and increased erosion.

**(2) Wind Erosion/Deposition**

The most vulnerable landforms to wind erosion/deposition are the sand dunes and other sandy landforms in the Thar. A closer look, however, indicates that the sandy landforms in the east are more stable than the similar landforms in the west. Rainfall gradient and wind strength are both responsible for the spatial variability in sand reactivation pattern.

The introduction of the tractor for deep ploughing, instead of the traditional animal-driven wooden plough, has increased the sand load manifold for the Aeolian processes in large parts of the desert, and accelerated the mobility of sand.

Increased destruction of the natural land cover in grazing lands for fuel and fodder and enlarging the frontiers of cultivation to less suitable sandy areas are also the responsible factors. In the foothills of the Aravali hill ranges along the wetter eastern part of the desert, such activities are also leading to accelerated water erosion, as manifested through the formation of rills and gullies.

The farmers are aware of headword progress of the gullies in the east, but do not believe that their agricultural activities hasten the process, unless tractors are used to loosen the soil. Many of them believe that the agricultural crop residues which they leave in the field are good sand binders and whatever land is being lost through gully erosion is a slow natural phenomenon. In other parts of the desert, farmers agree that deep ploughing with tractors, cultivation along dune slopes, or non-practising of long fallow systems and other traditional farming systems lead to accelerated sand movement and land degradation, but they have very few choices, as population pressure and economic consideration override environment consideration.

### (3) Mining

In western Rajasthan, about twenty major minerals and nine minor minerals are being mined. More than 90 per cent of the mine owners have open cast mining. The rest are underground mines. The area occupied by the mines is increasing and by 2000 AD 0.05 per cent of Jaisalmer district and 1.15 per cent of Jhunjhunu district are reportedly under mining activities.

The surface mining activity causes immediate degradation of land. The mining sites are abandoned after the excavation work is over, without adopting any reclamation measure. Mining on agricultural land, either surface or underground, reduces the productivity of land by way of excavation, disposal of debris and tailing. Mineral processing like grinding of limestone for cement industry, calcite and soapstone for ceramic industry, have three-fold adverse effects.

The fine dust, generated and released in the atmosphere, leads to surface scaling of the adjacent land after it settles down, consequently the infiltration rate is reduced and the run-off increases.

Mining activity restricts the sub-surface movement of water. With the removal of vegetation, the rate of evapotranspiration is reduced and as a result, there is a change in the hydrological balance in the area.

Due to this change, the perched water table rises and causes salinity. When the mining debris of minerals like ball clay, china clay, Fuller's earth, bentonite and gypsum are dumped on the sandy plain, a semi-impermeable surface layer is developed. These areas get flooded during the monsoon and gradually develop salinity. Sodium salt mining activity increases the surface salt concentration, causing total loss of vegetation.

### (4) Vegetation Degradation

One of the first casualties of desertification is natural vegetation. Degradation of natural vegetation is also one of its major causes. With increasing pressure on land vegetation, degradation is increasing at an alarming rate.

The common grazing lands around the villages are now some of the very severely degraded sites, as these are highly exploited and most neglected. Many good grazing lands have also been encroached upon for agriculture.

**Q29. What is social forestry? Explain its types. Give some examples of social forestry programmes.**

**Ans.** The National Commission on Agriculture, Government of India, first used the term 'social forestry' in 1976. It was then that India embarked upon a social forestry project with the aim of taking the pressure off the forests and making use of all unused and fallow land. Government forest areas that are close to human settlement and have been degraded over the years due to human activities needed to be afforested. Trees were to be planted in and around agricultural fields. Plantation of trees along railway lines and roadsides, and river and canal banks were carried out. They were planted in village common land, Government wasteland and Panchayat land.

Social forestry also aims at raising plantations by the common man so as to meet the growing demand for timber, fuel wood, fodder, etc, thereby reducing the pressure on the traditional forest area. This concept of village forests to meet the needs of the rural people is not new. It has existed through the centuries all over the country but it was now given a new character.

With the introduction of this scheme, the government formally recognised the local communities' rights to forest resources, and is now encouraging rural participation in the management of natural resources. Through the social forestry scheme, the government has involved community participation, as part of a drive towards afforestation, and rehabilitating the degraded forest and common lands.

This need for a social forestry scheme was felt as India has a dominant rural population that still depends largely on fuelwood and other biomass for their cooking and heating. This demand for fuel wood will not come down but the area under forest will reduce further due to the growing population and increasing human activities. Yet the government managed the projects for five years then gave them over to the village panchayats (village council) to manage for themselves and generate products or revenue as they saw fit.

Social forestry scheme can be categorised into following groups:

- **Farm forestry:** At present in almost all the countries where social forestry programmes have been taken up, both commercial and non- commercial farm forestry is being promoted in one form or the other. Individual farmers are being encouraged to plant trees on their own farmland to meet the domestic needs of the family. In many areas, this tradition of growing trees on the farmland already exists. Non-commercial farm forestry is the main thrust of most of the social forestry projects in the country today. It is not always necessary that the farmer grows trees for fuel wood, but very often they are interested in growing trees without any economic motive. They may want it to provide shade for the agricultural crops; as wind shelters; soil conservation or to use wasteland.

- **Community forestry:** Another scheme taken up under the social forestry programme is the raising of trees on community land and not on private land as in farm forestry. All these programmes aim to provide for the entire community and not for any individual. The government has the responsibility of providing seedlings, fertiliser but the community has to take responsibility of protecting the trees. Some communities manage the plantations sensibly and in a sustainable manner so that the village continues to benefit. Some others took advantage and sold the timber for a short-term individual profit. Common land being everyone's land is very easy to exploit. Over the last 20 years, large-scale planting of Eucalyptus, as a fast growing exotic, has occurred in India, making it a part of the drive to reforest the subcontinent, and create an adequate supply of timber for rural communities under the augur of 'social forestry'.
- **Extension forestry:** Planting of trees on the sides of roads, canals and railways, along with planting on wastelands is known as 'extension' forestry, increasing the boundaries of forests. Under this project, there has been creation of wood lots in the village common lands, government wastelands and Panchayat lands.
- **Agro-forestry:** Planting of trees on and around agricultural boundaries, and on marginal, private lands, in combination with agricultural crops is known as agro-forestry.

## Social forestry programmes

**Table 2.3: Social Forestry Programme**

| | |
|---|---|
| 1969-70 to 1979-80 | Social Forestry Plantations carried out through the State Scheme. |
| 1980-81 to 1984-85 | Word Bank Phase 1, first phase of Social Forestry called "Community Forestry Project" was implemented with assistance from the word Bank. |
| 1985-86 to 1992-93 | Word Bank Phase 2, second phase was implemented with assistance from the Word Bank and USAID. |
| 1993-94 to 1995-96 | Social Forestry plantations were undertaken under the state schemes. |
| 1996-97 to 2001-02 | Integrated Forestry Development Project (IFDP) with assistance from the OECF (Japan) |
| 2002-03 to 2003-04 | Social Forestry plantations were undertaken under the State Scheme |
| 2005-06 to 2011-12 | Social Forestry plantations were undertaken under the State Scheme |

**Q30. What do you understand by Aquatic Ecosystems? Describe types of an aquatic ecosystem.**

**Ans.** An aquatic ecosystem is a group of interacting organisms dependent on one another and their water environment for nutrients (e.g., nitrogen and phosphorus) and shelter. Familiar examples are lakes and rivers, but aquatic ecosystems also include areas such as flood plain marshes, which are flooded with water for only parts of the year. Seemingly, inhospitable aquatic ecosystems can sustain life.

Aquatic ecosystems refer to plant and animal communities occurring in water bodies. Aquatic ecosystems are classified on the basis of salinity into following two types:

**(1) Fresh water ecosystem**

Water on land which is continuously cycling and has low salt content is known as fresh water and its study is called limnology.

- Static or still water (Lentic), e.g. pond, lake, bogs and swamps.
- Running water (Lotic), e.g. springs, mountain brooks, streams and rivers.

*Physical characteristics*

Fresh waters have a low concentration of dissolved salts.

The temperature shows diurnal and seasonal variations. In tropical lakes, surface temperature never goes below 400C, in temperate fresh waters, never goes above or below 40$^0$C and in polar lakes never above 40C.

- In temperate regions, the surface layer of water freezes but the organisms survive below the frozen surface.
- Light has a great influence on fresh water ecosystems. A large number of suspended materials obstruct penetration of light in water.
- Certain animals float upto water surface to take up oxygen for respiration Aquatic plants use carbon dioxide dissolved in water for photosynthesis.
- Lakes and ponds are inland depressions containing standing water. The largest lake in the world is lake Superior in North America. Lake Baikal in Siberia is the deepest. Chilka lake of Orissa is largest lake in India.

Aquatic organisms can be floating in water or free swimming or sedentary (fixed), depending on their size and habit. Microscopic floating organisms such as algae, diatoms, protozoans and larval forms are called **plankton.** Rooted aquatic plants, fish, mollusk and echinoderms are bottom dwellers.

**(2) Marine ecosystem**

Marine ecosystem covers nearly 71 per cent of the earth's surface with an average depth of about 4000 m. Fresh water rivers eventually empty into ocean. Different kinds of organisms live at different depths of the sea or ocean.

Salinity of open sea is 3.6 per cent and is quite constant. The range of temperature variation is much less in the sea than on the land. Hydrostatic pressure due to water column increases with depth in oceans. It is 1 atm near the surface and 1000 atm at greatest depth. Animals in the deeper layers are adapted to the high pressure. Some marine organisms such as sperm whales and certain seals can dive to the great depths and swim back to the surface without difficulty. Tides, due to gravitational pull of the moon are a common feature of marine ecosystems.

Biodiversity of the marine ecosystems is very high as compared to terrestrial ecosystems. Almost every major group of animals occurs in the sea. Insects and vascular plant are completely absent in marine ecosystem. Maximum diversity of marine organisms is found in the tidal zone that is near the shore. Diatoms, algae, dinoflagellates and jelly fishes are some of the free floating life forms in oceans. Large crustaceans, molluscs, turtles and mammals like seals, porpoises, dolphins and whales are free swimming animals that can navigate. Bottom dwellers are generally sessile (fixed) organisms like sponges, corals, crabs and starfish.

**Adaptations:**

- Light weight animals and plants float in water and move with the water currents.
- Animals and plants in ocean are tolerant to high concentration of salts (osmoregulation). Osmoregulation is the process by which a constant osmotic pressure is maintained in blood.
- Swimming animals have streamlined body. Their body is laterally compressed.
- Deep sea forms show bioluminescence (they emit light).
- They are dependent for their food on the upper sea zones.

**Q31. Categorise aquatic organisms on the basis of their life form.**

**Ans.** The organisms in the aquatic ecosystem are unevenly distributed but can be classified on the basis of their life form or location into five groups.

- **Neuston:** These are unattached organisms, which live at the air-water interface such as floating plants and several types of animals. Some spend most of their lives on top of the air-water interface, such as water striders, while there spend most of their time just beneath the air-water interface and obtain most of their food within the water, e.g., beetles and back-swimmers.
- **Periphyton:** These are organisms, which remain attached or clinging to stems and leaves of rooted plants or substances emerging above the bottom mud. Usually sessile algae and their associated group of animals fall in this group.

- **Plankton:** The composition of plankton is highly volatile and may change in hours due to weather conditions, such as light exposure, wind, etc, as well as to changing currents. As such, plankton is not a good indicator of an ecosystem but a number of classifiers or modifiers are highly influential on plankton composition.
- **Nekton:** This group contains animals, which are swimmers. The nektons are relatively large and powerful as they have to overcome the water currents. The animals range in size from the swimming insects, which may be only about 2 mm long, to the largest animals that have lived on earth namely the blue whale.
- **Benthos:** The benthos or the benthic organisms are those found living in or on the bottom or benthic region of the water mass. They exhibit a variety of adaptations to the environment. The reason for this is that bottom is more heterogeneous habitat than either the open water or the surface and this diversity is reflected in the organisms. Practically every aquatic ecosystem contains well developed benthos. The adaptations of the organisms in the benthic community reflect the composition of the bottom, its stability or tendency to shift, and its depth.

**Q32. What are the factors that restrict productivity of aquatic habitats?**
**Ans.** Sunlight and oxygen are the two most important limiting factors of the aquatic ecosystems. Now we will consider some of the important limiting factors which exert controlling influence on productivity of aquatic ecosystems, namely sunlight, transparency, temperature and oxygen.

- **Sunlight:** Sunlight is a major limiting factor for water bodies, since light rapidly diminishes as it passes down the column of water. The upper layers of the aquatic ecosystems, up to which light penetrates and within which photosynthetic activity is confined forms the photic zone. The depth of this zone depends on the transparency of water.
- **Transparency:** Transparency affects the extent of light penetration. It is indirectly related to turbidity. Suspended particulate matters such as clay, silt and phytoplankton make the water turbid, consequently limiting the extent of light penetration and this photosynthetic activity in a significant way.
- **Temperature:** The water temperature changes less rapidly than the temperature of air because water has a considerably higher specific heat than air, that is larger amounts of heat energy must be added to or taken away from water to raise or lower its temperature. Since water temperatures are less subject to change, it follows that aquatic organisms have narrow temperature tolerance. As a result, even small changes in water temperatures

are a great threat to the survival of aquatic organisms than comparable changes in air temperature are in terrestrial organisms.

- **Dissolved oxygen:** Oxygen in the terrestrial ecosystems occurs in the atmosphere along with other gases in a certain fixed concentration however, in aquatic ecosystems it is dissolved in water, where its concentration varies constantly depending on factors that influence the input and output of oxygen in water. In fresh water, the average concentration of dissolved oxygen is 0.0010 per cent (also expressed as 10 parts per million or 10 ppm) by weight, which is 150 times lower than the concentration of oxygen in an equivalent volume of air.

**Q33. Differentiate between lentic and lotic fresh water ecosystem.**

**Ans.** Lentic ecosystem (also called the lacustrine ecosystem or the still water ecosystem) and lotic ecosystem (also called the riverine ecosystem) are two types of water ecosystems, the first dealing with still water ecosystems and the second dealing with flowing water ecosystems. Together, they are the two ecosystems that make up the study of freshwater ecology, also known as aquatic ecology.

**Lentic Water Features**

A lentic ecosystem entails a body of standing water, ranging from ditches, seeps, ponds, seasonal pools, basin marshes and lakes. Deeper waters, such as lakes, may have layers of ecosystems, influenced by light. Ponds, due to their having more light penetration, are able to support a diverse range of water plants.

**Lotic Water Features**

A lotic ecosystem can be any kind of moving water, such as a run, creek, brook, river, spring, channel or stream. The water in a lotic ecosystem, from source to mouth, must have atmospheric gases, turbidity, longitudinal temperature gradation and material dissolved in it.

Lotic ecosystems have two main zones, rapids and pools. Rapids are the areas where the water is fast enough to keep the bottom clear of materials, while pools are deeper areas of water where the currents are slower and silt builds up.

**Q34. What are wetlands? Discuss its components and importance.**

**Ans.** Wetlands are areas that periodically get inundated with water and support a flourishing community of aquatic organisms including frog and other amphibians. Swamps, marshes and mangroves are examples of wetlands. Wetlands are characterised by three main components:

- **Presence of water:** water is either at or near the land surface for some time. Some wetlands are continually flooded while others may simply have saturated soils.

- **Soil type:** wetland soils are called hydric soils and have characteristics which indicate they are different from nearby upland soils.
- **Vegetation type:** wetland plants, called hydrophytes, are adapted to life in wet conditions. Cattails, bulrushes and sawgrass are familiar hydrophytes.

**Importance**

Wetlands are important and valued environments for many reasons; some of them are listed below:

- They are highly productive ecosystems, and are able to capture energy and provide food for many animals.
- They provide important refuges for wildlife in times of drought.
- They are naturally beautiful places and provide opportunities for recreation activities such as boating, swimming, bushwalking and bird watching.
- They provide a natural water balance in the landscape and help to provide protection against floods.
- They have a role in providing water quality protection in the catchment by filtering pollutants such as sediments, nutrients, organic and inorganic matter and bacteria.
- They support a wide variety of flora (plants) and fauna (animals) and form different habitats and ecosystems.
- They provide nursery areas for fish, and breeding grounds for wildlife, particularly waterbirds.
- Wetlands provide vital habitat for some species of threatened fauna (animals).
- They provide refuge for migratory waterbirds that breed in the northern hemisphere in countries such as China and Siberia. Thousands of migratory waterbirds inhabit Australian wetlands each year.
- Many wetlands are of cultural significance to aboriginal people.

**Q35. What do you mean by Lake ecosystems? What are its characteristics?**

**Ans.** Lakes are inland bodies of water that lack any direct exchange with an ocean. Lake ecosystems are made up of the physical, chemical and biological properties contained within these water bodies. Lakes may contain fresh or salt water (in arid regions). They may be shallow or deep, permanent or temporary. Lakes of all types share many ecological and biogeochemical processes and their study falls within the discipline of 'limnology'. Lakes are superb habitats for the study of ecosystem dynamics: interactions among biological, chemical and physical processes are frequently either quantitatively or qualitatively distinct from those on land or in air. Because the boundaries between water and land, and water and air are distinct, there is tight coupling among many ecosystem components.

**(1) Thermal stratification:** The thermal is fairly pronounced during the summer season in most lakes of cold region. The thermal stratification is more during summer seasons primarily due to two reasons:

(a) Due to solar intensity that increases during summers, heating up the upper layer of water and the lower layers remain cool.

(b) Mixing of thermally stratified layers by winds. The various stratified layers are: Epilimnion, Metalimnion, Hypolimnion.

**(2) Winter Stratification:** During extreme winter's the surface layer of the water freeze and under these conditions, inverse stratification develops. The water beneath the ice develops warmth by absorbing solar radiations. At $4^{\circ}$C the water becomes heavy and dense and moves towards bottom where it mixes with bottom mud. This results in the higher temperature at bottom without the total stability being disturbed.

**(3) Over turn:** The circulation of water occurs twice a year, in autumn and spring called 'overturn'. This allows a though mixing of water, planktons, etc.

**(4) Light Stratification:** The penetration of light in water bodies is limited depending on the transparency of water and its ability to absorb light. On the basis of light penetration lakes become vertically stratified into two basic layers (1) the upper trophogenic zone, corresponding roughly to the photic zone. (2) tropholytic zone where decomposition is most active and which corresponds to the aphotic zone.

Between these two zones is the compensation depth – the depth at which light intensity is such that the photosynthetic production is just enough to balance respiratory losses and beyond which light penetration is so low that it is no longer effective. Generally, compensation depth occurs where light intensity is about 100 foot candles or approximately one per cent of full noon sunlight incident to the surface.

**(5) Oxygen Stratification:** In many lakes, the oxygen stratification nearly parallels to that of temperature during summer season. The quantum of oxygen is maximum of the surface which gradually decreases with depth.

**Q36. What do you mean by overturn? Also write its types.**

**Ans.** The summer or winter stratification is seasonal. Circulation of lake occurs twice a year, in the spring and autumn (fall) seasons by a process called overturn. This circulation is important for lakes which undergo stratification as it allows, through mixing of oxygen, phytoplankton and nutrients within the lake.

- **Spring overturn:** In spring and early summer season the increased solar radiation melts the ice cover, which as it attains a temperature of $4°C$, becomes dense and heavy and sinks to the bottom, displacing the lower water which moves up. This circulation of water is further helped by the prevailing summer winds and is called spring overturn.
- **Autumn (fall) overturn:** In autumn or early winter the air temperature falls, resulting in the cooling of the surface waters. When the surface water cools to $4°C$ it becomes dense and heavy and sinks to the bottom displacing the bottom warm water which rises to the surface. This mixing of the surface and bottom layers is further facilitated by strong winter winds and is called 'fall overturn'.

**Q37. Discuss the various salient features of marine ecosystem.**

**Ans.** Marine ecosystems are among the largest of Earth's aquatic ecosystems. They include oceans, salt marsh and intertidal ecology, estuaries and lagoons, mangroves and coral Marine ecosystems are among the largest of Earth's aquatic ecosystems. They include oceans, salt marsh and intertidal ecology, estuaries and lagoons, mangroves and coral reefs, the deep sea and the sea floor. There are following salient features of marine ecosystems:

**(1)** **Salinity:** The sea is salty and its salinity is fairly constant, averaging about 3.5 per cent usually written as 35 (parts per thousand). Sodium chloride is the main salt being 27 per cent while the rest are calcium, potassium and magnesium salts.

**(2)** **Light** is a limiting factor in the ocean as it contributes significantly to organic production and distribution of marine life. On the basis of the light penetration into two horizontal zones:

(a) The lighted photic or euphotic zone extending from the sea surface up to a depth of 200 metres, where sufficient light reaches to support photosynthesis. This photic zone, also called the epipelagic one.

(b) aphotic or lightless zone which distinguishable into three further sub-zones. (i) mesopelagic which extends from 200 metres to 1,000 metres. This zone is in semi-darkness as very little light penetrates it. (ii) bathypelagic zone which extends from 1,000 metres to 2,000 metres and where darkness is virtually complete, for humans though some fishes and crustacean do respond to dim light.

(c) abyssopelagic zone where permanent darkness prevails and where temperature is uniform at 3°C and hydrostatic pressure is enormous.

(3) **Temperature** like salinity remains almost constant in the oceans in contrast to the land of terrestrial ecosystems ranging from about 2°C in the polar seas to 32°C or more in the tropics.

(4) **Concentration of Nutrients:** The marine environment is low concentrations of dissolved nutrients, which since they occur in very little amount are measured in parts per billions (ppb) in contrast to salts, such as sodium chloride which is measured in parts per thousand (ppt).

(5) **Dissolved Gases:** The marine environment serves the gigantic reservoir of dissolved oxygen and carbon dioxide, which respectively help to regulate the composition of the air we breathe and the temperature of the atmosphere.

(6) **Alkalinity:** The sea is alkaline, as the electrical dissociation force of cations exceed that of anions. Further, it is buffered and has a pH of 8.2 normally, and so resists changes in pH.

(7) **Continuity:** The sea is a continuous body of water. All the oceans: Pacific,. Indian, Arctic and Antarctic are connected together.

(8) **Depth:** The sea is very deep varying in different regions. Generally, life extends to all depths but is confined more to the continental shelf and islands.

(9) **Currents:** The sea is in continuous circulation by means of currents. These may be either, wind driven surface currents of deeper currents, resulting from variations in temperature and salinity.

(10) **Waves and tides:** The sea is dominated by several kinds of waves and tides, which are produced by the pull of moon and sun.

**Q38. Discuss the terrestrial ecosystem in Indian context.**

**Ans.** India is a vast country and possesses many types of natural ecosystems.

**(1) Forests**

Forests in India can be classified in different ways, according to their position, atmosphere, weather condition, etc. Some of the common characteristics of various types of natural vegetation in India includes:

- tropical rain forests,
- tropical deciduous forests,
- temperate broad leaf forests,
- temperate needle leaf or coniferous forests,
- alpine and tundra forests, etc.

Apart from these, there are also some other types of forests are found in India like **tidal forests, Himalayan vegetation, rain forests of southern India, desert region,** etc.

### (a) Tropical rain forests

The tropical rain forests are playing an important role in natural vegetation in India. These types of forests include the tropical evergreen forests and tropical semi-evergreen forests and they are mostly found in places where there is plenty of rainfall and sunshine throughout the year. Growth of the trees is usually at its best where rainfall is in surplus of 200 cm, with a short dry season. Such types of forests are found within rainy slopes of the Western Ghats, plains of West Bengal and Orissa and north-eastern India. Trees grow very briskly in these forests and attain heights of about 60 m and above. The number of species in these forests is too vast and too assorted to utilise each one of them commercially. Ebony, mahogany and rosewood are the main trees of these forests.

### (b) Tropical deciduous forests

Tropical deciduous forests are also known as deciduous (whether it is moist or dry)forests because they cast leaves for about six to eight weeks in summer. They are also called the monsoon forests with all their grandeur and beauty. This is so because they form a natural cover approximately all over India, especially within regions having 200 and 75 cm of annual rainfall. Most of the tropical deciduous forests are found in the state of Kerala in India. Apart from Kerala, these forests can be found in the eastern slopes of Western Ghats and also in the north eastern parts of the peninsular plateau and in the valleys of the Himalayas. The tropical deciduous forests are pretty substantial, cost- effective and they demand a lot of maintenance, as they are less resistant to fire. These forests can be divided into moist and dry deciduous forests. The moist deciduous forests are most commonly found on the eastern slopes of the Western Ghats. They are also found in the region of Chota Nagpur plateau, covering east Madhya Pradesh, south Bihar, and west Orissa, Shiwaliks in the northern India. Important trees of these forests are teak, sal, and sandalwood.

### (c) Temperate broad leaf forests

It mainly occurs between 1500-2400 m altitudes in western Himalayas. Several species of Oak (Quercus) are found in these forests. Oak species are ever green in the Himalayan region. These species show peak leaf fall during summer but never become leafless. Height of the trees may be 25-30 m. Trees canopy is dense, herbaceous layer is least developed and grasses are generally lacking. The Oak forests are often rich in epiphytic flora.

### (d) Temperate needle leaf or coniferous forests

These type of forests are found in the Himalaya over 1700 to 3000 m altitude. These forests contain economically valuable gymnospermous trees like pine

(Pinus wallichiana) deodar (Cedrus deodara), Cypress (Cypressus torulosa), Spruce (Picea simthiana) and silver fir (Abies pindrow). Coniferous forests are taller 30-35 m and possess evergreen canopy of long needle like leaves. Canopy of these trees always remains green. In many species, it is cone-shaped.

**(e) Alpine and Tundra forests**

The alpine and tundra forests are another kind of natural vegetation in India. Vegetation growing at altitudes above 3600 m is usually known as alpine vegetation and it can be noticed that with the increment of the altitude, the plants show stunted growth. The trees like silver fir, pine, juniper and birch belong to this category. The alpine grasslands are mainly found at higher altitudes in this region. The people belonging to the tribal groups like Gujjar and Bakarwal make extensive use of this region. The vegetations like lichen and mosses are also found in high altitudinal regions.

- The **tidal forests** provide another variety of natural vegetation in India. They can be found along the coasts and rivers and they are enshrouded by mangrove trees that can live in both fresh and salt water. Sundari is a renowned mangrove tree, mainly found in the tidal forests and it is after this tree that the name Sundarban has been entitled to the forested parts of the Ganga-Brahmaputra delta.
- The **Himalayan vegetation** is one of the major kinds of natural vegetation in India. Thethick tropical forests in the eastern region of India have a sharp distinction with the pine and coniferous woodlands of the western Himalayas. Chir pine (*Pinus roxburghii*) grows throughout the northwest Himalayas, with the exception of Kashmir. Chilgoza (pine nut), oak, maple, ash (*Fraxinus xanthoxyloides*), etc also grow abundantly in the eastern Himalayas.
- The **rain forests of Southern India** are contributing hugely to the natural vegetation in India. The most luxuriant rain forests lie on the southwestern coast, in the state of Kerala. Here the lagoons are canopied by coconut trees and lead to the longest uninterrupted stretch of rain forests in the country. The Andaman and Nicobar Islands and the state of Arunachal Pradesh are some of the other regions with well preserved rain forests in India. Apart from that, dense sandal, teak and sisoo (*Dalbergia sissoo*) forests also flourish on the wet Karnataka plateau.
- The **Thar Desert** presents a wonderful picture of natural vegetation in India. The trees in this desert are short and stout, and stunted by the scorching sun. Cacti, *reunjha* (Acacia leucophloea), khejra (*Prosopis spicigera*), kanju (*Holoptelia*

*integrifolia*), Oak (*Calotropis gigantea*), etc. are common plants in this region. All the above mentioned varieties of forests and areas are contributing hugely to the natural vegetation in India.

**(2) Grasslands**

Grasslands are one of the intermediate stages in ecological succession and cover a part of the land on all the altitudes and latitudes at which climatic and soil conditions do not allow the growth of trees. In India, grasslands are found as village grazing grounds (Gauchar) and extensive low pastures of dry regions of western part of the country an also in Alpine Himalayas. Perennial grasses are the dominant plant community. In some regions, grasslands also support a variety of other herbaceous plants like sedges, legumes and members of the sunflower family.

Grasslands support a large number of herbivores from minute insects to very large mammals. Rats, mice, rodents, deer, elephant, dog, buffalo, tiger, lion, ferrets are some common mammals of grasslands. In the north east India, one horned rhinoceros is amongst the threatened animal of grassland is this region. A large number of avian fauna makes the grassland colourful.

**(3) Deserts**

The Thar desert in Rajasthan is an extension of the Sahara deserts through Arabian and Persian deserts. They extend from Punjab, Haryana, Rajasthan to Gujarat state. Indian deserts are divided into four main types:

- hills,
- plains with hills,
- marshes and,
- plains with sand dunes.

The distinct Rann of Kutch–Bhuj in Gujarat forms a separate zone with in Thar deserts due to its different climatic conditions. It represents vast saline flats. The region of sand dunes is most spectacular and covers an area of 100,000 sq. km nearly. It extends into Pakistan. The dunes are highly sandy and contain 0.12–0.18 mm size grain, 1.8 to 4.5 per cent of clay and 0.4–1.3 per cent of silt.

Since heat and light intensity are very high and sand dunes are shifting, these deserts can not support vegetation. There are only some thorn forests and dry open grasslands. Indira Gandhi canal which carries water through Punjab and Haryana enters into Rajasthan supports some vegetation. The main crops of desert are bajra, millet, wheat, barley, maize, jowar, guwar. Medicinal plants found here are mehndi, hak, isabgole and gugal. Indian deserts support many threatened species of birds and mammals, such as Asiatic lion, wild ass, bats, scaly ant eater, desert fox, Indian gazzel, four horned antelope , white browed Bushchat, Great Indian Bustard, Cranes and Sandgrouse. Gulf of Kuchch is distinguished by the presence of living corals, pearl oyster, sea turtles and a large number of migratory birds like kingfisher, cranes ibis and herons.

**(4) Mountains – The Himalayas**

**Distribution:** The Himalaya is a great range of mountains that spreads over a westnorthwest to east- southeast over a distance of about 2500 km covering Afganistan, Pakistan, India, Nepal, Bhutan and China. In India, it extends from the Indus trench below Nangaparbat in the west to Yarlungtsangpo-Brahmputra George below Namchebarwa peak in east. The Himalayas lying within India occupy nearly 5,31,250 sq. km area They cover about 16.6 per cent of India's total geographical area and are spread partially or completely over 12 states namely: Jammu and Kashmir, Himachal Pradesh, Uttaranchal, Sikkim, West Bengal, Arunachal Pradesh, Assam, Nagaland, Manipur, Tripura, Mizoram and Meghalaya. Himalayas are geographically divided into:

- the Eastern Himalayas or the Assam Himalayas: Out of the above the Eastern Himalaya has a greater diversity of ecosystems like, forests, grasslands, marshes, swamps lakes streams and rivers Eastern Himalayas consists of nearly 8000 species of the flowering plants. It has many primitive as well as many endemic plant species. Eastern Himalayas is known as centre of origin of cultivated plants. Many cereals, fruits and vegetables are cultivated here. E.g. Orchids, *Aster, Accasia, Albizzia, Delbergia* species (timber) and many legumes, etc.
- the Central Himalayas or the Nepal Himalayas
- the Western Himalayas: On the western Himalayas cold deserts of Ladakh support drought and cold resistant varieties of plants and animals, e.g. Yak.
- the North-West Himalayas or the Punjab Himalayas

Eastern Himalayas are one of the world and has large number of animals because of its varied ecological conditions, e.g. Pangolins elephants macaque languor civet.

**(5) Ghats**

Western and eastern ghats are also important ecosystems of India **Western ghats** also known as Sahyadri extend from Tapti river in north to Kanyakumari in south covering nearly 1,40,000 sq km parallel to the west coast of peninsular India. They pass through the states of Gujarat, Maharashtra, Goa, Karnataka, Tamilnadu and Kerala. These ghats are one of the richest biological resources and form distinct ecological and biogeographical region of India. Western ghats are one of 25 hot spots of the world. *Hot spots are the regions which show maximum biodiversity, richness of species and endemic forms.* These ecosystems are the threatened due to human interference. June- September are rainy months. The rainfall may vary from 100 to 500 cm. Soil is mainly red or black in most of the regions and rich in nutrients. 3500 species of flowering plants have been recorded from western ghats of which nearly1500 are endemic species. Nearly 209 species of fresh water fishes occur in these ghats of which 120 are endemic. Similarly out of 219 species of amphibians found here 106 are endemic.

**Eastern ghats** extend in north south-west strike in Indian peninsula covering an area of about 75000 sq. km They are spread through the states of Orissa, Andhra Pradesh and Tamilnadu. The eastern ghats do not form a continuous range because the great rivers Mahanadi, Godavari and Krishna cut across them. They are an assemblage of discontinuous ranges of hills, plateaus and basins. The climate of these ghats may be semiarid to semihumid with a rainfall ranging from 60 to 160 cm. The vegetation ranges from evergreen trees to that of dry savannas. The eastern ghats are affected by the human activity. Conservation of biodiversity here is a big issue today. Special measures are taken to protect this floristic zone. United Nations Conference on Environment held in Rio de Janerio in 1992 discussed the issue of conservation of this region.

**Q39. Discuss the aquatic ecosystem in India.**

**Ans.** Various aquatic ecosystems in India are as follows:

**Freshwater ecosystem**

Freshwater are terrestrial aquatic ecosystems. Lakes, flood ponds, reservoirs and rivers are its important components. The total freshwater area of India is about 7.6 million hectare.

- **Lakes** are naturally formed deep water bodies, e.g. Sultanpur lake, Batkal lake (Haryana).
- **Flood points** are the places that undergo periodic flooding as a river channel overflows with flood water, i.e. natural areas constituting shallow and seasonal water bodies. Bank of large rivers have flood points.
- **Reservoir** is man made areas holding water irrigation and human use. e.g, reservoirs formed by dams used for irrigation.
- **Rivers** are the flowing water bodies as you have studied in this lesson. For example river Yamuna, Ganga and Tapti, Krishna, Kaweri, Narmada, etc.

**Marine ecosystem**

India has a long coastline of about 8000 km stretching along nine states and two island chains. At the coast a number of rivers form estuaries at their conflu. nce with the sea.There are three gulfs - one on the east coast that is gulf of Mannar and two on the west coast, i.e. gulf of Kutchch and gulf of Khambhat.

The continental shelf (extension of land into the sea) is 200 m in depth but variable in width along the coast. The Indian ocean is the smallest of the three great oceans.

The tides are very important in determining the marine life. Nearly 14 species of sea grasses and 120 species of sea weeds are found along the coast. Representatives of almost all the invertebrate and vertebrate groups are found in the marine ecosystem. Corals are the most abundant and play a very important role. 199 species of corals are known from Indian Ocean. They make coral reefs which are home to a large number of other sedentary species like many molluscs, crustaceans and coelenterates. The biodiversity in a coral reef is comparable to that of a tropical rain forest. Sea shore provides feeding and breeding ground to a number of birds also. Sea crows, whales and dolphins are the mammals that have secondarily invaded the sea. Marine fisheries constitute a highly productive sector in India It is a source of food and employment to the coastal population.

**Q40. Define "Estuaries" and its features.**

**Ans.** An estuary is a place where a river or a stream opens into the sea. It is a partially enclosed coastal area at the mouth of the river where its fresh water carrying fertile silt and runoff from the land mixes with the salty sea water. It represents an ecotone between fresh water and marine ecosystem and shows a variation of salinity due to mixing of sea water with fresh water. Estuaries are very dynamic and productive ecosystems since the river flow, tidal range and sediment distribution is continuously changing in them. Examples of estuaries are river mouths, coastal bays, tidal marshes, lagoons and deltas.

**Features of Estuaries**

The physico-chemical properties of the estuaries have large variation in several parameters and this often creates stressful environment for organisms. This is the one cause that large organisms are less in number in this area than smaller organisms.

The most dominant feature of the estuarine environment is the fluctuation in salinity. Though salinity gradient exists sometime in an estuary but the pattern of gradient varies seasonally, with the topography, with the tides and with the amount of fresh water.

The estuaries are dominated by muddy substrates. The deposition of particles is also controlled by currents and size of particle. If the strong currents prevail, the substrate will be coarse (sand) whereas where waters are calm and the currents are weak only fine silt will settle out.

Another important variable is temperature. The temperature of estuary keeps on fluctuating, it heats up and cools down more rapidly under prevailing atmospheric conditions. The surface waters have the greatest temperature range and the deeper waters the smallest.

The wave action in the estuaries is small. As a result, there is deposition of fine sediments and development of rooted plants.

Currents in estuaries are caused primarily by tidal action and river flow. Currents are generally confined to channels, but velocities upto several knots can occur. The erosion and deposition in the estuaries are due to currents which is a natural cycle.

The water of estuaries is turbid because of the great number of particulates in suspension in the water. The turbidity is minimum near the mouth and increases with distance inland. One of the most important factors in estuary water is oxygen. Since, the solubility of oxygen in water decreases with increased temperature and salinity.

**Q41. Write a note on 'Thar Desert'. What are the conditions of plants and animals related to Thar Desert?**

**Ans.** The Thar Desert exhibited spectacular biological diversity because of its evolutionary history and geographical location. This is a extensive region of sandy desert in northwestern India and eastern Pakistan. The Thar Desert is about 805 km long and about 485 km wide. Rainfall is sparse averaging from 127 to 254 mm annually and temperature rises as high as 52.8°C in July.

### Plants

Ecologically, vegetation of the major part of Thar Desert region falls under the category of 'thorn forest type'. However, the natural vegetation cover has become progressively transformed due to prolonged and intense human interference. Nevertheless, natural vegetation makes a substantial contribution to the productivity of trees like **Khejri,** which are highly valued and conscientiously maintained. There are as many as 700 species of plants amongst which grasses alone account for 107 species. Large-scale destruction of natural vegetation from this part of the country is due to heavy pressure of overgrazing by livestock, making regeneration of plants process in the desert very difficult. Human activities and —more fundamental— underlying structural factors and material processes in our society are causing species to vanish at a rate unequalled since the doomsdays of the dinosaur. There's no time to waste. We must protect biodiversity now, for our next generation.

### Animals

Thar desert is fascinating. The Asiatic lion, used to inhabit the plains of Rajasthan, Punjab and Sind in the recent past. It is on record that the last lions occurring in the desert were shot during 1976. The cheetah now extinct in India was at one time found in the Kathiawad region. Similarly, leopards and caracal lynx, the wild boar, wild ass, Asiatic wolf, etc. have also met the same fate. Among other mammalian fauna, Indian gazelle, blue bull and black buck are also in the list of endangered animal species.

Predominant bird species are also very scanty, particularly in sandy habitats of western Rajasthan. The great Indian bustard, houbara, and lesser florican populations in the Thar Desert are dwindling as compared to that in the recent past. Pea-fowl, being a national bird, is well protected by people. Among reptiles, two species of crocodiles and turtles are now restricted to Jawai-dam in Sirohi district at the foot hills of Aravali. The large terrestrial reptile, the rock python found on the foothills of Aravali is also vanishing from the desert. Thus, looking at the past history of Thar desert, a large number of animals are at the verge of extinction and shme have vanished.

**Q42. What are the differences between oligotrophic lakes, eutrophic lakes, and mesotrophic lakes?**

**Ans.** Lakes of the world exhibit a great diversity of shape, size and combination of properties. However, on the basis of nutrient status and primary productivity they can be divided into three categories:

(1) Oligotrophic lakes
(2) Eutrophic lakes
(3) Mesotrophic lakes

Difference between these lakes are as follows:

**Table 2.4: Comparison of oligotrophic, eutotrophic and mesotrophic lakes**

| Criteria | Oligotrophic | Eutrophic | Mesotrophic |
|---|---|---|---|
| Depth surface area ratios | Oligotrophic lakes are deep often with steep sides. Their surface to volume ratio is low(surface area is small compared to depth). | Eutrophic lakes are shallow and their surface to volume ratio is high (surface area is large relative to depth) | Mesotrophic lakes are intermediate between the oligotrophic and eutrophic lakes. (surface area and depth are proportional). |
| Nutrient status | These lakes are poor in nutrients particularly nitrogen, phosphorous and organic matter. | These lakes are rich in nutrients such as nitrogen, phosphorous and organic substances. | They are mildly eutrophic and have characteristic features intermediate between the other two lakes. |
| Primary Production | Primary productivity in these lakes is low. | Primary productivity is high in these lakes due to presence of excess nutrients. | They contain moderate quantities of nutrients and have moderate primary productivity. |
| Species diversity | The number of organisms occurring here are low, though their species diversity is high. | The number of organisms, that is, biomass is high, though species diversity is low. | |
| Oxygen content | Oxygen content in such lakes is high and extends to the bottom. | Oxygen content here is low on the whole. | Oxygen content is medium. |
| Transparency of water body | Waters of oligotrophic lakes are transparent, appearing blue to green in sunlight. | Waters of eutrophic lakes arc cloudy. due to excess algal and plant growth. | Medium turbidity |

**Hello IGNOU Student,**

Do you want to get more marks which means good job, and better career opportunities?
Are you confused about where to study?
Do You know Gullybaba / GPH book is the only com pany started 15 years back by the Ex-IGNOU student and now provides No.1 IGNOU Self-help books across the globe?

We have created these ***Notes*** specially to help IGNOU Students.

We strongly recommend to read from ***GPH Books*** which contain complete material for exam preparation with previous year's question papers solutions.

You can order GPH Books on Gullybaba.com. Pay by "Cash on Delivery", Credit Card, Paytm, or Online Transfer and get home delivery by Govt. Postal Dept. after Lockdown.

# Community Ecology

## An Overview

A population consists of organisms of a particular species and has characteristics like natality, mortality, age structure, growth, dynamics, and so on. But when several populations share a common habitat and its resources, they interact among themselves and develop into a biotic community or simply, a community. Thus, a community is a larger unit than a population, since it includes more than one species population. Microorganism, plants and animals populations sharing a common habitat and interacting among themselves form an animal community and plant populations of an area form a plant community; but the concept of biotic community includes all populations of living organism of a common habitat, ranging from a tract of forest to the whole of the forest, from a small pond to a large lake, and so on.

The biological potential of each species population determines a tolerance range for environmental conditions. The range of environmental conditions which a tax on can tolerate is called its ecological amplitude. The composition of biotic community in any habitat determines the type of community, which survives and develops. The organisms of a community usually exhibit trophic (feeding) relationship among themselves. They also interact in sharing the space and there may be interactions at a reproductive and behavioural level. Animal populations differ in their trophic requirements and therefore a particular animal population. Many biological activities of plants, like periodicity, phenology, etc., are strong associated with animal activities and vice versa.

**Q1. What do you understand by ecological communities? Discuss its characteristics.**

**Ans.** An ecological community is defined as a group of actually or potentially interacting species living in the same place. A community is bound together by the network of influences that species have on one another. Inherent in this view is the notion that whatever affects one species also affects many others – the "balance of nature". We build an understanding of communities by examining the two-way, and then the multi-way, interactions involving pairs of species or many species.

**Characteristics**

There are following features of community:

- A community represents the biotic or living component of the ecosystem. If the non-living (abiotic) factors, together with the living (biotic) entities are considered, then we would be dealing with an ecosystem rather than a community.
- Communities are made up of organisms with interlocking food chains and each species depends on many other species in a community, which are taxonomically unrelated.
- A community may be of any size. A temperate forest of deodar trees is an example of a large community. Rotting log of wood harbouring many insects and worms represents a small community. So the size of a community may vary widely.
- It can be applied to any scale, that is, the earth as a whole can be considered as a large ecosystem, on the other hand, a bowl of water with various living organisms in it is an example of a small ecosystem. Similarly, a forest is a community, so is a rotting log in that forest containing fungus, insects like termites, and even mice. Similarly, a large number of microorganisms within the gut of termite that occurs in the rotting log of wood, also constitute a community.
- Some communities may be autotrophic, in the sense that they include photosynthetic plants and obtain their energy from the sun. Other communities such as those found in springs and caves are heterotrophic, as they depend upon organic material such as detritus as a source of energy.
- Interrelated with the idea of community is that of the ***stand.*** In some situations these two terms mean ***different*** things; and in some other situations these two terms mean the ***same*** thing, and are used interchangeably.

**Q2. Define the term "Gradient Analysis".**

**Ans.** Gradient analysis is a powerful technique to analyze for, and detect change in, the dynamics, structure, and function of ecosystems. Boundaries between zones or communities occur at distinctive locations along environmental gradients and are expected to be especially sensitive to environmental change. Gradient analysis can be performed at a range of scales, and allows integration and extrapolation of change across scales from those associated with communities to those of biomes. This review outlines the properties of gradients in space and time and uses. For example, the forests in the Rocky Mountain Physiographic Province to demonstrate constraints, the complex mosaics associated with distributional limits, transfers across boundaries, the role of disturbance, and threshold dynamics. A climate change scenario is developed to hypothesize future changes in boundary movements, community mosaics, and ecosystem properties along elevational and latitudinal gradients in the Rocky Mountain Province. Mechanistic explanations of ecological phenomena that are necessary for management require information on: (1) the physical environmental constraints operating on the ecosystem; (2) the biota that operate within those constraints; and (3) the interactions among the biota and between the biota and environment. The relative importance of these three elements differs between environments and along environmental gradients. Biota and their interactions may account for much of the variance in system structure and function in mesic environments, while abiotic factors may limit biotic activity in less favorable (arid) habitats. Plot studies that are analyzed as points along broader scale environmental gradients can provide quantitative information on the major driving variables, and broad scale analyses of environmental factors along the gradient generate the information for extrapolating between sites and across scales. Modeling that includes such spatial gradients provides the foundation for local to regional management programs.

**Q3. Write down the analytic character of bio-community.**

*Or*

**Describe and two qualitative characters of a plant community.**

**[Dec-2011, Q.No.-9]**

**Ans.** The characters, which are directly observed or measured in samples plots are called analytic characters. The analytic characters may be either qualitative or quantitative. The qualitative analytic characters are based on non-quantitative observations. For example, the species composition, stratification, phenology, association of species, etc. of vegetation. On the other hand, the quantitative analytic characters are measured in quantity. The major qualitative and quantitative analytic characters are described below:

**(1) Qualitative Characters**

The important qualitative characters are as follows:

***Floristic Composition***

One of the important qualitative characteristics of a community is its floristic composition. This broadly refers to the kind of species occurring in a community.

To study the Floristic composition of a community, the first thing done is to prepare a list of species comprising that particular community. In practice, it is nearly impossible to name each and every organism, as some of them are very minute. Amongst plants, usually the ***vascular*** plants are counted. In order to make a complete list, species appearing in different seasons are also considered. Although all the species in a community are significant:, but only a single species or a few species are often used in naming a community, because of its (their) abundance or dominance.

These lists give the idea about the following:

- ***One,*** the relationship of a particular species to the environment and to other species;
- ***Two,*** the habitat of different species,
- ***Three,*** the ecological amplitude of species, and
- ***Four,*** the present conditions and future trends of the community.

### *Stratification*

The stratification of a community is determined largely by the life-from of plants- their size, branching and leaves-which in turn influences and is influences by the vertical gradient of light. The stratification allows the plants to exploit the incoming radiation and the space to the maximum according to their differential requirements. The crowding effect is mitigated through adjustment in height.

A well developed coniferous and broad leaves forest has three principal layers of vegetation. From top to bottom, they are over-story stratum or mature forest canopy; understory stratum or intermediate forest canopy or shrub; and ground-story stratum or forest floor or herb layer.

### *Life-form*

A community has a characteristic structural composition of life-forms, viz., trees, shrubs, herbs, epiphytes, thallophytes, etc. Study of a community from the viewpoint of life forms can help in an understanding of functions of individual organisms in a community.

Raunkiaer (1909, 1928, 1934) gave a classification of life forms which is based upon the overwintering parts or the location of organs that can survive summer drought or other unfavourable conditions. In other words, it is the unfavourable environmental condition that, determines the life forms and also the position and degree of protection to perennating buds. According to him, the height of the perennating buds reflected adaptation to climate. He has assumed that the vegetation of the hot tropics represents the primitive life from and that of colder regions represent the more highly evolved forms.

*According to Raunkiaer there are five life forms:*

- **Phanerophytes:** The perennating buds in this case are present on erect shoots much above the ground and are least protected.

They are abundant in the tropics and their number progressively decreases as we proceed from tropics to polar region.

- **Chamaephytes:** These plants are found in cold region and at higher latitudes. The perennating buds and shoot apices are borne very close to the ground.
- **Hemicryptophytes:** They are also found in cold regions. Aerial parts die at the onset of unfavourable conditions. Stolons may or may not be present. Perennating buds are presents at the ground level.
- **Cryptophytes:** Perennating buds are always below the ground level or are submerged in water.
- **Therophytes:** These are annuals which complete their life-cycle from seed to seed during the favourable season of the year. They have a period of few weeks to few months. They are usually found in deserts.

***Dispersion and Sociability***

The dispersion refers to the distribution of the individuals in the horizontal space. This distribution may be uniform, random, or clumped (grouped) as shown in fig. 3.1. The sociability expresses the relation of individuals to each other and indicates the closeness between individuals. Braun-Blanquet (1932) recognised five arbitrary categories of sociability:

$S_1$ - plants growing singly.

$S_2$ - plants growing in small groups.

$S_3$ - plants occurring in small patches.

$S_4$ - plants forming large patches.

$S_5$ - plants occurring in essentially continuous populations.

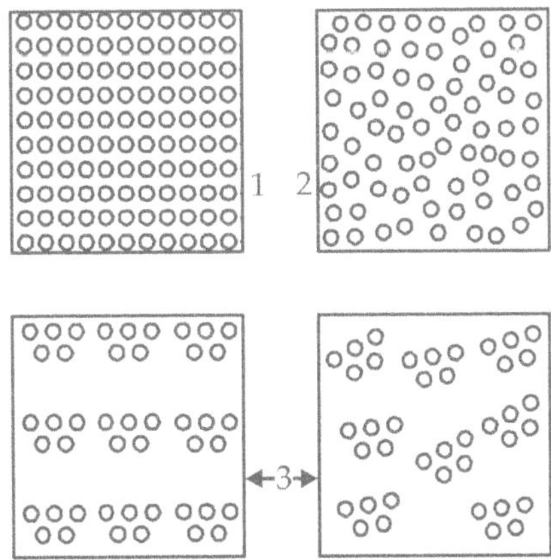


**Fig. 3.1**

### *Vitality*

It is concerned with the normal growth and reproduction ability of the species which helps it in maintaining its position in the community. The vigour indicate the state of health. The vigour of a species in field may indicate the end or the beginning of a new stage of succession, a change in soil moisture, attack by parasites, effect of grazing, etc. Various authors have recognised three to five categories of vitality. These are:

$V_1$ - plants which germinate but die soon without reproducing,

$V_2$ - plants which inger after germination but cannot reproduce,

$V_3$ - plants which reproduce but only vegetatively,

$V_4$ - plants which reproduce sexually but are uncommon,

$V_5$ - plants which reproduce sexually and grow regularly.

### *Association of Species*

It is the growing together of two or more species in close proximity to one another as a rather regular occurrence; for example Boswellia serrata and Dendrophthoe falcata in the Aravalli mountain of south-eastern Rajasthan. Association of species may be brought about by the similarity in ecological amplitudes of two or more species; similarity in geographical ranges; differences in life-forms so that extensive competition can be avoided; dependence of one species upon another for shade, or for food as parasites; dependence for protection from grazing. Association may be so pronounced that a certain species may indicate the presence of other species in the stand.

## Quantitative Characters

The important qualitative characters are as follows:

### *Frequency*

It is concerned with the homogeneity of the occurrence of the individuals of a species within an area. It is expressed as the percentage occurrence of individuals of a species in a number of observations. It is the degree of dispersion in terms of percentage occurrence.

The distribution of species is rarely uniform or regular in an area. Variation is cause by many influences, such as micro-habitat conditions of topography or soil, vegetative propagation, quantity and dispersal of seeds time of invasion, grazing, activity of rodents, loss by insects or diseases. As a result, some areas may have higher frequency while others may have lower frequency. Such differences are more pronounced in irregular topography or where soil varies within short distances.

Frequency is calculated by finding the percentage number of plots or samples in which a species occurs divided by the number of plots studied.

$$\text{Frequancy} = \frac{\text{Number of plots in which species occurs}}{\text{Total number of plots sampled}} \times 100$$

### *Density*

Frequency does not give correct idea of the distribution of any species, unless it is correlated with other characters, such as density, etc. Density represents the numerical strength of a species in the community. The number of individuals of a species per unit area is its density. It is calculated as follows.:

$$\text{Density} = \frac{\text{Number of individuals of a species}}{\text{Area sampled}}$$

*Or*

$$= \frac{\text{Total number of individuals of a species in all the sampling units}}{\text{Total number of sampling units studied}}$$

### *Cover*

Cover is the area occupied by a plant and can be expressed as either basal cover or canopy cover. The basal cover is the land area occupied by the cross-section of the stem, and canopy cover is the total land area under the canopy of a plant. The basal area can be only a small fraction of the total land area under a community, but the canopy cover of a single species may be several times the total land area because of overlapping canopies. Stratification in a forest causes increase in canopy cover by more than 150-200 per cent of the ground area. On the basis of foliage cover in a community the species are grouped into five classes:

Class A - Species with 5 per cent foliage cover or less.

Class B - Species with 6-25 per cent cover

Class C - Species with 26-50 per cent cover

Class D - Species with 51-75 per cent cover

Class E - Species with 76-100 per cent cover

Plants with greater canopy cover are capable of intercepting more solar energy and cause deeper shade, which influences the plant distribution of the ground flora.

### *Height of plants*

The height of plants usually indicates their vigour, and a measure of the environmental conditions. It is a very good indicator of their general performance and therefore can be employed as a criterion of the success of species in various habitats. It is sometimes difficult to secure accurate measurements because the height attained by the stem and leaves varies with individual plants of the same species growing under similar conditions.

Height measurements have given us many interesting and important results, for example, interspecific competition between Artimisia tridentata and range grasses, resulted in 4 inch tall Agropyron cristatum, but 7 inch tall where competition was lacking (Robertson, 1947).

### *Weight of Plants*

Weight is one of the most important quantitative characteristics of plants. The total weight of food substances, protoplasm and other substances constitutes the forage value of the herbage. Most of the researches on weight have been done on the forage parts, but since the seventies, some work has been done on the weight of stem and branches. Very meagre amount of work has been done on root system probably because of the difficulty of sampling and exploiting the entire root system.

**Q4. What are the synthetic characteristics of biotic community?**

*Or*

**Describe any two synthetic characters of a plant community.**

**[June-2012, Q.No.-9]**

**Ans.** Data are collected from analytic characteristic result in tentative grouping of stands into associations, on the basis of synthetic characteristics, which are as follows:

### Presence and Constancy

The uniformity of a species in number of stands of the same type of community is denoted by the terms presence and constancy. If a species is found in 15 to 25 stands in a type of community its presence or constancy is 60 per cent. The term constancy is used if sample areas are of equal size and the term presence is used if the sample areas vary from stands to stands. Species are classified into five classes of constancy. These classes are:

Class I - 1-20 per cent of the sampling units of a community

Class II - 21-40 per cent of the sampling units of a community

Class III - 41-60 per cent of the sampling units of a community

Class IV - 61-80 per cent of the sampling units of a community

Class V - 81-100 per cent of the sampling units of a community

The species that occur in over 80-90 per cent or in more sampling units are called constant species. These species are important as they characterise and help to distinguish a community type. The species belonging to class IV and V indicate two possibilities: i) the species have a wide ecological amplitude and are therefore capable of growing in various micro-habitats, and ii) the various sampling units are very similar in environmental conditions, so that species of narrow amplitude can grow in all of them.

### Fidelity

Fidelity refers to the degree to which a species is restricted in its occurrence to a particular kind of community. The species with low fidelity occur in a number of different communities, and species with high fidelity are restricted to few or only one community. The following five fidelity classes can be recognised:

*(A) Characteristic species (Character, faithful species)*

**Fidelity 5:** Exclusive, completely or almost completely restricted to one kind of community

**Fidelity 4:** Selective, occurring most frequently in one kind of community, but also, though rarely, in other kinds

**Fidelity 3:** Preferential, occurring more or less abundantly in several kinds of communities but with optimum conditions for abundance and vitality in one kind of community.

*(B) Companion Species*

**Fidelity 2:** Indifferent, occurring without pronounced affinity or preference for any particular kind of community

*(C) Accidental Species*

**Fidelity 1:** Strange, rare and accidental intruders from another community or relicts from an earlier stage of succession

Some species cannot grow or are not found in other communities, because species differ in their ecological amplitude or in their capacity to tolerate a wide range of ecological conditions. Some species are able to associate with others, whereas others are not.

### Dominance

It is a characteristic of vegetation, which expresses the predominating influences of one or more species in a stand so that the population of other species is more or less repressed, or is reduced in number and vitality. Dominants are those species which are highly successful in a particular habitat. Cover and population density are the chief qualities determining dominance, but parameters like frequency, height, life form and vitality arc also important. The dominants exercise a controlling influence in the habitat while modifying the microhabitat which permits the growth of many different species which otherwise cannot survive in the absence of dominants.

### Physiognomy and Pattern

Physiognomy is the general appearance of vegetation as determined by the growth, form of dominant species. It may be considered a synthetic character because the appearance is based on a number of qualitative characteristics such as the kind of dominant species, life form, population density, cover, height, sociability, stratification, and association of species. For example, if we look at a community where large trees are dominant and some shrubs are also present we would immediately say that it is a forest. Similarly, on the basis of appearance one can identify a community as grassland or desert community.

Pattern refers to whether the vegetation occurs in the form of groups or clumps of individuals or in any other non-random arrangement.

### Frequency

This term refers to the degree of dispersion of individual species in an area, and is usually expressed in terms of percentage. Frequency can be studied by sampling the study area at several places at random or in a desired pattern, so that the site is covered adequately and the names of the species that occur in each sampling unit are recorded. To determine the frequency of a species. Consider a species that occurs in five sampling units out of a total of 20 sampling units, then its frequency (F) is 25 per cent. It is calculated by the following formula:

$$F = \frac{\text{Number of sampling units in which that species occurred}}{\text{Total number of sampling units studied}} \times 100$$

A species most abundantly spread all over the area will have chance of occurring in all the sampling units, and therefore, its frequency will be 100 per cent. A poorly dispersed species, with large number of individuals aggregated in one place will have a chance of occurrence in only a few sampling units and its frequency value will be low. Thus, a high frequency value shows a greater uniformity of its dispersion.

### Importance Value Index (IVI)

In any study of community, the quantitative value of each of the frequency, density, and cover has its own importance. But the total picture of ecological importance cannot be obtained by any one of these alone. For instance, frequency gives an idea as to how a species is dispersed in an area but we do not get any idea about its number or the area covered. Density gives an idea about the numerical strength and so on. To have an overall picture of ecological importance of a species with respect to the community structure, the percentage values of the relative frequency, relative density and dominance are added together and this value out of 300 is called the Importance Value Index (IVI) of the species.

The IVI as such, gives the composite picture of sociological status of a species in a community but it does not provide an idea of relative values of frequency, density and dominance.

### Species Diversity

It is one of the most important and basic characteristics of a community. There are various ways of measuring species diversity, the simplest is to enumerate the number of species present in a given area. This is relatively easy to achieve for plants, and large or sedentary animals but it is generally difficult to enumerate the various insect species accurately. For large areas such as forests, islands, etc., it may take many years to prepare a reasonable estimate of species numbers. Assessment of species diversity on the basis of species list is not fully satisfactory because drawing of an exhaustive and accurate species list is often an involved exercise. And, unless an elaborate exercise is undertaken there is a good possibility that a number of species may be left out. Since so many species in a sample are likely to be rare, we should not ignore this fact while measuring diversity.

For example, compare two imaginary samples of 100 individuals each with two species A and B. The details of number of species of each sample are given in Table 3.1.

**Table 3.1: Number of Species in Two Sampling**

| Simple | Number of Species | |
|---|---|---|
| | A | B |
| I | 50 | 50 |
| II | 99 | 1 |

In sample I there are 50 individuals of A and 50 individuals of B, but in sample II there are 99 A and 1 B. Is the diversity of these two samples really same? If we choose to measure diversity as the numbers of species present in each sample then the answer is yes, but most ecologists would consider the community with 50A and 50B to be more diverse than the one with 99A and 1B.

To determine species diversity, the most widely used index is Shannon's Index of Diversity (H') and it is calculate as below:

$$H' = \sum_{i=1}^{i=S} pi \ \log_e \ pi$$

H' = Index of species diversity

S = Number of species

P = Proportion of the total sample belonging to the ith species (in rank), which is calculated by dividing the number of individuals in species i by the total number of individuals in the sample.

e = base of natural logarithms $(\log_e p_i = 2.302 \times \log_{10} p_i)$

(Remember that $\sum_{i=1}^{i=S}$ means that — add up the following expression, for values of i from i = 1 to i = S).

The larger the value of H', the greater the uncertainty about predicting the next species to be encountered and so the greater the diversity. Let us now compare the two samples I and II, each of 100 individuals, and see whether sample I has higher index of diversity H' or sample II?

**Sample I:**

$$H' = -\left[(0.50 \times \log_e 0.50) + (0.50 \times \log_e 0.50)\right]$$

$$= -\left[2(0.50 \times -0.69)\right] = 0.69$$

**Sample II:**

$$H' = -\left[\left(0.99 \times \log_e 0.99\right) + \left(0.01 - \log_e 0.01\right)\right]$$
$$= -\left[\left(0.99 \times -0.01\right) + \left(0.01 \times -4.61\right)\right]$$
$$= -\left[(-0.01) + (-0.05)\right]$$
$$= 0.06$$

Sample I has the higher index of diversity.

**Q5. What do you understand by succession? What are the kinds of succession?**

*Or*

**Briefly describe the different kinds of succession.**

**[June-2012, Q.No.-12(a)]**

**Ans.** Succession is the 'birth' of an ecosystem and subsequent 'ageing' process of its biotic and abiotic features. Odum (1971) preferred to call this orderly process as ecosystem development. He defined it in terms of the following three parameters: (1) It is an orderly process of community development that involves changes in species structure and community processes with time; it is reasonably directional and therefore, predictable. (2) It results from modification of the physical environment by the community, that is a succession is community controlled even through the physical environment determines the pattern, the rate of change, and often sets limits as to how far development can go.

**Characteristics of Succession**

Ecological succession is characterised by the following features:

- It tends to progress from unstable biotic community to stable biotic community, i.e. complete adjustment with the environment.
- Its seral stages are so regular and directional that an ecologist can often predict the sequence of future communities.
- In successive seral stages, there is a tendency towards an increase in species diversity, total biomass, niche specialisation and humus content of the soil.
- It tends to progress from simple food chains to complex food webs.
- The habitat tends to modify from aquatic or dry conditions to mesic (moderately wet) conditions.
- Succession of plant and animal communities occurs side by side. However, plant succession is easily visible.

**Kinds of Succession**

Succession may be of the following types:

***Primary succession***

A succession developing on newly emerged land or water is termed a primary succession. This succession starts in the areas of extreme conditions and the process terminates after a long series of intermediate stages.

### *Secondary Succession*

A succession developing following a fire or similar major disruption to an established community is called a secondary succession. Secondary succession has fewer stages than the primary succession and the climax is reached very quickly.

### *Autotrophic Succession*

Autotrophic succession is characterised by the early and continued dominance of autotrophic organisms like all kinds of lower and higher green plants. It starts in a predominantly inorganic environment and the energy flow is maintained indefinitely.

### *Hetrotrophic Succession*

It involves the predominance of heterotrophic organisms like fungi, bacteria and animals at the initial stages. Such a succession begins in a medium rich in organic matter.

### *Autogenic Succession*

It involves replacement of one community by another due to modification of the environment by the communities themselves. There seems to be a very reasonable point in considering succession as a characteristic of the community itself, because the community acts on the habitat and tends to make the area or the habitat less favourable for itself but more favourable for other communities.

### *Allogenic Succession*

It is the replacement of one community by another due to forces other than the effects of communities on the environment.

### *Induced Succession*

Activities such as overgrazing, frequent scrapping, shifting cultivation or industrial pollution may cause succession. In agriculture, man makes an effort to stop the normal developmental series of a community and to maintain it at a certain point. He prevents the invasion of a field sown with some crop by other plants, that is, the so-called 'weeds'. Agricultural practices are retrogression of a stable state to a young state by man's deliberate action. In a natural stable state, the community respiration balances community production and there is a little lift, which can be harvested. Therefore, man tries to control the succession in such a way that a managed steady state is maintained, which is different from a natural steady state and wherefrom a good amount is harvested.

### *Retrogressive Succession*

It means a return to simpler and less dense or even depauperate form of community from an advanced or climax community. Most of our natural forests are degrading into shrublands, savanna or even more depauperate desert like stands by the severity of grazing animals brought from the surrounding villages. Extensive removal of wood, leaves and twigs also leads to retrogressive succession.

*Cyclic succession*

It refers to repeated occurrence of certain stages of succession wherever there is an open condition created within a large community. In some forests, the juvenile plants of the dominant plants forming overstory are found in the understory at an arrested stage of growth. As soon as an old tree dies, the juvenile plants of the same species, on getting adequate light and space, suddenly show active growth and cover the open canopy space.

**Q6. Describe the various steps involved in the process of succession. [June-2012, Q.No.-13(b)]**

*Or*

**Write a short note on Nudation. [Dec-2012, Q.No.-5(a)]**

**Ans.** Succession is a universal process by which all communities develop from beginning or bare areas to maturity. It is directional, that is, it has a beginning and an end. The beginning is characterised by certain pioneers, which gradually change as time passes and the end product is the final stable community, so to say the climax community of that area, which is capable of self-perpetuation and which is in equilibrium with the physical environment. The complete process of succession involves the following sequential steps, which follow one another:

**Nudation**

Production or creation of bare areas are the initial causes of succession. Bare areas may be produced in a variety of ways, for example, *erosion* by the action of water, wind, gravity and ice. *Water* may produce a bare area that is entirely without plants along a stream bank. *Wind* brings about land slides especially in sandy soil resulting in bare areas. *Gravity* produces bare areas by pulling down material freed by weathering on the steep slopes of hills. *Glaciers,* ice and snow cause extensive deposits, presenting an extreme condition for rock succession. *Volcanoes* produce bare areas by deposits of lava, such bare areas are characteristic features of Yellowstone National Park. *Fire* caused by lightening in vegetation creates a bare area for colonisation. Bare areas may occur as a result of increased water content of the substratum. *Man* is the most destructive of the biotic factors and destroys vegetation over the largest areas.

**Invasion**

It is the movement of one or more organism from one area into another, which is already occupied by other organisms. It is going on at all time and in all directions. The invasion includes following three steps: (1) ***Plant migration*** - the movement of plants from one area to another constitutes plant migration. Plants must migrate to that area where nudation has taken place. (2) ***Ecasis***—Migration must be followed by ecasis before invasion can be said to have completed. Ecasis is the adjustment of the plant to a new home. (3) ***Aggregation***—After the ecasis of the migrators, the development of families and colonies is due to aggregation.

**Competition**

It occurs between individuals of different species or between individuals of about the same size and having the same general environmental requirements such as water, light, gases, etc. Competition tends to produce plant diversity in both structure and function in most vegetational types. Such diversity in both structure and function in most vegetational types. Such diversity leads to higher yield of plant material per unit area of land surface, because of greater utilisation of the available resources. There is no competition between a parasite and the host.

**Reaction**

Competition results in reaction. When plants grow together and complete for the necessary factors, they profoundly react upon the place in which they grow. The area once fully lighted becomes more or less densely shaded. If it was wet, the large amount of water absorbed from the soil and lost through transpiration makes it drier. If it was dry, the accumulation of humus by the decay of dead roots, stems and leaves adds to the water retaining power of the soil. The area gradually becomes moister. The vegetation checks the wind movement of the soil where seedlings grow. Owing to shade, temperature becomes lower and the moisture content of the air in the vicinity of the plants increases. The soil becomes richer due to the accumulation of humus, bacteria, fungi, etc., and thus more favourable for plant growth. As a result, the vegetation is kept in a dynamic state and succession proceeds towards the climax.

**Coaction**

Coaction refers to the influence of two or more species or individuals upon each other. Coaction upon woody plants is less frequent, but they are not without importance. Plant parasite or animals may retard succession by destroying certain kinds of plants; grazing animals often produce this effect. Fire which may be either biotic or a climatic factor is largely destructive though it may be only retarding in its effect.

**Stabilisation**

The progressive invasion typical of succession produces stabilisation. The dominant species of the climax prevent the entrance into the community, of many new species of plants. The adjustment between the dominant species of a climax and environment approaches so near to perfection that the community is relatively stable.

**Q7. How ecological succession can be illustrated in different habitats?**

***Or***

**Enumerate the successive changes during hydrosere and Xerosere. [Dec-2010, Q.No.-3 (c)]**

*Or*

**Describe the various changes in the characteristics of ecosystems during the process of succession. [Dec-2011, Q.No.-13(a)]**

**Ans.** Ecological succession can be best illustrated by studying the following examples in different habitats:

### (1) Hydrosere (Aquatic Succession)

The various stages in a hydrosere are well studied in ponds, pools or lakes of a limited area (fig.3.2). In a man-made pond, where the soil has been dug out, there are little or no nutrients in the sub-stratum below the water and the water itself does not contain any nutrients. Due to this fact, this stage is characterised by a bottom barren of plant and animal life. In such a new and virgin pond, hydrosere starts with the colonisation of some phytoplanktons, which forms the pioneer plant community and finally terminates into a forest (the climax community). The complete process of hydrosere includes the following stages:

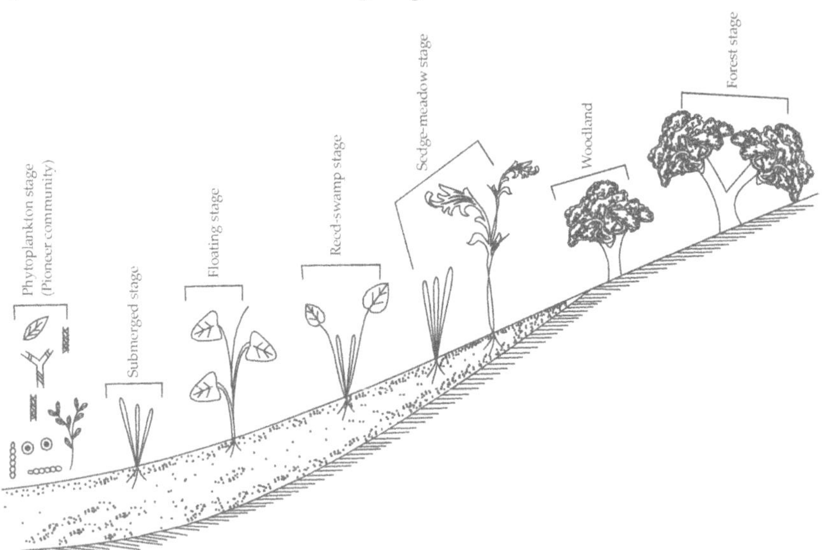


**Fig 3.2: Hydrosere in a Pond Ecosystem**

#### *Phytoplankton stage*

During the pioneer stage of succession, algal spores may be brought by wind along with soil particles and deposited on the water. The unicellular and colonial phytoplanktonic forms begin to multiply and quickly become the pioneer colonisers. In the presence of traces of phosphorus in the medium, large blooms of blue-green algae appear as they could utilise atmospheric nitrogen. Later on filamentous algae like Spirogyra and Oedogonium appear.

### *Submerged stage*

As a result of death and decomposition of planktons, and their mixing with the silt, brought from the surrounding land by rain water and by the wave action of pond water, there develops a soft mud at the bottom of the pond. This new habitat which tends to be a bit shallower and where light penetration may now occur easily becomes now suitable for the growth of roots submerged hydrophytes like Vallisneria, Ceratophyllum, Potamogeton, Hydrilla, Utricularia, etc., on the shallow regions where light reaches the bottom in sufficient quantity. The death and decay of these plants further contribute to the enrichment of the substratum. The water level also decreases making the pond more shallower. This new habitat now replaces these plants giving way to another type of plants, which are of floating leaf type.

### *Reed-swamp stage*

This is also known as amphibious stage as the plants are rooted but most part of their shoot remains exposed to air. Species of Scirpus, Typha, Sagittaria, Phragmites, Cyperus, Fimbristylis and Polygonum, etc. are the chief plants of this stage. They have well-developed rhizomes and form a very dense vegetation. The water level is by now very much reduced and finally becomes unsuitable for the growth of these amphibious species.

### *Sedge-meadow stage*

Due to successive decrease in water level and further changes in the substratum species of some Cyperaceae and Gramineae such as Carex, Juncus, Cyperus and Eleocharis colonise the area. They form a mat-like vegetation towards the centre of the pond with the help of their much branched rhizomatous systems. As a result, of high rate of transpiration, there is much rapid loss of water, and sooner or later the mud is exposed to air. Thus, mesic conditions approach the area marshy vegetation disappears gradually.

### *Woodland stage*

By the time of disappearance of marshy vegetation, soil becomes drier for most time of the year. This area is now invaded by terrestrial plants, which are some shrubs. By this time, there is much accumulation of humus with rich flora of micro-organisms. Thus, mineralisation of the soil favours the arrival of new tree species in the area.

### *Forest stage*

This is the climax community of hydrosere succession. In tropical climates with heavy rainfall, there develops tropical rain forest, there develops tropical rain forest, where as in the temperate region, there develops mixed forest. In tropical regions and moderate rainfall, there develops tropical deciduous or monsoon forests. Since the particular type of trees can tolerate the environmental conditions they create, the forest cover which becomes stabilised.

### (2) Xerosere (Psammosere)

Under arid conditions, succession is a very slow process, mature soils are slow to develop and easy to destroy. Accumulation or organic matter is very slow and leaching processes are limited by the scanty precipitation. Because of the serious large scale destruction of the original vegetation, it is very difficult to form a clear notion of what the climax ought to be and its theoretical reconstruction is possible only after comprehensive investigations on the phytosociology of the arid regions. The existing vegetation on sandy plains and dunes are due to the extreme degradation of natural vegetation through cultivation, overgrazing, lopping and burning. Under such conditions, it is extremely difficult to infer the hypothetical order of succession.

In arid zones, successional process is usually faster in the initial stage, but becomes very slow after the first few phases. Extensive ecological studies in western Rajasthan for the last two decades have led to build up the probable successional stages (Saxena, 1977) on various habitats, which are described as follows:

#### *Hills*

The denuded rocks, in initial stages are colonised by tough grasses and forbs, e.g., Oropetium thomaeum, Tragus biflorus, Enneopogon brachystachys, Melanocencharis jacquemontii, Lepidogathis trinervis and Blepharis sindica. With the accumulation of substratum shrub species such as Euphorbia caducifolia, Grewia tenax, Zizyphus nummularia get foothold.

Simultaneously, higher grass species such as Eleusine compressa start dominating. The shrub species pave the way for the tree species, e.g., Maytenus emerginatus, Morringa cancansis and Cordia gharaf. If these species remain undisturbed, they appear to end up ultimately in the climax community to reach its climax with Schima nervosum. The slow buildup of the soil arrests the grassland community to the Eleusine stage only. In the higher rainfall zone, Hackelochloa, Bothriochloa and Branchiaria maintain the disclimax for Sehima nervosum type of grassland.

Flat alluvial plains with loamy sand to sandy loam soils get the invasion of Aristida, Melanocenchris, Tephrosia, Indigofera and Crotalarial in the early stage of colonisation. Under protection perennial grasses and undershrubs gain the upper hand in 3-4 years. If the area continues to be undisturbed spiny species, e.g. Zizphus and Capparis gather ascendency, which simultaneously culminates into the climax stage of Prosopis cineraria.

#### *Lithosere*

It is a typical xerosere and it occurs on bare rocks. Lithosere includes the following stages:

(1) **Crustose lichens stage:** The lichens of this stage are species of Rhizocarpon, Rinodina and Lecanora. They produce some acids

which bring about weathering of rocks. The dead organic matter of lichens becomes mixed with the small particles of rocks. However, this process is very slow. These lichens are than replaced by foliose type of lichens.

(2) **Foliose lichens stage:** They appear on the substratum partially built up by the crustose lichens. This community includes species of Parmelia, Dermatocorpon etc, which have large leaf-like thalli. They can absorb and retain more water and are able to accumulate dust particles which help in the further build up of the substratum. Thus, some humus becomes accumulated. The weathering of rocks and its mixing with humus result into the development of a fine thin soil layer on rock surface, and thus there is a change in the habitat.

(3) **Moss Stage:** The development of thin soil layer on rock surface, especially in the crevices, favours the growth of some such xerophytic mosses as species of polytrichum, Tortula and Grimmia. At their successful growth, they compete with the lichens. Due to their death and decay, there is further addition of organic matter in the soil. The thickness of the soil layer now increases.

(4) **Herbs stage:** Due to more extensive growth of mosses there accumulates more soil and there are added more minerals to it due to leaching out from the overlying vegetation. This changed habitat favours the growth of some herbaceous weeds which are chiefly the annuals, in turn being followed by some biennials and perennials. Due to their growth and death there is much more accumulation of humus in soil together with further weathering of rock. Thus, habitat changes with decreasing xeric conditions. This stage is constituted by such shallow rooted grasses as Aristida, Festuca, Poa, Solidago, etc., which in turn are replaced by shrubs.

(5) **Shrub stage:** Due to much accumulation of soil, the habitat becomes suitable for shrubs which start migrating in the area. These are species of Rhus, Phytocarpus, etc. They overshadow the herbaceous vegetation. The soil is further enriched by this dense shrubby growth. These in turn are finally replaced by trees which make up the climax community.

(6) **Forest stage:** Some xerophytic trees species invade the area. Further weathering of rocks and increasing humus content of the soil favour the arrival of more trees and vegetation finally becomes mesophytic. Thus, there develops finally a forest community.

### *Plagiosere*

It refers to deflected succession, that is, the normal development of the vegetation is prevented by anthropogenic influences. However, the normal development is not completely checked. The anthropogenic influences may be in the form of grazing or fire or some other factors, for example, the succession towards a forest may be directed towards a grassland community by grazing. In the deflected succession in Marshland, Fenland and Bogland in England, there operates a master factor continuously and results in an deflected climax vegetation, that is, the climax communities that develop in the above localities are a deviation from the normal course of development and such climax communities as we find in Marshland, Fenland and Bogland are therefore plagioseres.

**Q8. Describe various models of succession.**

*Or*

**Describe the three models of succession with the help of diagrams.**
**[Dec-2011, Q.No.-13(b)]**

**Ans.** There are two main points of debate in successional mechanism; one, whether the effects of early species on the environment is the critical factor determining succession of species; or whether what matters most are life history characteristics of species, such as longevity. Below, we describe three mechanisms, the first one emphasises on environmental modification, while the other two emphasise on the life-history characteristics.

### The Facilitation Model

The first model is the classical theory of succession, called the facilitation model, which postulates an orderly hierarchical system of change in the community from pioneer species towards climax species (Figure 3.3 a). The classical theory of succession was elaborated by Frederic E. Clements, who developed a complete theory of plant succession that included the monoclimax hypothesis. The biotic community, according to Clements, is a highly integrated superorganism. It shows development through a process of succession to a single end point in any given area—the climatic climax. The development of the community is gradual and progressive, from simple pioneer communities to the ultimate, or climax, stage. This succession is due to biotic reactions only—the plants and animals of the pioneer stages alter the environment in ways that favour a new set of species, and this cycle recurs until the climax is reached. According to Clements view, development through succession in a community is therefore analogous to development in an individual organism. Secondary succession differs from primary succession in having a seed bank from plants that occur later in succession, so that late succession species are already present in the early stages of secondary succession (Figure 3.3 a, b). Secondary successions should also lead over time to the climatic climax.

The key assumption of the classical theory of succession is that species replace one another because at each stage the dominant species modify the environment to make it more suitable for other species. Thus species replacement is orderly and predictable and provides directionality for succession, leading finally to the climax community. These characteristics led Joe Connell and Ralph Slatyer to call this the facilitation model of succession—the early species in succession facilitate the arrival of the later species.

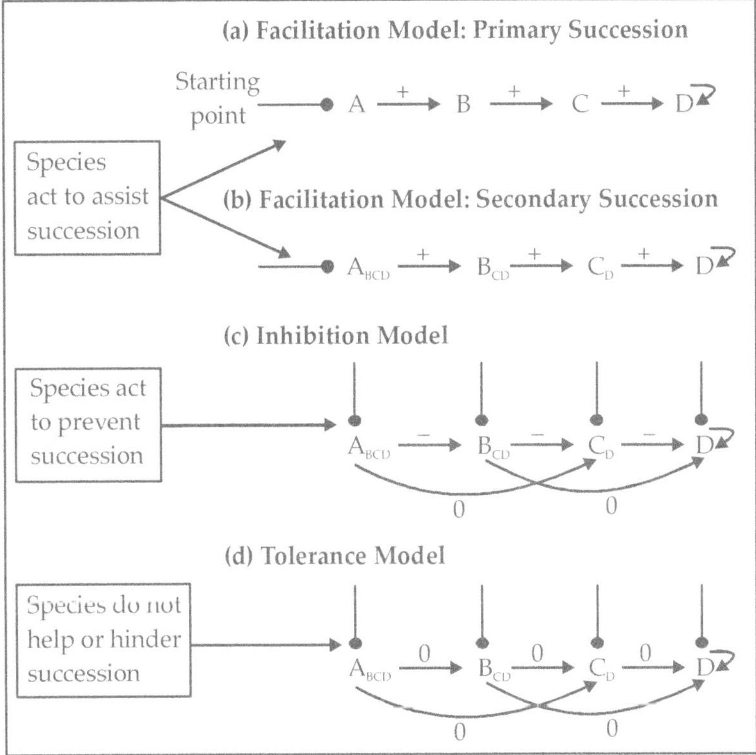


**Fig. 3.3: Conceptual models of Succession.**

The capital letters A-D represent hypothetical vegetation types or dominant species: subscript letters indicate that species are present as minor components or as propagules. Black arrows represent vegetation sequences in time; blue lines represent alternative starting points for succession after disturbance. Circular arrows indicate that the species replaces itself, + = facilitation, - = inhibition, 0 = no effect. In these simplified sequences species D would be the climax species. (Modified after Noble 1981.)

In Clements' view, the climax community in any region is determined by climate. Other communities may result from particular soil types, fire or grazing, but these subclimaxes are understandable only with reference to the end point of the climatic climax. Therefore, the classification of communities must be based on the climatic climax, which represents the state of equilibrium for the area.

**The Inhibition Model**

A second major hypothesis of succession was proposed by Frank Egler in 1954, who called it initial floristic composition. In this view, succession is very heterogeneous because the development at any one site depends on who gets there first. Species replacement is not necessarily orderly because each species excludes or suppresses any new colonists (Figure 3.3 c, b). Thus succession becomes more individualistic and less predictable because communities are not always converging towards the climatic climax, in contrast to what the classical theory of succession predicts.

Egler's hypothesis of initial floristics actually contained two ideas. Part of his hypothesis has been called the inhibition model of succession. The species present early in succession inhibit the establishment of the later species (Figure 3.3 c). No species in this model is competitively superior to another. Whichever plant colonises the site first holds it against all comers until it dies. Succession in this model proceeds from short-lived species to long-lived species and is not an orderly replacement because chance always determines which species gets there first. This model has been called the pre-emptive initial floristics model to emphasise that the first species at a site pre-empt the course of succession.

**The Tolerance Model**

Frank Egler's initial floristics model can also describe the third major model of succession proposed by Joe Connell and Ralph Slatyer, who called it the tolerance model. This model is intermediate between the facilitation model and the inhibition model. In the tolerance model, the presence of early successional species is not essential—any species can start the succession (Figure 3.3 d). Some species are competitively superior, however, and these eventually come to predominate in the climax community. Species are replaced by other species that are more tolerant of limiting resources. Succession proceeds either by the invasion of later species or by a thinning out of the initial colonist, depending on the starting conditions. The tolerance model includes Egler's emphasis on the initial colonisers as a major influence on how succession proceeds.

The critical distinction among the three hypotheses is in the mechanisms that determine subsequent establishment. In the classical facilitation model, species replacement is facilitated by the previous stages. In the inhibition model, species replacement is inhibited by the present residents until they are damaged or killed. In the tolerance model, species replacement is not affected by the present residents.

The utility of these three models of succession is that they immediately suggest experimental manipulations to test them. Removing or excluding early colonisers, transplanting seeds or seedlings of late succession species into earlier stages, and other experiments can shed light on the mechanisms involved in succession.

**Q9. Discuss the Trends in Succession.**

**Ans.** Succession is a definite aspect of change in ecosystem and by analysing the trend in it, we can know why succession takes place. The succession may initiate on a bare or nude area initially colonised by very small plants and finally the large woody trees. The early stages of succession are characterised by very few species, less dry weight and dependence on abiotic sources for nutrition. The net primary production is greater than respiration and the food chains are short as well as grazing. The higher stages of succession are characterised by larger diversity in species, increase in bio-mass, substratum rich organic matter. The simple food chains are replaced by more complex ones. Thus, we see that the trend proceeds from simple stages to further complex and lasting ecosystem, thereby reducing wastage of energy and supporting a greater bio-mass.

**Some common trends in succession:**

- The species composition changes continuously during the succession, but change is usually more rapid in the earlier stages than in the later ones.
- The total number of species represented increases initially, then sometimes declines slightly, and finally becomes more or less stabilised in the older stages. This trend applies particularly to the heterotrophs, whose variety is usually much greater in the later stages of the succession.
- Net primary productivity (the amount of energy converted into products of photosynthesis by autotrophs, and available to heterotrophs) increases until it reaches a stable high level.
- The store of inorganic nutrients held in the organisms and soil of the ecosystem increases, and an increasing proportion of this store is held in the tissue of plants.
- Both the total biomass in the ecosystem and the amount of non-living organic matter increase during the succession until a more stable stage is reached.
- The height and massiveness of the plants in the community increase and lead to greater differentiation of vertical strata.
- The food webs become more complex, and the relations between species in them become better defined or more specialised. As a result, the efficiency of resource utilisation at the various levels usually rises.

**Q10. What are the various factors that influence community organisation?**

***Or***

**Write short note on niche, keystone and dominant species.**

***Or***

**Justify the statement "Organisms occupying the same habitat can belong to different nitches".** **[Dec-2011, Q.No.-8(a)]**

*Or*

**Describe with appropriate examples the role of Keystone species.** **[June-2012, Q.No.-8(a)]**

*Or*

**How are Keystone species different from that of dominant species?** **[June-2012, Q.No.-8(b)]**

**Ans.** The various factors that influence community organisation are as follows:

### Habitat

Habitat is the physical environment in which an organism lives. Each organism has particular requirements for its survival and lives where the environment provides for those needs. The environmental requirement of an elephant would be a forest. You would not expect an elephant in the ocean nor would you expect a whale in the forest? A habitat may support many different species having similar requirements. For example, a single ocean habitat may support a whale, a sea-horse, seal, phytoplankton and many other kinds of organisms. The various species sharing a habitat thus have the same 'address'. Forest, ocean, river, etc. are examples of habitat.

The features of the habitat can be represented by its structural components namely (i) space (ii) food (iii) water (iv) and cover or shelter.

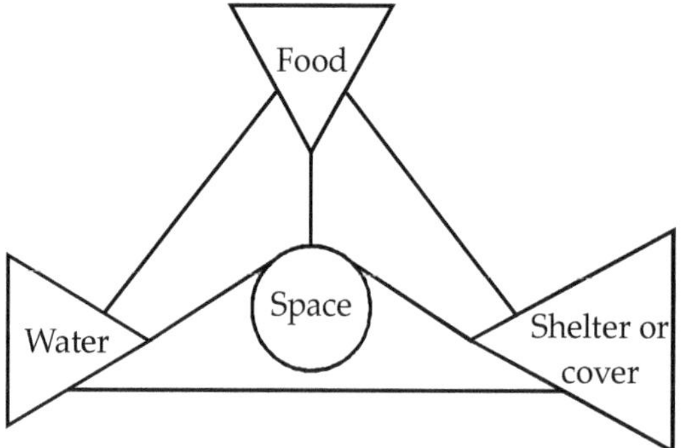


**Fig. 3.4: Structural components of a habitat**

### Niche

In nature, many species occupy the same habitat but they perform different functions. The functional characteristics of a species in its habitat is referred to as "**niche**" in that common habitat. So for example, the food niche occupied by a fox in a woodland is the tope predator, squirrels occupy the large tree-dwelling herbivore niche, and rabbits fill the large ground and burrow-living herbivore niche. Habitat of a species is like its 'address' (i.e. where it lives) whereas niche can be thought of as its "profession" (i.e. activities and responses specific to the species). The term niche means the sum of all the activities and relationships of a species by which it uses the resources in its habitat for its survival and reproduction.

A niche is unique for a species while many species share the habitat. No two species in a habitat can have the same niche. This is because if two species occupy the same niche they will compete with one another until one is displaced. For example, a large number of different species of insects may be pests of the same plant but they can co-exist as they feed on different parts of the same plant. The most important resources in the niches of animals are food and shelter while in case of plants, they are moisture and nutrients (phosphorous and nitrogen).

### Keystone Species

When the activities of a species determines community structure that species is called **keystone species**.

Example of a keystone species could be of the African elephant. By their feeding habits elephants destroy shrubs and small trees and push woodland habitats towards open grassland. Large mature trees can be destroyed by elephants feeding on their bark. As more grasses invade the woodland habitats, the frequency of fires increases, which accelerates the conversion of woods to grassland. This works to the disadvantage of the elephant, because grass is not a sufficient diet for elephants and they begin to starve as woody species are eliminated. However, other ungulates that graze the grasses are favoured by the elephants' activities. Thus in this community elephants play an important role in shaping the community organisation.

Keystone species may be relatively rare in natural communities or may not be easily recognised. At present, few terrestrial communities are believed to be organised by keystone species, but in aquatic communities keystone species may be common.

### Dominant Species

These are recognised by their greater number or more biomass and in general, are described separately for each trophic level. Dominance is related to the concept of species diversity. We may define community dominance index as follows:

Community dominance index = percentage of abundance contributed by the two most abundant species.

$$= \frac{y_1 + y_2}{y}$$

where $y_1$ = abundance of most abundant species

$y_2$ = abundance of second most abundant species

$y$ = total abundance for all species

Abundance may be measured by density, biomass or productivity.

Dominance is not always closely related to diversity. Dominant species are usually assumed to be competitive dominants. For example, of the many invertebrates species present in a rotting log community, many species may be dominant at least once but none would be dominant in every log.

Dominance can be achieved in three ways: (i) the first species to reach a new resources like in a rotting log, may become dominant, (ii) a species may become dominant by specialising on one part of a resource set that is widely distributed, and (iii) a species may generalise so that it could use a wide variety of resources.

## Stability

It is a dynamic concept that refers to the ability of a system to absorb change and return back from disturbance. Following figure explains the concept of stability in an ecosystem. The black ball represents the community on a surface which represents environmental conditions. In (a) the community is stable as the system will return back to point I after disturbance. In (b) the community is locally stable but if perturbed beyond a limit it will move to other positions of relative stability (II and III). In (c) large disturbances will cause extinction of some species and recolonisation by newer species.

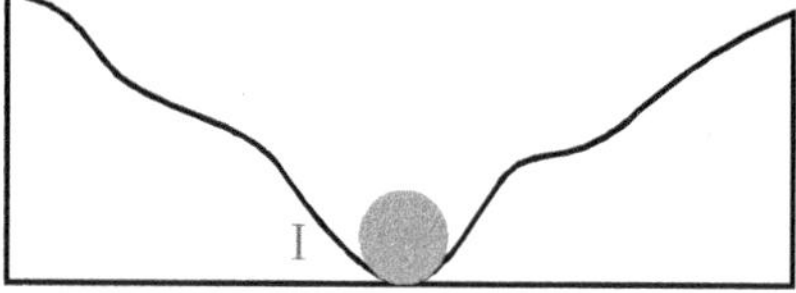


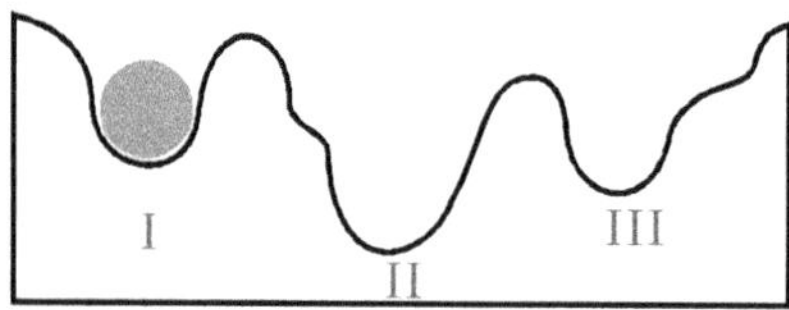


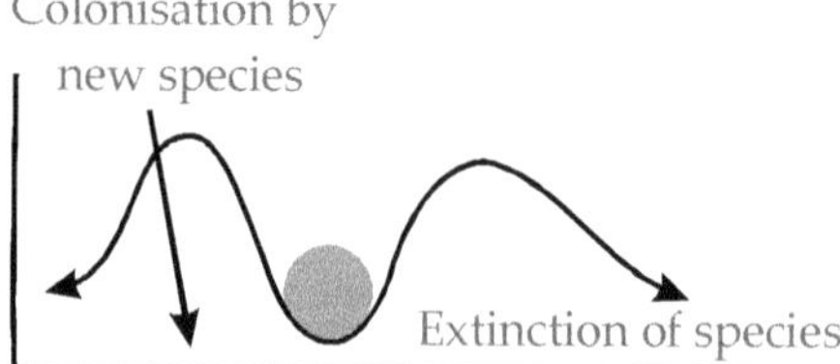


**Fig. 3.5: Stability concept in an ecosystem**

Thus, stability is dynamic concept but is equilibrium is centered. There must be one or more equilibrium limits or points at which the system remains when faced with a disturbing force. Stability may be local or global. Local stability is the tendency of the system to return to its original position from a small disturbance; gaps in forests filling it with similar species of trees are examples of local stability. Global stability is the tendency of a community to return to its original condition from all possible disturbances. Resistance is a measure of the degree to which a system is changed from an equilibrium state after disturbance. Resilience is the speed with which a perturbed system returns to equilibrium. A rapid return is an evidence of high resilience.

Natural communities are products of evolution where non-random combination of interacting species are produced in which diversity and stability are related.

**Q11. Define the various interspecific and intraspecific interactions.**

**Ans.** Individuals in a species population interact amongst themselves – intraspecific interactions as well as with individuals of other species population – interspecific interactions. Some have minimal influence on one another while some such as parasites and their hosts, predators and their prey, have very distinct and immediate relationships. At an individual level, these relationships can be harmful or beneficial; at a population level they can reduce, stabilise or enhance the rate of population growth.

The effects of these interactions can be positive, negative or neutral. **Neutral interactions** (OO) have no affect on the growth of population. **Positive interactions** (+ +) benefit both populations and if the relationship is mutually detrimental then the **interaction is negative** (– –). When one species maintains or provides a condition necessary for the welfare of the other but does not affect its own well being by doing so, the interactions is called **commensalisms** (O+). The interaction (O–), in which one species reduces or adversely affects the population of another but remains unaffected itself is called **amensalism**. An example may be the release of toxic substances by one organism that inhibits the growth and survival of another. This is known as allelopathy. An example is juglone a chemical substance released into the soil by black walnut tree which suppresses the growth of other plants near it. Amensalism may be considered as a form of competition.

Ecologically more important than amensalism and commensalisms is the relationship which benefits both population (+ +). Such interactions are termed **mutualism**. For example, bacteria present in termites and stomachs of ruminant animals help in the digestion of cellulose. The bacteria get a warm environment and help their host to extract nutrients. The nitrogen fixing bacteria Rizobium found in the root nodules of leguminous plants are another common example of mutualism.

Negative interactions are **competition** (– –), which is detrimental to populations of both species and **predation** and **parasitism** (– +), in which the population of one species benefits at the expense of another. Parasitism involves one organism's feeding on another and the prey or 'host' is seldom killed outright. The host survives, though its fitness is reduced and when it dies, it is due to reduced resistance to other infections. Familiar parasites are tapeworm, fleas, plasmodium and numerous other diseases causing microorganisms.

**Q12. What is Predation? Explain co-evolution of Predator-Prey System.**

**Ans.** Predation is an interaction between species in which one species uses another species as food. Predation is a process of major importance in influencing the distribution, abundance, and diversity of species in ecological communities. Generally, successful predation leads to an increase in the population size of the predator and a decrease in population size of the prey. These effects on the prey population may then ripple out through the ecological community, indirectly changing the abundances of other species. One example of such indirect effects of predation involves the trophic cascade.

**Co-evolution of Predator-Prey System:** To survive the predator must feed and the prey must avoid becoming food. Because if the prey becomes exterminated then the predator will naturally starve. How is this stable predator-prey relationship maintained? One may suggest that natural selection changes the characteristic of both so that their interactions produce populations stability. Prudent predators would kill and eat individuals that have crossed the reproductive age, the weak and the young. Young individuals in nature have a high death rate due to one cause or another. In the wolf-moose example many moose in the breeding age group are 'tested' by the wolves and quickly ignored because they are difficult to catch and kill.

Evolutionary change in two or more interacting species or coevolution occurs most tightly when predators regulate the prey population. In some predator-prey systems where the predator does not regulate the size of the prey population evolutionary pressures are reduced. Much of the stability we see in nature probably results from continued coevaluation of predators and prey. Foolish predators that kill all their prey, exist for a short time in evolution, with the result that we are left today with highly selected predator-prey systems.

**Q13. What do you understand by herbivory? Discuss.**

**[June-2011, Q.No.-6(c)]**

*Or*

**Describe the relationship of plants and herbivores.**

*Or*

**Write a short note on Defence mechanism in plants.**

**[Dec-2012, Q.No.-5(b)]**

**Ans.** Herbivory is just a special kind of predation. Predation on plants by herbivores involves defoliation and consumption of fruits and seeds.

Defoliation is the destruction of plant tissue like leaves, bark, stem, roots, etc. Even though plants may persist and regenerate, defoliation has an adverse effect. Plant biomass is decreased, removal of leaves and subsequent death of some roots reduce the vigour of the plant; its competitive ability and its fitness. In case of seed predation, even if only a few seedlings survive then seed predation has no real impact; only if seeds are removed from an expanding population, then seed predation reduces the rate of increase. On the other hand if consumption of seeds is a mechanism for dispersal of seeds then predation works to the advantage of the herbivore. We all realise that plants cannot move so to 'escape' from herbivores they must evolve some clever adaptation. Thus, herbivores can be important selective agents on plants. Some of these adaptations are:

### Defence Mechanisms in Plants

Some plants use mechanical means to discourage predation. The sharp spines of cacti, the thorns in the rose bush, leathery leaves of oak trees are some examples. Plants may use a variety of chemical weapons that we are only just starting to appreciate. These chemicals are known as ***secondary plant substances.*** These substances are by-products of the primary metabolic pathways in plants.

Secondary plant substances are not waste or excretory products but have an ecological role as anti-herbivore components, and have rapid turnover rates in the metabolic pool. Some of these chemicals are familiar to us, species like cinnamon and cloves are phenylpropanes; peppermint oil, and catnip are terpenoids; nicotine, opium, marijuana and caffeine are alkaloid secondary plant substance.

Defence mechanisms in plants may be of two types:

- **Quantitative:** That are most expensive and not easily mobilised. They are most effective against the specialist herbivores. Tannins and resins concentrated near the surface of the leaves, in barks and in seeds are examples. They form indigestible complexes with leaf proteins, reduce the rate of assimilation of dietary nitrogen, and the ability of gut microorganism to break down leaf protein and lower the palatability.
- **Qualitative:** Present in low concentration (less than 2 per cent of dry weight). Examples are alkaloid and cynogenic compounds that interfere with metabolism. These compounds can be synthesised quickly at low cost, are effective at low concentrations and are readily transported to the site of attack. They can be shuttled about in the plant from growing tips to leaves, stems, roots and seeds and they can be transferred from seed to seedling. They protect the plants from generalist herbivores.

### Herbivore Countermeasures

Animals try to overcome plant defences by evolving mechanisms to render them harmless. The coevolution of plants and animals can thus occur. For example, a milkweed (Asclepias curassavica) containing a chemical that affects vertebrate heartbeat is not eaten by cattle. But certain insects eat it without any harmful effect. In fact, they set apart the poison in their bodies as a chemical deterrent to predation.

### Hervibore Interactions

The plant-herbivore interaction is thought to be of the predator-prey type, in which the predator (animal) gains and the prey (plant) looses. But it may not always be so. It can be mutualistic in which both benefit. A very interesting example is seen in the ant-acacia system. The swollen thorn acacia provides ants a place to live and food to eat and the ants in turn provide protection to the plant by attacking any herbivore that attempts to eat the plant. The ants thus reduce herbivore destruction and serve as a living defence mechanism.

**Q14. What do you understand by competitions within organism of community? Discuss its result.**

*Or*

**Explain the different types of competitions within organism of community.**

*Or*

**With the help of suitble examples brieflydiscuss different types of competitions within a population. [Dec-2010, Q.No.-5(a)]**

**Ans.** Competition is the use or defence of a resource by one individual that reduces the availability of that resource to other individuals. In other words, competition is the use or defence of food source, living space, or mates so that others cannot have it. There are two main types of competition: intraspecific and interspecific competition.

Intraspecific competition is the competition between organisms of the same species. Usually competing over mating rights. For example: male deer with fight for the right to mate with a female. The male that wins the fight gets to mate and the loser has to fight a different male or wait another year to mate. This insures that the healthiest individual best adapted to their environment will pass on their genes to offspring at a greater rate than individual less fit. Intraspecific competition is one of the driving forces of evolution. Evolution is the change in a species over time. This change occurs by mutations that may occur that can cause a species to become better adapted to their environment.

An example of intraspecific completion is plants of same species (e.g. trees that grow very close together vie for sunlight and soil nutrients. Hence, these plants competing for limited resources such as soil nutrients and water are affected, particularly their growth and structure. Some plants that cannot obtain much sunlight tend to bend towards the sun. Other plants adapt by growing taller or developing bigger roots.

Interspecific competition is competition between organisms of different species. Interspecific competition is often less intense than intraspecific competition because individuals of different species do not compete for exactly the same kinds of food, space, or mates. An example of interspecific competition is the competition between predators for the same kind of prey. The competitive exclusion principle states that two competitors cannot coexist on the same limiting resource. Meaning that if the availability of a resource such as food decreases, two competitors cannot compete for that same resource. Both competitors will be negatively affected by the decrease resource. Organisms can develop behaviour to limit the effects of competition. For example three species of warblers (birds) eat similar types of food and can occupy the same forest, but they differ in their feeding pattern. One feeds from the tops of trees, another from the middle and the last feeds on the bottom portion of trees. Another behaviour that has developed to limit the effects of competition is diurnal and nocturnal animals. Diurnal organisms sleep at night and are active in the daylight. Nocturnal organisms sleep during the day and are active at night. Such behavioural adaptations greatly reduce, but do not entirely eliminate the competition for food.

An example of *interspecific competition* is between lions and tigers that vie for similar prey. Another example is a farm of rice paddies with weeds growing in the field.

**Competition in Laboratory population**

Although species with small niche differences are able to eco-exist in a community, those with identical niches cannot, even if only one shared resource is in short supply. Competition becomes so intense that one species is finally eliminated. Greater number of offsprings of the 'winner' species with better suited traits gradually displace members of the less efficient species. This is known as the competitive exclusion principle. It was first demonstrated in the laboratory by G.F. Gause (1934) in mixed cultures of closely related paramecium species. Although each population survived when grown individually, only one survived when grown together with a fixed amount of food (Fig. 3.6).

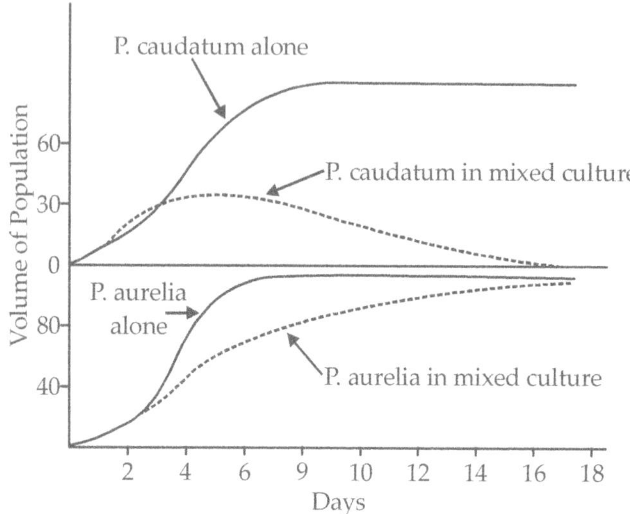


**Fig. 3.6: Competition between two species of paramecium.**

Competition between species does not always lead to expansion of one population and restriction of another. Gause showed in another experiment that when two different species of paramecia P. aurelia and P. bursaria occupy the same tube, both survived because P. aurelia could feed on the yeast suspension in the upper layers of the fluid whereas P. bursaria could feed on the yeast in the bottom layers. This difference in the feeding behaviour between these species allowed them to coexist. It was thus demonstrated that two or more similar species can live together only if their niches differ.

## Competition in Natural Populations

If the laboratory results apply to populations in nature, there is a wide range of opinion on the importance of the competitive exclusion principle. Although this principle has been repeatedly demonstrated in laboratory experiments, it is not the rule in nature or rather it is not easy to see in natural communities.

There are two situations where competitive exclusion would not be expected to occur:

(1) When the critical resource is in abundance. For example, six species of the leafhopper Erythoneura can live on the same tree and feed on the same leaves. Not only are their habitats and food source same but their life cycle phases are similar. Apparently competitive exclusion is avoided because of an abundance of resources.

(2) When environmental conditions are unstable and change frequently. There is just not enough time for one species to replace the other during the short period when resources become

limited. For example, in oceans and temperate lakes, changes sometimes occur so suddenly that there is no time for one species of phytoplankton to increase so much in numbers so as to exclude the other, despite intense competitions for limited nutrients. Because steady changes take place during primary and secondary succession, competitive exclusion has not been seen in communities undergoing succession.

Another reason why the process of competitive exclusion may go unnoticed in nature is that is takes time for one species to exclude another. If researchers are unable to observe the community continuously then they may miss the process entirely.

**Results of competition**

Competitive exclusion is not the only outcome of competition. Sometimes a shared resource can be partitioned in such a way that potential competitors use different portions of the resource. For example, let us take a hypothetical case of 4 species of birds that live in a similar habitat. They would feed on different position in the canopy and thus avoid competition. In addition to partitioning of space, a shared resource may be exploited at different times.

These are example of resource partitioning. A study involving closely related species of birds to test Gauses' hypothesis was done on the cormorant (Phalacrocorax carbo) and the shag (P. aristotelis). These species occur in similar habitats and appear to have a wide niche overlap. They are both cliff nesters and eat fish. It was shows that cormorant nests chiefly on flat broad cliff edges and feeds chiefly in shallow estuaries and harbours; the shag nests on narrow cliff edges and feeds mainly out at sea. Thus because of these differences competition is minimised.

A similar partitioning of resources exists among plants. Species of plants cultivated together exploit different soil depths: Some have shallow fibrous roots that draw water from the soil top. Another species may have sparsely branched taproot that extends to an intermediate depth. Yet another may have a taproot that is moderately branched in the upper layers but develops primarily below the rooting zone of the other species.

In addition to spatial partitioning, a shared-resource may be exploited at different times. This is known as temporal partitioning. An example can be seen in grasslands where a species of buttercup Ranunculus grows only in early spring before competing perennial grasses begin to grow.

Another alternative to competitive exclusion is character displacement where intense competition affects evolution, leading to displacement or change in a characteristic rather than extinction of a species. An example is seen in the forests of Europe, where six species of a small bird called titmice (Parus) coexist because each species has a slightly different beak size. These differences in beak size prevent any two species from seeking the same food in the same feeding area. For example, titmice with longer beak catches larger insects. Biologists have found out that, all the six species evolved from an identical ancestor and that variations in beak size are the result of character displacement.

**Q15. Define population. What are the major features of population?**

**Ans.** 'Population' is defined as a group of freely interbreeding individuals of the same species present in a specific area at a given time. For example, when we say that the population of a city is 50,000, we mean that there are 50,000 humans in that city. However, all populations of humans living in any part of the world constitute the species ***Homo sapiens.***

A population has traits of its own, which are different from those of the individuals forming the population. An individual born and dies but a population continues. It may change in size depending on birth and death rates of the population. An individual is either female or male, young or old but a population has a sex ratio and age structure, which means, the ratio of male to female in the population and the various age groups into which the population may be divided.

The characteristics of any population depends on:

- density of the population,
- natality (birth rate),
- mortality (death rate),
- dispersion,
- age distribution
- growth form.

**Density**

The number of individuals per unit area at a given time is termed as **population density**. The density of species varies from time to time and from one place to another. For example, you may notice more plant and animal species in the garden during the monsoon season. Density of a particular organism in a region is determined by selecting random samples of a particular dimension size called quadrant from that region.

In case of large, mobile animals like tigers, leopards, lions, deer etc, the density may be determined by counting individual animals directly or by the pugmarks (foot imprints) left by the animals in a defined area. Pugmarks of each individual animal is unique and different from one others. Study of pug marks can provide the following information reliably if analysed skillfully:

- Presence of different species in the area of study.
- Identification of individual animals.
- Population of large cats (tigers, lions, etc.).
- Sex ratio and age (young or adult) of large cats

Counting of human population is called **census** and is carried out by the Indian government every 10 years. In census, however each individual is physically counted.

## Natality

The rate at which new individuals are born and added to a population under given environmental conditions is called **natality**. Birth, hatching, germination and vegetative propagation cause an increase in the number of individuals in a population.

In case of humans, natality or birth rate is usually expressed in terms of births per thousand per year.

## Mortality

Loss of individuals from a population due to death under given environmental conditions is called **mortality**. The number of individuals dead in a year is calculated for obtaining the mortality rate or death rate. Mortality rate in human population may be expressed in terms of number of persons dead per thousand per year.

## Population Dispersion

Population dispersion or Population distribution is the observation of where individuals are found in a habitat. How individuals "disperse" themselves. There are three main types of dispersion: **clumped**, **uniform** and **random**.

- **Clumped Dispersion:** It is the tendency for populations to be found in tight clusters, dispersed across a large landscape. In between these population hubs, very few to no individuals are usually found. This sort of a dispersion can be caused by a number of factors. Some species cluster together for protection, while others group around natural resources necessary to their survival.
- **Uniform Dispersion:** It is the tendency for populations to be found evenly distributed about their habitat. This is generally caused by a species ability to survive anywhere in their habitat - they use the resources found immediately around them, and spread out as to use all of the available resources.
- **Random Dispersion:** It is the tendency for populations to be found randomly about their habitat. In immobile species, this is usually caused by their ability to live anywhere in a given habitat, except, they are limited to growing wherever they are first set root (which is usually caused randomly, from spores drifting in the wind to seeds falling and tumbling on the ground). In motile populations, individuals are able to move about their habitat, so that at any given instance, they can be found anywhere about their environment.

## Age distribution

Natural populations include individuals of all age groups. It, therefore, becomes necessary for us to consider age distribution of a population. Age distribution refers to the proportions of individuals of different age groups in a population. The population may be broadly divided into three age groups:

- pre-reproductive group: comprising of juvenile individuals or children,
- reproductive group: consisting of individuals capable of reproduction ,
- post-reproductive group: contains aged individuals who are incapable of reproduction.

A rapidly growing population will usually contain a large proportion of individuals in the reproductive age group; a stationary population (where there is no increase or decrease in population) contains an even distribution of all age groups, and a declining population contains a large proportion of old or post-reproductive age of an individuals.

### Population Growth

The growth, stability or decline in number of individuals in a population is influenced by its relation with the environment.

Populations have characteristic patterns of growth with time, which is depicted by population growth curves. Two basic forms of population growth curves can be identified. (i) 'J' shaped growth curve and the (ii) 'S' shaped or sigmoid growth curve.

**Q16. "Growth is the fundamental feature of the population which is limited by the carrying capacity of our environment and population size is regulated by various density factors". Discuss.**

*Or*

**Explain carrying capacity with the help of suitable diagram.**

**Ans.** Growth is the most fundamental dynamic feature that a species population displays. Size of a population depends upon the balance between natality and immigration which remove them. If natality and immigration exceed mortality and emigration, population will grow, if these are equal population will remain same size, i.e. static and if death and emigration exceed population will decrease. For example, the size of a population of mice in a field seems to vary little from year to year despite the fact that these organisms produce so many offsprings that their population could increase greatly from one year to the next. The size of such type of natural populations is limited by environmental factors. Now consider another example of *Paramecium caudatum* population studied by Russian ecologist G.F. Gause to see how rapidly population could increase if nothing stopped their growth. Every few hours a well nourished Paramecium divides to form two new individuals. Gause set up tubes containing sufficient bacteria for food and introduced one paramecium into each. If nothing checked the growth of paramecium, population showed exponential growth, that is as time went on the number of individuals added in each time period kept on increasing. When this type of increase in population size is graphed on a linear axis, the exponential growth is plotted as a curve that shows steep growth. When the population size is plotted on a logarithmic axis, the exponential growth plots as a straight line (see Fig. below (a) and (b))

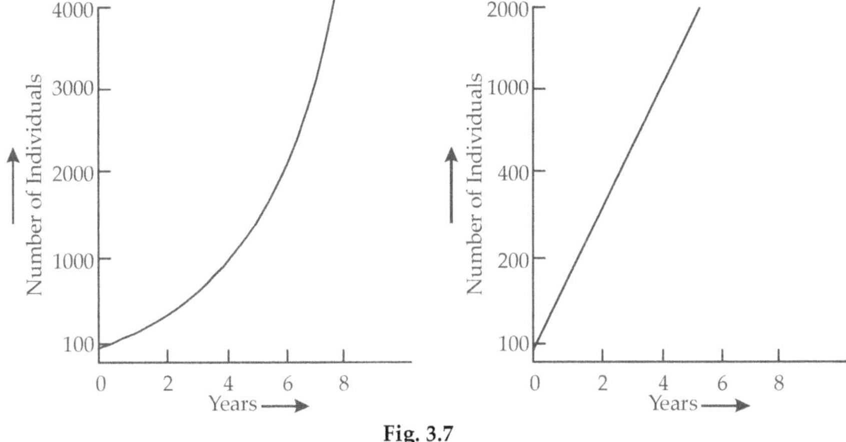


**Fig. 3.7**

This type of exponential growth can be expressed in the form of following equation

$$\frac{dN}{dt} = \gamma mN$$

where N is the number of individuals in a population, $\frac{dN}{dt}$ is increase (or change) in number of individuals per unit time and $\gamma m$ is the maximum rate of population growth per individual and is known as innate capacity for increase or biotic potential of the population. This is achieved when environment does not impose any limitations, i.e. food and space are superabundant and there is no interference from the members of other species.

**Carrying Capacity**

The number of individuals in a natural population varies with time. If the size of a population declines too drastically due to some reason, it may become extinct, but may later be re-established by immigration from other populations. On the other hand, increase in size of a population is not infinite since the carrying capacity of the environment always imposes a restriction upon it.

Carrying capacity of a population is the maximum population size that can exist in a habitat or ecosystem over a long period of time without detrimental effects to either population, habitat, or ecosystem.

Accordingly, such type of population growth can be explained by following logistic equation and the curve plotted is called logistic curve.

$$\frac{dN}{dt} = \gamma m\, N\left(\frac{K-N}{K}\right)$$

Where N = population Number

$\frac{dN}{dt}$ = Change in Number per unit time

$\gamma m$ =innate capacity for increase

K = Carrying Capacity

The term $\left(\frac{K-N}{K}\right)$ indicates how much of the resources are still available to populations. When N is much less than K, the term $\left(\frac{K-N}{K}\right)$ come s approximately 1 and the equation becomes $\frac{dN}{dt} = \gamma m\, N$ (equation for exponential growth). As N almost becomes equal to K, the term $\left(\frac{K-N}{K}\right)$ is almost zero and $\frac{dN}{dt}$ i.e. the growth rate also becomes zero.

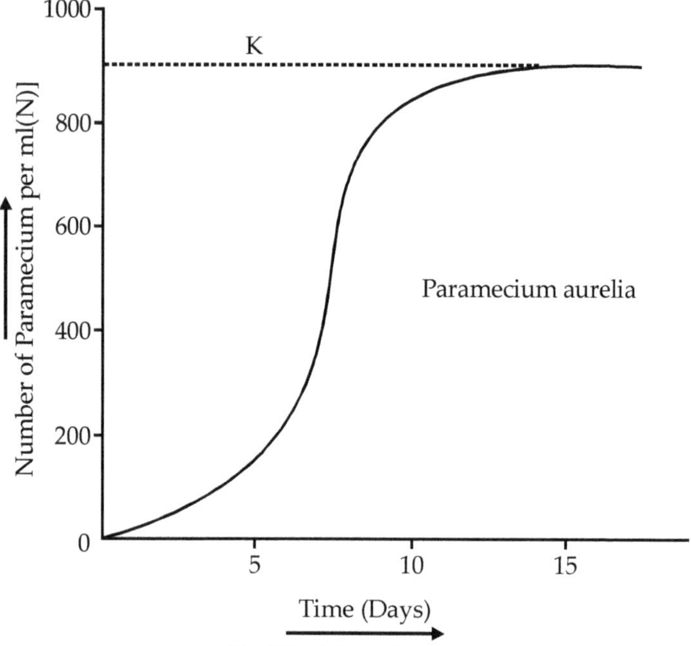


**Fig. 3.8: S shaped curve**

Another type of population growth curve called J-shaped curve is obtained when the density of organisms increases rapidly and then stops abruptly as environmental resistance or other limits become effective more or less suddenly. Carrying capacity is determined by various factors including predation, competition and climatic conditions. All factors which limit a population growth are collectively known as the ***environmental resistance*** to population growth.

There are two ways of keeping a population below the carrying capacity:

(1) Density dependent factors

(2) Density independent factors

### Density Dependent Factors

The density dependent factors are intrinsic or biotic factors and they depend on interactions between individuals within same population or populations of different species. Density dependent factors may stabilise the population at the level determined by carrying capacity of the environment. The important density dependent factors are reproductivity, immigration, competition for resources, predation, parasites, and diseases. The contribution of these factors may vary from species to species.

Competition can be between individuals of same species called ***intraspecific competition*** and between individuals of different species called ***interspecific competition.*** Generally, members of the same species need same resources and are bound to compete for them.

### Density Independent Factors

Density independent factors are the extrinsic factors, which tend to regulate the density of a population in ways that are not correlated with its density. Environmental factors such as bad weather and scarcity of space, pollution, etc. are some factors. A hurricane, a severe winter, or a drought may kill most of the individuals in a population irrespective of its density. In a bad weather only some individuals may be able to shelter from it; if the number of shelters is limited. Thus, only a fraction of a large population will be protected. However, we cannot pinpoint one or two factors and say that they determine the size of a particular population. Often the sizes of natural populations are affected by many different factors whose interactions can be complex.

**Q17. What are the factors that affecting biotic potential?**

**Ans.** Biotic potential differs from one species to another, e.g., bacterial populations can grow faster than population of oak trees. The rate of reproduction of any individual can be increased in any or all of three following ways:

- By producing a large number of offsprings each time it reproduces,
- By having a long reproductive life, and
- By reproducing as early in life as possible.

Of these three factors, the last one is most important. A bacterium neither lives for a long time nor produces many offsprings each time it reproduces. Its reproductive potential is higher than that of a dog because most bacteria can reproduce within an hour after being formed by cell division, whereas a dog is not able to reproduce until it is at least 6 months old. So we can say that shorter the generation time of a species, the higher its reproductive potential. In case of organisms with equal generation time, the number of offsprings produced determines which has higher potential for population growth. Thus the population of a plant that produces 100 seeds a year can potentially grow faster than the population of a plant that produces 10 seeds a year. However, with longer pre-reproductive period, number of offsprings produced does not affect much the biotic potential of a population.

**Q18. Give the evolutionary implications of natural regulation.**

**Ans.** Many changes in abundance can be attributed to changes in extrinsic factors such as weather, disease or predation. But some changes in abundance are the result of changes in the genetic properties of the organisms in a population. Such evolutionary changes are produced by the genetic feedback mechanism. It is believed by the biologists that natural population regulation has its foundation in the process of evolution.

Illustrate the type of systematic changes by a simple model which could be involved in the genetic feedback mechanism. Consider a two-species system of one plant and one herbivore, and to make the model simple, let us focus on only one gene on one chromosome in the plant. The hypothetical gene has a major effect on

- The ability of the plant to survive in its environment and
- The palatability of the plant to the herbivore. Two different alleles (A and a) occur at the hypothetical gene locus, and the properties of the genotypes are as shown in Table 3.2.

**Table 3.2: Genotype of Plants**

| | AA | Aa | aa |
|---|---|---|---|
| Ability of plant to survive | Good | Poor | Very poor |
| Palatability to herbivores | High | Low | Very low |

Thus, plants of genotype AA are to survive very well but attract many herbivores because they are desirable foods. Each plant genotype can support only a limited number of herbivores before it is killed by overgrazing. Finally, we assume that the reproductive rate of the herbivore will be affected by the genotype of plant on which it lives, so that highly palatable plants are best for herbivore reproduction.

There is an example of genetic changes of this type playing a role in population regulation. The Hessian fly population was reduced drastically in Kanas after 1942 when resistant varieties of wheat were introduced. The herbivore population of Hessian flies was significantly reduced by changing the genetic makeup of the wheat plant.

Self-regulatory populations present yet another problem no covered by the genetic feedback mechanism. Self-regulation is clearly a desirable adaptation for any population that has the potentially of destroy its resource.

**Q19. What do you mean by population pyramid? What are the different types of population pyramid?**

*Or*

**What is meant by age pyramid? Compare the different types of age pyramids. [Dec-2010, Q. No.-4 (a)] [June-2012, Q.No.-7]**

**Ans.** The population pyramid is a method of visually presenting the population data of a given group. They are used to show the age and sex distribution in a population, and can be used to assess potential trends in the population in the future. These charts use a paired-bar chart, with two sets of data lined up next to each other, with the youngest members of the population listed at the bottom and the oldest at the top, forming a roughly triangular or pyramid shape. Three varieties of these charts are currently in use.

- Expansive Pyramids: Expansive pyramids typically represent populations with high fertility rates and below-average life expectancies. They show larger numbers or percentages of younger age groups, and each successively older group is represented by a smaller bar. This pyramid type is typically applied to many Third World countries, and areas of Latin America.
- Constrictive Pyramids: Much the opposite of expansive pyramids, constrictive pyramids show lower numbers or percentages for younger people and larger numbers for adults than do expansive pyramids. These pyramids typically reflect populations with a large number of adults and a longer average life expectancy, like those found in the United States and some European countries.
- Stationary Pyramids: Stationary pyramids are the middle ground, displaying relatively equal numbers and percentages for almost all age groups involved. These models usually reflect nations with a very even age/sex distribution. Several European countries fall under this population model.

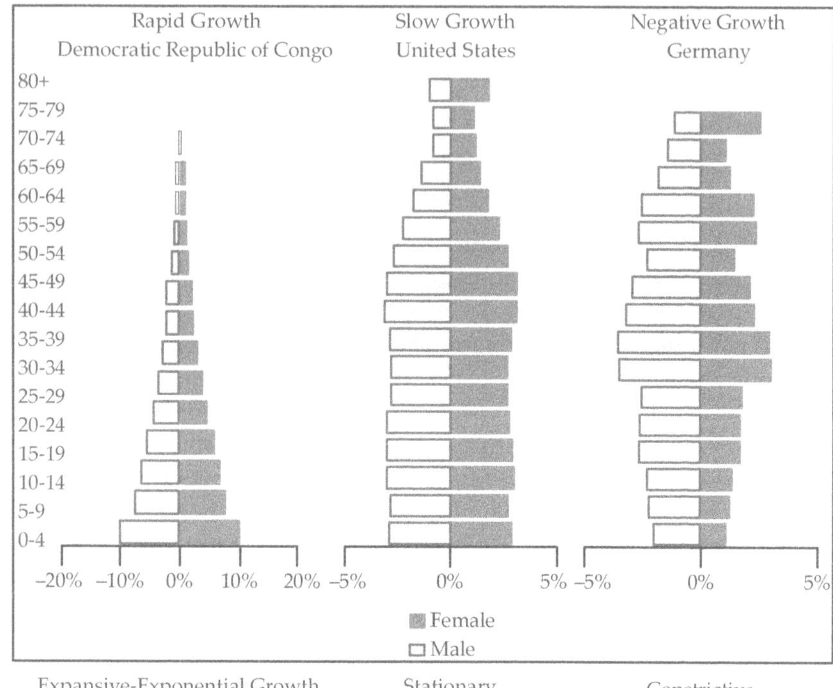


**Fig. 3.9: Three types of population pyramid**

**Q20. State the ways of population dispersal.**

**Ans.** Population dispersal is the movement of individuals in or out of the habitat. This movement can be grouped into following there categories.

### Emigration

Emigration literally means the one way outward movement. Generally, it is the result of overcrowding. This is generally regarded as an adaptive behaviour that regulates the population in a particular habitat and avoids its exploitation. Moreover, such movement provides opportunities for inter-breeding with other populations leading genetic diversity and adaptability. Continued emigrations are rare; however, when they occur, the result is depopulation. In such cases, equilibrium is maintained by enhancing the reproductive ability as well as decreased mortality among the population. It is exhibited by migratory locust, lemming, grouse, snowy owl, and grey squirrel.

### Immigration

Immigration is just opposite to emigration. It can be defined as one way inward movement. As a result, over-population is caused, followed by high mortality among immigrants. It reduces reproductive capacity of the individuals.

Rapid or large scale immigration or emigrations are more likely to have pronounced effects than the small or gradual dispersal movements. The introduction of a large number of bluegill fingerlings into a pond where the bluegill population has reached its carrying capacity, resulted into decreased growth rate and smaller size of the fish.

**Migration**

Migration is the periodic departure and return of a population. It is best developed in insects like butterflies, dragon-files, fishes like eels, and in several birds and mammals. Migratory movements are controlled by circadian, lunar and tidal rhythms as well as seasonal variations.

The reasons for migration generally are the requirements of food, shelter or reproduction. Unexploited habitats and resources are thus utilised by these populations. However, it may cause mortality during dispersion, nevertheless protects the individuals from intraspecific-competition. Bird Migration still remains a mystery of endurance and navigation.

Dispersal is much influenced by the presence or absence of the barriers and the vagility or inherent power of movement. Vagility is often greater than commonly realised. Although birds and insects are noted for their ability to 'get around', many plants and lesser forms of animals show greater dispersal powers.

# Human and Ecology

## An Overview

Nearly every activity a person does affects the ecosystem, either positively or negatively. The magnitude of these effects can vary depending on the type of ecosystem a person lives in or where they are at any given moment. Increased fossil fuel emissions and excessive fertilizer applications have resulted in regional and global effects, which present new challenges in the way we can sustainably coexist with nature.

Population increases can affect multiple ecosystems, often simultaneously. For example, as coastal regions become home to more and more people each year, homes and shopping centers are constructed, existing roads are widened and new roads are constructed.

Fossil fuel combustion has increased over the past several decades as the population has continued to climb and more homes have become multi-car households. This has increased the amount of carbon dioxide in the atmosphere and has exacerbated the greenhouse effect

Because we as a species exert such an influence on our surrounding ecosystems, making smart lifestyle choices can lessen the detrimental impact on the environment, and even reverse some of the recent trends. Cutting back on our reliance on oil, such as by biking or walking instead of driving, would lower the amount of carbon dioxide emitted into the atmosphere, as well as other ozone-destroying chemicals.

**Q1. List the major adaptations in primates that ultimately led to the first *Homo* species.**

*Or*

**What are trends in human evolution in relation to environment?**

**Ans.** Homo sapiens belong to the mammalians order primates, which also includes tree shrews, tarsiers, lemurs, lorises, monkeys and apes. The most distinct primate adaptations are found in the development of the nervous system and parts of the brain which are responsible for greater muscular dexterity and intelligence.

Adaptations led to the upright posture and bipedal locomotion characteristic of human beings today. Primates have 5 digits (fingers and toes) on each limb with at least one digit opposable to the rest, to help in grasping the tree limbs or food. The digits end in sensitive pads with nails rather than claws.

As the trees receded the arboreal habitat must have become overcrowded and less desirable. Perhaps the climatic changes produced a decline in fruit yields. What happened really, was that as the niche of dense forests receded, another one that of savanna expanded. The adaptations that enabled primates to grasp tree branches eventually led to the ability to make and handle tools and to perform delicate manipulations requiring hand-eye co-ordination. This evolution of the nervous system is linked to the arboreal or tree-dwelling life style of early primates. An animal living on trees requires muscle dexterity to jump from branch to branch and a keen and sharp vision. In most primates both eyes face forward and therefore, see the same thing; the two superimposed images provide **stereoscopic vision** or ability to perceive depth. During evolution, the snout of primates became progressively shorter.

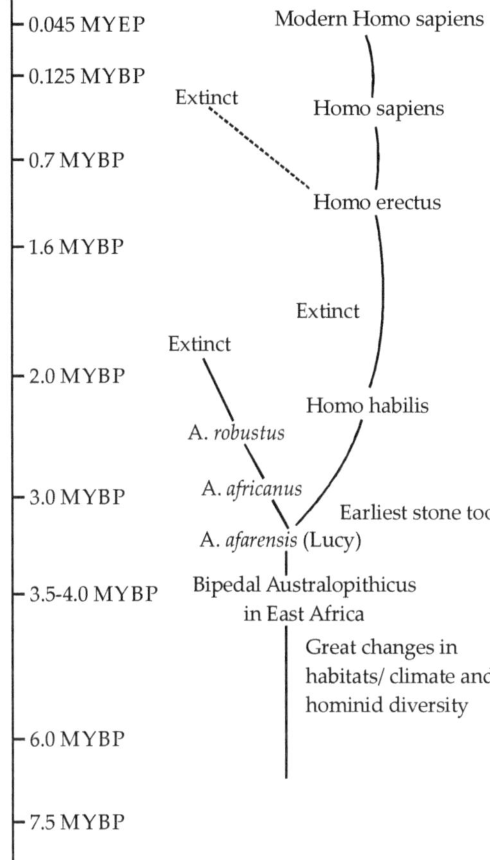


**Fig.4.1 Plausible pattern of human evolution and some famous ancestors of modern man in time (MYBP is million years before present)**

Sometime after *Australopithecus afarensis* about 500,000 to 1000,000 year ago Homo erectus appeared as the first species in fossil records to live a human type of existence. Home sapiens appeared sometime as recently as 100,000 to 40,000 years ago. Homo sapiens survived as a result of the competitive advantage it gained due to better developed brains and tools.

Changes in the outward appearance of our human ancestors were slow and subtle. The further evolution of the species was favoured by intraspecific co-operation and culture leading to a gradual increase in reproductive success. Humans can swim, run, climb, but there are other organisms that can do it much better. However, no other species can do all we can. Because of the cooperative interactive way of life only one of us had to invent the wheel for all of us to use it.

Archeological records of human campsites indicate that early humans started out as small bands of hunters who supplemented kills with foraged and gathered edible items. The hunter-gatherer cultures allowed humans to exploit agriculture, once it was discovered about 10,000 years ago.

As food energy moves from one trophic level to another about 90per cent of the available energy is lost with each transfer. It remains true to this day that a vegetarian diet can support many more people than if the crop was fed to sheep and these sheep were eaten by humans.

This gave humans greater opportunities for inventiveness and development of technologies which have greatly influenced the survival and growth of human population.

**Q2. Write a note on historical perspective of Human Population.**

**Ans.** Anthropologists believe the human species dates back at least 3 million years. For most of our history, our distant ancestors lived a precarious existence as hunters and gathers. This way of life kept their total numbers small, probably less than one crore (10 million). However, as agriculture was introduced, communities evolved that could support more people. World population expanded to about 30 crore (300 million) by AD 1 and continued to grow at a moderate rate. But after the beginning of Industrial Revolution in 18th century, living standards rose and widespread famines and epidemics diminished in some regions and population growth accelerated. The population climbed to about 76 crore (760 million) in 1750 and reached 100 crore (1 billion) around 1800.

In 1800, the vast majority of the world's population (86per cent) resided in Asia and Europe, with 65 per cent in Asia alone. By 1900, Europe's share of world population had risen to 25 per cent, fueled by the population increase that accompanied the Industrial Revolution. Some of this growth spilled over to the Americas, increasing their share of the world total.

In 2000, the world had 610 crore (6.1billion) human inhabitants. This number could rise to more than 9 billion in next 50 years. For the last 50 years, world population multiplied more rapidly than ever before, and more rapidly than it will ever grow in the future.

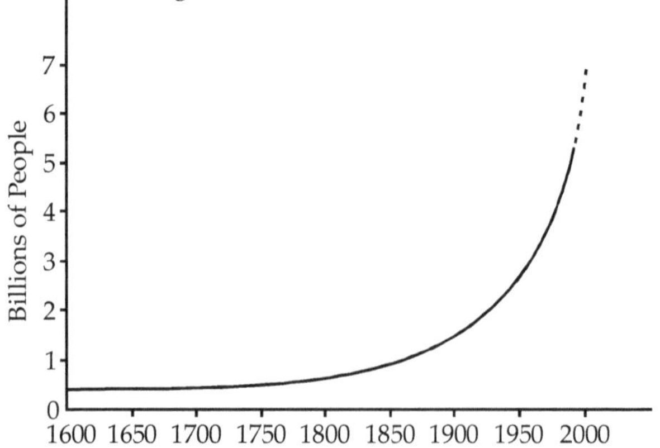


**Fig. 4.2: Growth of the Human population during the past 400 years**

**Q3. Discuss the Exponential growth and Age-Sex Distribution in human population growth.**

**Ans. Exponential growth**

Exponential growth can generate enormous numbers in a short time. For example, if the doubling time for the world's population is 40 years then at this rate by 2090 the population will be 32 billion persons.

Exponentially growing animal populations can overshoot the carrying capacity of their habitat; similarly, in the terms of some resources, the human population will exceed the capacity of these resources. As the population grows exponentially, the demands for resources such as water, food, fertilisers, housing and medical care, minerals, etc., also grow exponentially and similarly the wastes, organic and inorganic released, and the consequent its environment is polluted. Thus, even small reductions in exponential growth rates are important contributions towards efforts to maintain the human population within the earth's carrying capacity.

**Age-Sex Distribution**

Population pyramids are often viewed as the most effective way to graphically depict the age and sex distribution of a population, partly because of the very clear image these pyramids present.

A population pyramid also tells how many people of each age range live in the area. There tends to be more females than males in the older age groups, due to females' longer life expectancy.

Population pyramids can be used to find the number of economic dependents being supported in a particular population.

Age structure in a population is important because individuals vary in their age and many functional aspects are linked with age. Infants and older people have higher rates of mortality as compared to individuals of intermediate ages. According to this we divided a into three sub groups.

- Prereproductive
- Reproductive
- Post reproductive

**Q4. What are the impacts of population growth on environment?**

**Ans.** The enormous increase in human population is making the future of humans insecure. It is estimated that 5 million people lived in the world at the time when agriculture begin about 12000 years ago. The population of our country alone is now well over one billion.

With growing population, requirement for space, shelter, and commodities have exerted enormous pressure on the environment. To provide for these, land use has change dramatically.

**Clearing land for cultivation to grow more food**

Forests and natural grasslands have been converted to farmlands. Wetlands have been drained and arid lands have been irrigated. These changes have been made to grow more food and more raw materials. But in doing so, the natural resources have been depleted and the landscapes have undergone drastic changes. For example, forests have been cleaned over large for cultivation of agriculture crops. Many mangrove forests known to reduce erosion and stabilise shorelines have been cleared use for growing food crops to meet the needs of the growing population.

**Water scarcity**

Water received as rainfall, flows into rivers, lakes and other water bodies. Some of it seeps into the ground and reaches the ground water. At certain depth of the soil, all the pore spaces between soil particles are saturated with water. This depth is called **Water Table**. The water table may remain stable if the drawn from the ground water is replenished by the seepage of the rain water. But if water withdrawal exceeds beyond the rate of replenishment of the ground water table keep on receding and resulting in drying out of wells. In many areas, excessive withdrawal has depleted ground water resources causing acute water scarcity.

**Need for human settlements**

Apart from excessive land use changes for growing food, large population means greater requirement for shelter. To make houses for so many, stones and other building materials have to be quarried more rocks have to be blown off and more water to be used.

**Need for transport**

Elaborate network of transport is required to fulfil the growing need of teeming millions. Various modes of transports have been developed which consume growing quantities of fossil fuels such as coal, gas and petroleum, polluting the atmosphere.

**Need for various commodities**

Articles of everyday use such as plastic vessels, mugs, buckets, etc., agricultural implements, machinery, chemicals, cosmetics etc are manufactured in factories. The raw materials and fossil fuels and water needed to run industries for manufacturing these products lead to their depletion. Rapid industrialisation has also led to pollution from dumping of industrial effluents into rivers and other water bodies. Rapid industrialisation has caused much damage to the environment. Mining activities have depleted stock of mineral resources particularly fossil fuels. Present day industrial civilisation is becoming a burden on nature and it is time for us to learn to live in harmony with nature.

**Slum development**

Over populated areas result in congested roads and slum formation which lack basic amenities like drinking water, drainage, waste disposal, lack of hygienic conditions and filthy environment create potential conditions for public health problems including spread of epidemic diseases. Discharge of untreated effluents and throwing of waste into water 'bodies have polluted most of the lakes and rivers.

**Pollution resulting from overpopulation**

Holy rivers Ganga, Yamuna and other are suffering from pollution due to discharge of effluents from industries, human settlements, bathing, washing of clothes and throwing of garbage into the river.

**Q5. What do you understand by the term 'demographic transition'? Explain the role of demographic transition in the variation in population growth in different regions.**

**Ans.** The term demographic transition is used for the process whereby high levels of mortality and fertility— in other words, high death and birth rates— slowly but irreversibly drop too much lower levels. It is a long and drawn-out process that can take many decades, even a century or more.

The pattern of population growth is not a definite indicator of the region where it exists. The industrialised nations of the world which possess sufficient wealth have experienced a slow birth rate as compared to the less developed countries of the world. This is attributable to the phenomenon called 'demographic transition' and it takes place in four phases:

- **The pre-industrial stage:** where the living conditions are very hard and so the high birth rate negates the affect of high death rate.
- **The transitional stage:** where death rate is low because of better sanitation and healthcare. The food production is also high.
- **The industrial stage:** where birth rates fall as people who have migrated to cities understand the advantages of rearing small families, in an expanding economy.
- **The post-industrial stage:** where birth rate and death rate are equal. The population growth at this level becomes zero.

However, if the economic growth leads to zero population growth, then the economic development taking place in the developing nations should reduce population growth. But this is not fully true in the modern world as the population growth in developing nations is quite high. This is mainly because the rapid growth in population of these countries far surpasses the capacity to enhance standard of living of the people. The lack of education and sufficient resources thus is unable to check population growth and so demographic transition needs to take form in other ways, especially through population control.

As a result of demographic transition the more developed nations are now growing at the rate of 0.6 per cent per year with a doubling time 118 years. In less developed countries better healthcare and improved sanitation led to a steady decline in death rate without bringing down the birth rates sufficiently. Consequently populations have continued to increase rapidly.

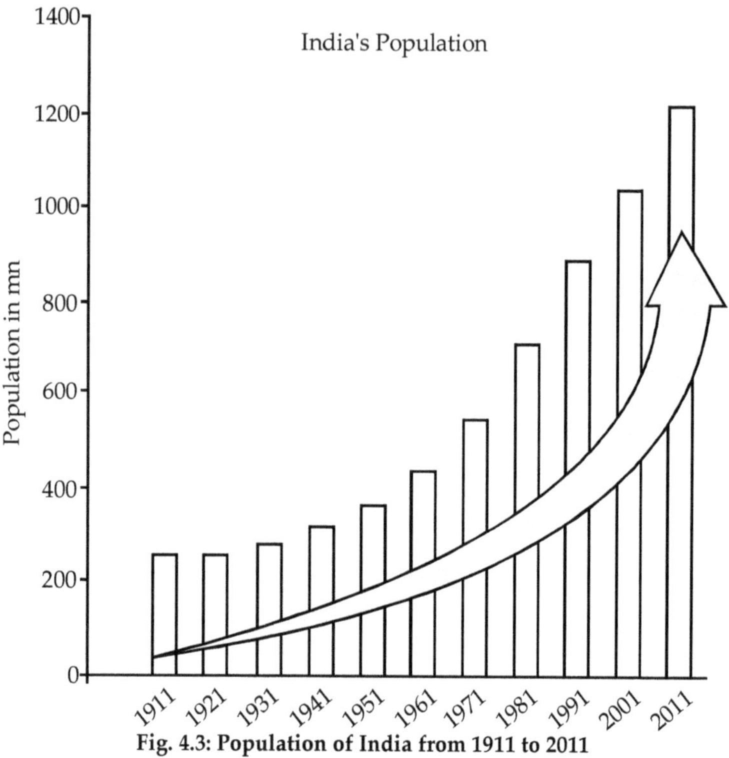


**Fig. 4.3: Population of India from 1911 to 2011**

**Q6. Define overpopulation. Also explain its types.**

**Ans.** Overpopulation refers to when an organism's numbers exceed the carrying capacity of its habitat. In common parlance, the term usually refers to the relationship between the human population and its environment, the earth.

Overpopulation is not solely a function of the size or density of the population. Overpopulation can be determined using the ratio of population to available sustainable resources. If a given environment has a population of ten, but there is food or drinking water enough for only nine, then that environment is overpopulated; if the population is 100 individuals but there is enough food, shelter, and water for 200 for the indefinite future, then it is not. Overpopulation can result from an increase in births, a decline in mortality rates due to medical advances, from an increase in immigration, a decrease in emigration, or from an unsustainable biome and depletion of resources.

Over Population can be divided into two parts:

- People Over-population
- Consumption Over-population

**(a) People Over-population:** It is the situation where the numbers of people are more than the availability of food, water and essential resources, which means that the population growth exceeds the economic growth. This type of over-population results in the degradation of the renewable resources and has a harmful effect on the environment.

**(b) Consumption Over-population:** It is the situation where small number of people use large quantum of resources in a disproportionate manner. This results in the depletion of the resources and the degradation of environment at a much higher rate.

**Q7. Describe world population prediction.**

*Or*

**Write short note on projection of population growth between 2000 to 2050.**

**Ans.** World population is projected to grow from 6.1 billion in 2000 to 8.9 billion in 2050, increasing therefore by 47 per cent. The average annual population growth rate over this half-century will be 0.77 per cent, substantially lower than the 1.76 per cent average growth rate from 1950 to 2000. In addition, growth is projected to slow the further the projections go. For 2000-2005, the annual growth rate is estimated at 1.22 per cent; by 2045-2050, it will be only 0.33 per cent. Although growth rates will fall, the annual increase in world population will remain large: 57 million a year on average between 2000 and 2050.

This is smaller than the 71 million people added annually between 1950 and 2000 but still substantial. It means that, on average each year for 50 years, world population will expand by about as many people as now live in Italy. The increase, over 50 years, will be more than twice the current population of China, or more than twice the current population of all more developed regions combined. Although population growth will eventually subside, and a variety of countries will see little or no population growth, for the world as a whole the next 50 years can hardly be characterised as demographically tranquil.

The estimate for the 2000 population, based on a greater number of well-executed national censuses than ever before, may well be more accurate than most estimates of current world population that have been made in the past. Projected figures for the near term (say up to around 2010) benefit from the accuracy of base data and are unlikely to be off by much. Projected figures for 2050, in contrast, are much less certain. To hedge its bets, the 2002 Revision includes alternative projection scenarios, particularly high-growth and low-growth scenarios, according to which world population would reach 10.6 billion or 7.4 billion by 2050 (figure 1). Between the high and low scenarios, average annual growth rates for 2000-2050 range from 1.12 to 0.40 per cent, and annual increments range from 91.3 to 26.8 million.

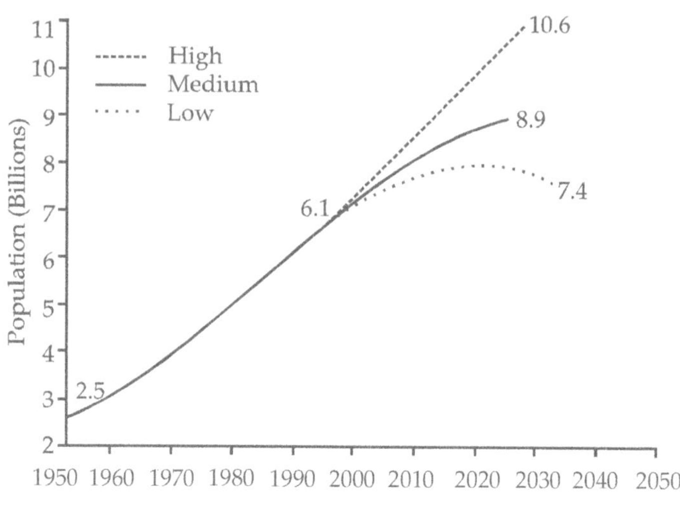


**Fig. 4.4**

**Q8. Discuss the degradation of ecosystems. What are the causes of degradation?**

*Or*

**How does overgrazing affect the ecology of an area?**

**[Dec-2010, Q.No.-2(b)]**

**Ans.** The degradation of ecosystems is an environmental problem that diminishes the capacity of species to survive. This degradation occurs in different ways and is manifested in a reduction in the richness of the ecosystems as well as their biological diversity, and in the goods and services, they can offer, thereby affecting indigenous and migratory species. The degradation of ecosystems due to overexploitation of their resources, though serving a short-term economic goal, has had direct negative effects on social welfare in the medium and long-terms.

The important causes that have lead to the degradation of the ecosystem are:

**Deforestation:** One of the main causes that contribute to the degradation of ecosystems is the deforestation due to the advance of the agriculture frontier and inappropriate forest exploitation. More lands are deforested for commercial agriculture and live-stock rearing, and due to overexploitation of forest for wood and energy.

**Land:** At a lower scale, another problem is the uncontrolled fires used to prepare land for agricultural activities or to remove forest for the development of stock rearing areas. This practice eliminates the organic covering of the land, making it more susceptible to erosion by both wind and water. In addition, the fire's cause health problems and detract from the aesthetic value of the landscape.

Accidental or natural fires are another case in point. They affect areas of natural forest. In the Upala and Los Chiles cantons, in Costa Rica, some 10,000 hectares were burned between 1998 and 1999. This problem is even more serious in the Nicaraguan territory of the basin.

**Urbanisation:** The construction of roads without proper drainage measures or in territories subject to penetration and settlement are high-stress factors for ecosystems, especially those which are highly fragile as a result of their weather conditions and the nature of their soil and water.

**Mining:** Mining and the extraction of construction materials without taking measures to cushion the impact cause drastic changes in the natural landscape while degrading its valuable ecosystems.

**Wetlands:** Wetlands are very fragile ecosystems that are being severely affected, causing a reduction in the number and diversity of the species of terrestrial flora, birds, reptiles, mammals, fish, and crustaceans. This problem results from excessive exploitation of wildlife species either to feed the population, to trade their furs, or to trade live species, and from sedimentation, which causes changes in water quality, thereby significantly affecting the reproduction of aquatic species that live and/or reproduce in the wetlands.

**Overfishing:** The use of inappropriate fishing techniques endangers the existence of certain species, altering the food chain of aquatic fauna and consequently deteriorating the aquatic ecosystems. This is the case of the bull shark that is now hard to find in Lake Nicaragua or in the San Juan River. In some cases, the introduction of exotic species endangers the existence of indigenous species with a high cultural value. Such is the case of the guapote, whose numbers are being reduced by the introduction of tilapias. The deterioration of ecosystems is exacerbated by the lack of an institutional presence in the territory, be it for technical or economic reasons, or a combination of both. As a result, laws on the regulation and control of natural resource use are not enforced. The participation of civil society in controlling the use and exploitation of natural resources is limited and, in many cases, very timid or markedly apathetic.

**Overgrazing:** It is a term, which refers to the phenomenon wherein the pressure on a patch of land arising out of the grazing of herbs and shrubs by animals is so high that the land cannot replenish the lost cover in a reasonable period of time. This causes soil-erosion and desertification. In heavily grazed areas the soil becomes loose and thus the water-retention capacity is lost. As a result, of this deforestation, the rainfall in such areas decline making them prone to famine and rendering the soil infertile permanently. This phenomenon is on a sharp rise in India as the cattle count is increasing at a much faster pace than can be supported by the existing vegetation cover present in grazing lands. Thus the cattle carrying capacity has been thoroughly superseded, causing frequent famines and resulting in rapid deforestation.

Overgrazing damages a wide range of ecosystem properties, and is not simply confined to primary producer species. The primary impact is on the plant community, but changes therein will affect higher trophic levels, decomposers, the soil system and the physical environment of the whole ecosystem. Although some ecosystems exploited for grazing have a high degree of resilience to grazing pressure, other are inherently fragile. Grassland ecosystems in semi-arid and arid environments are especially vulnerable. Generally, overgrazing is likely to cause permanent change to the affected ecosystem. In some instances, the resulting damage to the ecosystem may be catastrophic.

**Agriculture:** With the ever increasing process of population growth it has become essential for humans to increase their agricultural activities manifold, so as to have enough food to meet the hunger needs of humans. This means implementation of superior scientific methods of farming, which may have severe adverse effect on the ecological balance. To support rapid food production man has today resorted to use of various insecticides, pesticides etc, which have a degrading effect on soil. Also the availability of land is made by extensive deforestation, which also destroys the natural habitat of so many organisms. In the process the soil management becomes improper leading to problems of soil-erosion, desertification, etc. thus it can be said that the extensive growth in agricultural activities are proving to be extremely detrimental in the long-run, as they thoroughly interfere in the maintenance of ecological balance by nature.

**Other Causes:** Natural enemies like termites, pests and several kinds of diseases affect the forests adversely. There is also massive destruction of forests because of floods and fires. Some forest fires are not natural, but they are due to deliberate burning of trees by smugglers. Defence activities like preparing ditches and bunkers, movement of heavy armoury and their testing and use, also affects the ecosystem considerably.

**Q9. Define wildlife. What are the major risks related to wildlife?**

*Or*

**What are the various threats to wildlife? [Dec-2012, Q.No.-12(a)]**

**Ans.** Wildlife is a very general term for life in ecosystems. Deserts, rainforests, plains, and other areas—including the most built-up urban sites—all have distinct forms of wildlife.

It is all non-domesticated plants, animals, and other living things. Domesticated wildlife is plants, animals, and other living things that have been removed from nature and raised in an environment that is more or less controlled. Domestication, act of taming, or controlling, wild plant and animal species and producing them for human benefit, is performed often and has an impact on the environment, both positive and negative.

(i) **Selective Destruction:** The process of selective destruction of any species in a region, to achieve a particular goal can also have destructive effects. This is because the nature has its own method of maintaining the natural equilibrium between the flora and fauna of a region. If this is artificially disturbed, it definitely results in environmental degradation.

**(ii) Domestication:** Man has today domesticated a large percentage of animals, which are in any way useful to him. However this is not a healthy sign as native wildlife of a particular region is capable of better utilisation of native plant life of the region, as compared to the domestic cattle. This results in conversion of fertile areas in to deserts, due to improper and imbalanced grazing.

**(iii) Hunting and Export:** The hunting is mainly of three types, i.e.

(a) Commercial hunting which is undertaken for profit resulting from sale of the animal fur, etc.

(b) Subsistence hunting which is undertaken for provision of food to humans; and

(c) Sport hunting undertaken for the recreation of humans.

However hunting can be of any type, but results in the endangerment to the species being hunted. The peculiar examples are tigers, cheetah, snow leopard, rhinoceros, whales, etc. which are all hunted for commercial purposes.

**(iv) Introduction of New Species:** In the process of expansion of human territories, man has advertently or inadvertently carried with him various species of animals to new geographical areas. This has resulted in their competition for survival with the existing native species. This has in many cases caused population explosion in several areas and has sometimes killed the existing specie in totality.

**(v) Pets, Medical Research and Zoos:** The animals and plants throughout the world are tamed to be confined to zoos and are used at a large scale for research in biology and medicine. The process of taming of the animals and removal of plant species from their natural habitat causes a severe threat to their existence. The animals also get killed in large numbers in laboratories facing human experimentation and many a times becomes incapable of successful reproduction in captivity. This endangers their survival and causes extinction.

**(vi) Elimination of disturbance of wildlife habitats:** The process of removal of living area of any species known as the removal of habitat. In such a case, the species forced to either migrate to a new habitat or face the risk of death. In the former case the new area might pose threat of co-existence with other species and competition may eliminate them. If there is no risk of co-existence the species may still succumb to predation, starvation or diseases. The destruction of habitat occurs due to deforestation , drainage of wetlands, overgrazing, urbanisation, extensive agriculture, mining, development projects, etc. water and soil pollution also cause severe loss of habitation to the aquatic life and soil microorganisms.

(vii) **Pesticides:** As the human population grows uncontrolled the need to produce grains at a faster pace becomes a necessity. The rampant danger to crops appears in the form of pests. Thus scientists have extensively worked to produce pesticides to prevent crop deterioration. However these have resulted in severe damage to the animal life as well. This is because large varieties of pesticides, which do not get dissolved or destroyed rapidly, once sprayed on land, get consumed y the worms and small in sects in the soil. These are in turn eaten by the birds, which then get prone to reproductive failure and egg shell thinning. This endangers their very existence.

**Q10. What is meant by "conservation of wildlife"? Discuss the various kinds of measures required for species conservation.**

*Or*

**Describe five important measures for the conservation of a wildlife species. [Dec-2012, Q.No.-12(b)]**

**Ans.** Conservation refers to the preservation of wild plants and animals in natural ecosystems, gardens or zoos, detached from their natural environment. Today, wildlife conservation is a total concept and it not only involves plants and animals, but also the microorganisms, soil and other physical elements of the environment in which they live or on which they depend.

**Measures for Species Conservation:** Several types of actions needed for species conservation are described below:

- **Habitat Conservation:** It is the major factor in the extinction of plants and animals. If the ecological considerations are kept in mind during urban and other developments, the damage to the habitat can be prevented considerably.
- **Providing Critical Resources:** Another way to improve the habitat of a threatened species is to determine which resource is limiting the population size and to provide more of that resource.
- **Captive Breeding:** Species which, are reduced to dangerous levels need more intensive management and one strategy is their captive breeding. It means, the eggs from the nests of endangered

birds are taken and hatched in captivity. Such attempts have been successful with California condor and several species of cranes. Some species such as Cheetah, Pandas, Cranes, Bats and Penguins are not inclined to breed in captivity. So techniques like artificial insemination and many others are used.

A major goal of captive breeding programme is the eventual release of species back into the wild. It has been found that the individuals that are released are special vulnerable.

- **Development of Reserves:** Establishment of Biological reserves, National parks, Forest reserves, Wildlife refuges and Biosphere reserves are effective means of preserving wildlife species. Such reserves are mostly established in the naturally functioning ecosystems. Therefore, it is easy to manage them. An important aspect about these reserves is that more than one endangered species can be protected in the same area.
- **Controlling Introduction of Alien Species:** The individuals of alien species may affect the other species by preying on them, providing tough competition for food or destroying their habitat. The alien species can also cause a population explosion of exiting species by killing off their natural predators.
- **Reducing Pollution:** Pollution of various kinds has affected the survival of living beings, particularly the wildlife in various ways. Pollution is the product of modern civilisation and this problem continues to grow. So, development of effective methods to curb pollution, change in practices to avoid the generation of pollutants is called for.
- **Research and Documentation:** First, list of endangered species are established by various national and international agencies. Another important action used to save an endangered species is the compilation of information about it. Information is also gathered about the way of breeding, area required, food and climate in order to survive. It is also important to know why the population has been reduced to the danger point.
- **Legal Actions:** Several legal approaches have been used to preserve species. One is to enact laws regulating the killing of members of certain species, with severe penalties for breaking the law. These laws may be very effective. Those, who are caught with a dead deer and do not carry a tag or ones who killed out of season are fined heavily.

  Nations signed the Convention on International Trade in Endangered Species (CITES) which prohibits all trade of endangered species or their products.
- **Public Participation and Awareness:** The awareness in public is of paramount importance to preserve wildlife and conserve

their natural habitat. This is needed so as to achieve control in pollution, commercial hunting, habitat destruction, deforestation, desertification, energy consumption, etc.

**Q11. Discuss the concept of extinct species and threatened species.**

***Or***

**Distinguish between extinct and threatened species.**

***Or***

**What are various categories of threatened species? Write one or two lines about each. [June-2012, Q.No.-12(a)]**

**Ans. Extinct Species**

A species becomes extinct when the last existing member dies. Extinction therefore becomes a certainty when there are no surviving individuals that are able to reproduce and create a new generation. A species may become functionally extinct when only a handful of individuals survive, which cannot reproduce due to poor health, age, sparse distribution over a large range, a lack of individuals of both sexes (in sexually reproducing species), or other reasons.

Ultimate fate of every species is extinction but after industrialisation this rate has increased tremendously. The extinct species only exist in museums and photographs. The most noted example of extinct species is passenger pigeon.

**Threaten Species**

Threatened species are native species that is at risk of becoming endangered in the near future. It may have a declining population or be exceptionally rare. Like endangered species, the cause of its rarity is variable, but may be due to threats such as habitat destruction, climate change, or pressure from invasive species.

Several plant and animal species are threatened by the possibility of being on the verge of extinction but the seriousness of this threat varies. International Union of Conservation of Nature (IUCN) has categorised threatened species into four categories which are:

- **Endangered:** A species is considered endangered when its numbers are few and its homeland is very small, or both and if special protection is not given it may become extinct. For example, the lion –tailed monkey from rain forests and Sholas of south India.
- **Rare:** These are those species whose number is few or they live in such small areas or such unusual environment (endemics), that they could quickly disappear. The Great Indian Bustard (*Ardeotis nigriceps* ) is an example of rare species of India.
- **Depleted:** These are the species whose numbers are greatly reduced from those of the recent past, and they are continuing

to decrease. It is the continued decrease, which is the main cause of concern. Animals/plant in this category can quickly change to a rare or endangered category. In the past few years, the fur of the clouded leopard (*Neofelis nebulosa*) was sold illegally in Kashmir markets.

- **Indeterminate:** Those species that seem to be in danger of extinction but their true information regarding their status is not known are the indeterminate species. The snow leopard (*Leo uncia*) was classified as indeterminate species in 1968, and was declared endangered in 1970. You probably know that the snow leopard is hunted for its thick beautiful fur.

**Q12. Briefly explain the following terms:**

**(i) The Red Data Book**

**Ans.** The Red Data Book was first issued in 1966 by the IUCN's Special Survival Commission as a guide for formulation, preservation and management of special listed.

The original IUCN Red Data Book threat categories have been widely applied to hundreds of thousands of taxa of animals, plants, and fungi. Note that these categories refer to the conservation status of an organism *in the wild*, not to its presence in cultivation or captivity.

In this Book, information for endangered mammals and birds is more extensive than for other group of animals and plants, coverage is also given to less prominent organisms facing extinction.

The pink pages in this publication include the critically endangered species. As the status of the animals changes, new pages are sent to the subscribers. Green pages are used for those species that were formerly endangered, but have now recovered to a point where they are no longer threatened. With passing time, the number of pink pages continue to increase. There are pitifully few green pages.

**(ii) The Appiko Movement**

**Ans.** In Kannada language 'appiko' means 'to hug'. This movement started in the Salkani forest in the Uttar Kannada region of the Karnataka State. Here logging contracts were given to private contractors. The result was that many more trees were cut than actually permitted. This resulted in various problem to the people living nearby, (i) soil erosion, (ii) siltation of streams and rivers, (iii) scarcity of fuel wood and (iv) animal fodder made the local youth council to start the 'appiko' movement in 1983. The local youth and women hugged the trees. (It is the women and children, specially girls who have the burden of fetching fuel wood, fodder and water). The movement spread to other districts in the State. After a sustained struggle of 38 days, the people won the battle. The State Government cancelled the trees felling permission.

**Q13. How wildlife plays valuable role in human life?**

**Ans.** If we were of the opinion that cultivated plants and domesticated animals is what wildlife consists of, we are mistaken. Wildlife, in fact, comprises of the innumerous varieties of wild plants, animals, fungi and microorganisms that exist on our planet earth, rather than just cultivated plants and domesticated animals. Knowingly or unknowingly, we largely depend on this wildlife for every elementary requirement in our life. The food we eat, the clothes we wear, the medicines we consume, a variety of building materials used for construction, numerous chemicals used for manufacturing our necessities, all are extracted from the wildlife existing around us. It plays a significant role in human life for the following reasons:

- **Economic Significance:** Wildlife resources provide people with a wide variety of direct economic benefits. Some of which are: as source of food, spices, flavouring agents, scents, soap, cooking oil, lubricating oils, waxes, dyes, natural rubber, medicines and several other important materials. Most of the plants that supply 90 per cent of the world's food today were domesticated from wild plants in the tropics. Besides providing direct benefits, many wildlife species benefits us indirectly. As many insect species carry out pollination for many food and non-food species. Predatory insects, parasites, and disease-causing bacteria and viruses are increasingly used for the biological control of various weeds and insect pests, thus helping reduce losses of crops and trees.
- **Medicinal Value:** About 40 per cent of all drugs used throughout the world have active ingredients extracted from plants and animals. The worldwide annual sales of drugs based on naturally derived chemicals amount to at least $40 billion. Aspirin, which is probably the world's most widely used drug, was developed according to a chemical "blueprint" supplied by a compound extracted from the leaves of tropical willow trees. Penicillin is produced by a fungus and certain species of bacteria produce other life saving antibiotics such as tetracycline and streptomycin. Thanks to those antibiotics and more than 1000 other drugs, diseases like typhoid fever, scarlet fever, bubonic plague, diphtheria, syphilis and gonorrhoea can be treated more effectively. Certain flowering plants also produce medicinal compounds. For example, quinine is used to treat Malaria (from the cinchona tree); digitalis is used to treat chronic heart trouble (from the foxglove plant); and morphine and cocaine are used to reduce pain (from the opium poppy plant and the coca shrub respectively). Drugs that have been extracted from plants are used to treat leukemia, several forms of tumors, cancer, various heart ailments, and hypertension (high blood pressure).

Therefore, the discovery of other life saving drugs depends on the survival of microorganisms, plants and animals that some persons might consider to be insignificant. Furthermore, fewer than 5,000 of the earth's 2,20400 species of flowering plants have been analysed by scientists for the presence of valuable drugs.

- **Medical Research:** Many animal species are used to test drugs and vaccines and to increase our understanding of human health and disease. The nine-banded armadillo for example is being used to study leprosy and prepare a vaccine for this disease. This disease has been a curse to humankind since ancient times and a cure has been difficult to find, because the bacteria that cause the disease grow in humans but not in laboratory conditions. This was a major problem in developing a vaccine. However, in 1971 it was discovered that the bacteria flourished in the nine-banded armadillo. Fortunately, that species is with us. Scientists now have a good opportunity to study and perhaps someday to conquer leprosy. Similarly, the Florida manatee, an endangered mammal, is being used to help understand haemophilia.
- **Genetic Reservoir:** Despite the present and future economic and health importance to human beings, very little is known about most of the earth's 1.7 million identified species. Less than 1 per cent of the earth's identified plant species have been thoroughly studied to determine their possible usefulness. Loss of this biological and genetic diversity reduces our ability to respond to new problems and opportunities—as though we have thrown away millions of gifts without unwrapping them.

  The maintenance of large gene pool is also of great interest to agriculturists. All domestic crops and livestock's originated from native plants and animals. And those native species are still needed to provide the new genetic characteristics that we need to help solve our present and future food production problems. For example, the new varieties of wheat and rice, which have significantly increased food production in the recent years, have been produced by breeding experiments that utilised thousands of native and domesticated varieties of rice and wheat.
- **Ecological Significance:** Wildlife plays an essential role in the ecological and biological processes that are yet again significant to life. The normal functioning of the biosphere depends on endless interactions amongst animals, plants, and microorganisms. This, in turn, maintains and enhances human life further. To add on, these ecological processes are vital for agriculture, forestry, fisheries and other endeavors that support human life. Besides, there are several biological processes wherein

wildlife plays a key role, such as pollinisation, germination, seed dispersal, soil generation, nutrient cycling, predation, habitat maintenance, waste breakdown, and pest control.

- **Aesthetic and Recreational Significance:** Many wild species are a source of beauty, wonder, joy and recreational pleasure for large number of people. Observing leaves change colour in autumn, smelling the aroma of wild flowers, watching an eagle soar overhead are some of the pleasurable experiences that are unexplainable and even not bought with money.

All of us, the believers in conservation should save our natural resources, both living and non-living and should be obligated to pass on something better than what we have received, to the future generation.

**Q14. Discuss the effects of air pollution leading to:**

**(i) Global warming**

**Ans.** Atmospheric gases like carbondioxide, methane, nitrous oxide, water vapour, and chlorofluorocarbons are capable of trapping the out-going infrared radiation from the earth. Infra-red radiations trapped by the earth's surface cannot pass through these gases and to increase thermal energy or heat in the atmosphere. Thus, the temperature of the global atmosphere is increased. As this phenomenon of increase in temperature is observed in green houses, in the botanical gardens these gases are known as green house gases and the heating effect is known as green house effect. If greenhouse gases are not checked, by the turn of the century the temperature may rise by 5°C. This will melt the polar ice caps and increase the sea level leading to coastal flooding, loss of coastal areas and ecosystems like swamps and marshes, etc.

**(ii) Ozone depletion**

**Ans.** The stratosphere has an ozone layer which protects the earth's surface from excessive ultraviolet (UV) radiation from the Sun. Chlorine from chemicals such as chlorofluorocarbons (CFCs) used for refrigeration, air conditioning, fire extinguishers, cleaning solvents, aerosols (spray cans of perfumes, medicine, insecticide) cause damage to ozone layer chlorine contained in the CFCs on reaching the ozone ($O_3$) layer split the ozone molecules to form oxygen ($O_2$). Amount of ozone, thus gets reduced and cannot prevent the entry of UV radiation. There has been a reduction of ozone umbrella or shield over the Arctic and Antarctic regions. This is known as ozone hole. This permits passage of UV radiation on earth's atmosphere which causes sunburn, cataract in eyes leading to blindness, skin cancer, reduced productivity of forests, etc. Under the "Montreal Protocol" amended in 1990, it was decided to completely phase out CFCs to prevent damage of ozone layer.

**Q15. What do you understand by water pollution? Discuss its various causes.**

**Ans.** Water pollution means contamination of streams, lakes, seas, underground waters or oceans by substances, which are harmful to living things. Water is necessary for life on earth. Water pollution occurs when a body of water is adversely affected due to the addition of large amounts of materials to the water. When it is unfit for its intended use, water is considered polluted.

Water pollution is any chemical, biological, or physical change in water quality that harms living organisms or makes water unsuitable for desired uses. Water pollution can come from single (point) sources, or from larger and dispersed (non-point) sources.

**(1) Point sources** discharge pollutions at specific locations through drain pipes, ditches, or sewer lines into bodies of surface water. Examples include factories, sewage treatment plants (which remove some but not all pollutions), underground mines, and oil tankers. Because point sources are located in specific places, they are fairly easy to identify, monitor, and regulate. Most developed countries have laws that help to control point-source discharges of harmful chemicals into aquatic systems. In most developing countries, there is little control of such discharges.

**(2) Non-point sources are** broad and diffuse areas, rather than points, from which pollution enter bodies of surface water or air. Examples include runoff of chemicals and sediments from cropland, livestock feedlots, logged forests, urban streets, parking lots, lawns, and golf courses. We have made little progress in controlling water pollution from non-point sources because of the difficulty and expense of identifying and controlling discharges from so many diffuse sources.

Agricultural activities are by far the leading cause of water pollution. Sediment corded from agricultural lands is the largest source. Other major agricultural pollutions include fertilisers and pesticides, bacteria from livestock and food processing wasters, and excess salt from soils of irrigated cropland. Industries facilities are a second major source of water pollution; they emit a variety of harmful inorganic and organic chemicals. Mixing is the third biggest source. Surface mining disturbs the land, creating major erosion of sediments and runoff of toxic chemicals.

A 2007 study by Purdue University (Indiana, USA) researchers found that parking lots are a major source of non-point pollution for rivers and lakes because of grease, toxic metals, and sediments that collect on their impervious surface. Because parking lots also disrupt the hydrologic cycles by preventing rain from soaking into the ground, they can worsen local flooding and erosion.

Climate change from global warming will also contribute to water pollution in some areas. In a warmer world, some regions will get more precipitation and other areas will get less intense downpours will flush more harmful chemicals, plant nutrients, and microorganisms into waterways and prolonged drought will reduce river flows that dilute wastes.

Following table lists the major types of water pollutants along with examples of each and their harmful effects and sources.

**Table 4.1: Major Water Pollutants and their Sources**

| Type/Effects | Examples | Major sources |
|---|---|---|
| Infectious agents (pathogens) cause diseases | Bacteria, viruses, protozoa, parasites | Human and animal wastes |
| Oxygen-demanding wastes deplete dissolved oxygen needed by aquatic species | Biodegradable animal wastes and plant debris | Sewage, animal feedlots, food processing facilities, pulp mills |
| Plant nutrients cause excessive growth of algae and other species | Nitrates ($NO_3^-$)and phosphates ($PO_4^{3-}$) | Sewage, animal wastes, inorganic fertilizers |
| Organic chemicals add toxins to aquatic systems | Oil, gasoline, plastics, pesticides cleaning solvents | Industry, farms, households |
| Inorganic chemicals add toxins to aquatic systems | Acids, bases, salts, metal compounds | Industry, households, surface runoff |
| Sediments disrupt photosynthesis, food webs, other processes | Soil, silt | Land erosion |
| Heavy metals cause cancer, disrupt immune and endocrine systems | Lead, mercury, arsenic | Unlined landfills, household chemicals, mining refuse, industrial discharges |
| Thermal pollution make some species vulnerable to disease | Heat | Electric power and industrial plants |

**Q16. What is noise pollution? Describe its two sources and two effects on human health. How to control over noise pollution?**

**Ans.** Noise is one of the most pervasive pollutants. A musical clock may be nice to listen during the day, but may be an irritant during sleep at night. Noise by definition is "sound without value" or "any noise that is unwanted by the recipient". Noise in industries such as stone cutting and crushing, steel forgings, loudspeakers, shouting by hawkers selling their wares, movement of heavy transport vehicles, railways and airports leads to irritation and an increased blood pressure, loss of temper, decrease in work efficiency, loss of hearing which may be first temporary but can become permanent in the noise stress continues. It is therefore of utmost importance that excessive noise is controlled. Noise level is measured in terms of decibels (dB). WHO (World Health Organisation) has prescribed optimum noise level as 45 dB by day and 35 dB by night. Anything above 80 dB is hazardous.

Noise pollution is a growing problem. All human activities contribute to noise pollution to varying extent. Sources of noise pollution are many and may be located indoors or outdoors.

**Indoor sources** include noise produced by radio, television, generators, electric fans, air coolers, air conditioners, different home appliances, and family conflict. Noise pollution is more in cities due to a higher concentration of population and industries and activities such as transportation. Noise like other pollutants is a by product of industrialisation, urbanisation and modern civilisation.

**Outdoor sources** of noise pollution include indiscriminate use of loudspeakers, industrial activities, automobiles, rail traffic, aeroplanes and activities such as those at market place, religious, social, and cultural functions, sports and political rallies. In rural areas farm machines, pump sets are main sources of noise pollution. During festivals, marriage and many other occasions, use of fire crackers contribute to noise pollution.

**Effects of noise pollution**

Noise pollution is highly annoying and irritating. Noise disturbs sleep, causes hypertension (high blood pressure), emotional problems such as aggression, mental depression and annoyance. Noise pollution adversely affects efficiency and performance of individuals.

**Prevention and control of noise pollution**

Following steps can be taken to control or minimise noise pollution-

- Road traffic noise can be reduced by better designing and proper maintenance of vehicles.
- Noise abatement measures include creating noise mounds, noise attenuation walls and well maintained roads and smooth surfacing of roads.
- Retrofitting of locomotives, continuously welded rail track, use of electric locomotives or deployment of quieter rolling stock will reduce noises emanating from trains.
- Air traffic noise can be reduced by appropriate insulation and introduction of noise regulations for takeoff and landing of aircrafts at the airport.
- Industrial noises can be reduced by sound proofing equipment like generators and areas producing lot of noise.
- Power tools, very loud music and land movers, public functions using loudspeakers, etc should not be permitted at night. Use of horns, alarms, refrigeration units, etc. is to be restricted. Use of fire crackers which are noisy and cause air pollution should be restricted.
- A green belt of trees is an efficient noise absorber.

**Q17. Explain the major Gaseous air pollutants and their sources and harmful effects.**

**Ans.** Generally, gaseous pollution is caused by the burning of fuels. Gaseous air pollutants constitute an important overall component of both outdoor and indoor air and are recognised to cause health effects, essentially in individuals with pre-existing disease. Following table lists some pollutants, their sources and harmful effects.

**Table 4.2: Gaseous air pollutants: their sources and effect**

| Pollutant | Source | Harmful effect |
|---|---|---|
| Carbon compound ($CO$ and $CO_2$) | Automobile exhaust burning of wood and coal | • Respiratory problems<br>• Green house effect |
| Sulphur compounds ($SO_2$ and $H_2S$) | Power plants and refineries volcanic eruptions | • Respiratory problems in humans<br>• Loss of chlorophyll in plants (Chlorosis)<br>• Acid rain |
| Nitrogen compound ($NO$ and $N_2O$) | Motor vehicle exhaust atmospheric reaction | • Irritation in eyes and lungs<br>• Low productivity in plants<br>• Acid rain damages material (metals and stone) |
| Hydrocarbons (benzene, ethylene) | Automobiles and petroleum industries | • Respiratory problem<br>• Cancer causing properties |
| SPM (Suspended Particulate Matter) (Any solid and liquid particles suspended in the air, (flush, dust, lead) | Thermal power plants, Construction activities, metallurgical processes and automobiles | • Poor visibility, breathing problems<br>• Lead interferes with the development of red blood diseases and cancer.<br>• Smog (smoke & fog) formation leads to poor visibility and aggravates asthma in patients |
| Fibres (Cotton, wool) | Textile and carpet weaving industries | • Lung disorders |

**Q18. Discuss the various effects of water pollution.**

**Ans.** The effect of water pollution depends on the type of pollutants presents in water. Pollutants bring about physical and chemical changes that make the water unfit for drinking and harmful to aquatic life. The main effects of pollutants are mentioned below:

**(1) Effects on aquatic ecosystem**: Presence of organic and inorganic wastes present in water decreases the dissolved $O_2$ (DO) content of the water. Water having DO content below 8.0 mg $L^{-1}$ may be considered as contaminated. Water having DO content below 4.0 mg is considered to be highly polluted. DO content of water is important for the survival of aquatic organisms. A number of factors like surface turbulence, photosynthetic activity, consumption by organisms and decomposition of organic matter are the factors, which determine the amount of, DO present in water.

The higher amounts of organic waste increase the rates of decomposition and consumption, thereby decreases the DO content of water. The demand for is directly related to increasing input of organic wastes and is expressed as biological oxygen demand (BOD) of water. 'BOD is a measure of oxygen required by aerobic decomposers for the biochemical degradation of organic materials (i.e. bio-degradable materials) in water.' It is expressed in milligrams of oxygen per litre of water. The higher value of BOD indicate low DO content of water. Since BOD is limited to biodegradable materials only, therefore, it is not a reliable method of measuring pollution load in water. Chemical oxygen demand (COD) is a slightly better mode used to measure pollution load in water. It is the measure of oxygen equivalent of the requirement for oxidation of total organic matter (i.e. biodegradable and non-biodegradable) present in water. Polluted water effects aquatic ecosystem in the following ways:

(i) The contamination of water bodies by pollutants reduce DO content, thereby, eliminates sensitive organisms like plankton, molluscs and fish, etc. However, a few tolerant species like Tubifex (annelid worm) and some insect larvae may survive in highly polluted water with low DO content. Such species are recognised as indicator species for polluted water.

(ii) Biocides, polychlorinated biphenyls (PCBs) and heavy metals, such as Hg, Pb, Cd, Cu, As, etc. directly eliminate certain species of organisms.

(iii) Hot waters discharged from industries, when added to water bodies, lowers its DO content.

**(2) Biological Magnification:** 'The phenomenon through which certain pollutants get accumulated in tissues in increasing concentration along the food chain is called biological magnification. 'Many of the pesticides are non-degradable and their residues have long life. The organochlorine compounds such as DDT, some other pesticides, radionuclides, etc. are the most persistent pesticides. Once they are absorbed by an organism, they cannot be metabolised and broken down or excreted out. These pollutants get accumulated in fat containing tissues of the organisms. A classic example of biological magnification is the accumulation of DDT in the tissues of organisms of aquatic food chain.

DDT is an insecticide, which is sprayed on water bodies to check the growth of mosquitoes. After regular spraying of DDT for few years in long islands in USA, the population fish eating birds began to decline. Later, it was found that the concentration of DDT had increased 800 times in the phytoplankton relative to the concentration in water, zooplankton contained about 5 times higher concentration than phytoplankton, different fishes had 9-40 times greater concentration than the zooplankton and birds contained about 25 times higher DDT concentration relative to than in fishes.

**(3) Eutrophication:** The addition of inorganic compounds and decomposition of organic wastes in water bodies increase the nutrient content of water. It causes profuse growth of algae especially the blue green algae, and may totally cover the water surface. This type of algal growth is called algal bloom. The algal bloom often release toxins in water, and inhibits the growth of other algae. Aquatic animals (e.g. fishes) may also die due to toxicity or lack of oxygen. 'The process of nutrient enrichment of water, which often lead to the loss of species diversity is called eutrophication.

**(4) Effects on human health:** A number of health hazards are caused due to various types of pollutants present in water. The important human health hazards relate to water pollution are as follows:

(a) The water polluted with sewage usually contains pathogens like virus, bacteria, parasitic protozoa and worms. The sewage contaminated water, therefore, is a source of water borne diseases like jaundice, cholera, typhoid, amoebiasis, etc.

(b) The water contaminated with heavy metals can cause serious health problems. Mercury compounds in waste water are converted by bacterial action into extremely toxic methyl mercury, which can cause numbness of limbs, lips and tongue, deafness, blurring of vision and mental derangement.

A crippling deformity called Minamata disease due to consumption of fish captured from mercury contaminated Minamata Bay in Japan was detected in 1952. Water contaminated with cadmium can cause itai-itai disease also called ouch-ouch disease (a painful disease of bones and joints) and cancer of lungs and river. The compounds and lead cause anaemia, headache, loss of muscle power and bluish line around the gum.

**(5) Hazards of ground water pollution:** Ground water get contaminated due to seepage from industrial wastes and agricultural runoff.

(a) Presence of excess nitrate in drinking water is dangerous for human health and may be fatal for infants. It reacts with haemoglobin to form non-functional methaemoglobin, and impairs oxygen transport. This condition is called methaemoglobinemia of blue baby syndrome.

(b) Excess fluoride in drinking water causes teeth deformity, hardening of bones and stiff and painful joints (skeletal fluorosis).

(c) Over exploitation of ground water may lead to leaching of arsenic from soil and rock sources and contaminate ground water. Chronic exposure to arsenic causes black foot disease. It is causes diarrhoea, peripheral neuritis, hyperkeratosis and also lung and skin cancer.

**Q19. Define air pollution. What are the effects of air pollution on living organism and plants?**

**Ans.** Air pollution is a result of industrial and certain domestic activity. An ever increasing use of fossil fuels in power plants, industries, transportation, mining, construction of buildings, stone quarries had led to air pollution. It may be defined as the presence of any solid, liquid or gaseous substance including noise and radioactive radiation in the atmosphere in such concentration that may be directly and indirectly injurious to humans or other living organisms, plants, property or interferes with the normal environmental processes.

**Effects of air pollution on living organisms**

Our respiratory system has a number of mechanisms that help in protecting us from air pollution. The hair in our nose filters out large particles. The sticky mucus in the lining of the upper respiratory tract captures smaller particles and dissolves some gaseous pollutants. When the upper respiratory system is irritated by pollutants sneezing and coughing expel contaminated air and mucus. Prolonged smoking or exposure to air pollutants can overload or breakdown these natural defences causing or contributing to diseases such as lung cancer, asthma, chronic bronchitis and emphysema. Elderly people, infants, pregnant women and people with heart disease, asthma or other respiratory diseases are especially vulnerable to air pollution.

Cigarette smoking is responsible for the greatest exposure to carbon monoxide. Exposure to air containing even 0.001 per cent of carbon monoxide for several hours can cause collapse, coma and even death. As carbon monoxide remains attached to haemoglobin in blood for a long time, it accumulates and reduced the oxygen carrying capacity of blood. This impairs perception and thinking, slows reflexes and causes headaches, drowsiness, dizziness and nausea. Carbon monoxide in heavy traffic causes headaches, drowsiness and blurred vision.

Sulfur dioxide irritates respiratory tissues. Chronic exposure causes a condition similar to bronchitis. It also reacts with water, oxygen and other material in the air to form sulfur-containing acids. The acids can become attached to particles which when inhaled are very corrosive to the lung.

Nitrogen oxides especially $NO_2$ can irritate the lungs, aggravate asthma or chronic bronchitis and also increase susceptibility to respiratory infection such as influenza or common colds.

**Effects of air pollution on plants**

When some gaseous pollutants enter leaf pores, they damage the leaves of crop plants. Chronic exposure of the leaves to air pollutants can break down the waxy coating that help prevent excessive water loss and leads to damage from diseases, pests, drought and frost. Such exposure interferes with photosynthesis and plant growth, reduces nutrient uptake and causes leaves to turn yellow, brown or drop off altogether. At a higher concentration of sulphur dioxide majority of the flower buds become stiff and hard. They eventually fall from the plants, as they are unable to flower.

Prolonged exposure to high levels of several air pollutants from smelters, coal burning power plants and industrial units as well as from cars and trucks can damage trees and other plants.

**Q20. Define soil pollution. What are the sources of soil pollutions? How to control soil pollutions?**

**Ans.** Addition of substances, which adversely affect the quality of soil or its fertility is known **as soil pollution.** Generally, polluted water also pollute soil. Solid waste is a mixture of plastics, cloth, glass, metal and organic matter, sewage, sewage sludge, building debris, generated from households, commercial and industries establishments add to soil pollution. Fly ash, iron and steel slag, medical and industrial wastes disposed on land are important sources of soil pollution. In addition, fertilisers and pesticides from agricultural use, which reach soil as run-off and land filling by municipal waste are growing cause of soil pollution. Acid rain and dry deposition of pollutants on land surface also contribute to soil pollution.

**Sources of soil pollution**

***Plastic bags:*** Plastic bags made from low density polyethylene (LDPE), is virtually indestructible, create colossal environmental hazard. The discarded bags block drains and sewage systems. Leftover food, vegetable waste, etc. on which cows and dogs feed may die due to the choking by plastic bags. Plastic is non- biodegradable and burning of plastic in garbage dumps release highly toxic and poisonous gases like carbon monoxide, carbon dioxide, phosgene, dioxine and other poisonous chlorinated compounds.

***Industrial sources:*** It includes fly ash, chemical residues, metallic and nuclear wastes. Large number of industrial chemicals, dyes, acids, etc. find their way into the soil and are known to create many health hazards including cancer.

***Agricultural sources:*** Agricultural chemicals especially fertilisers and pesticides pollute the soil. Fertilisers in the runoff water from these fields can cause eutrophication in water bodies. Pesticides are highly toxic chemicals, which affect humans and other animals adversely causing respiratory problems, cancer and death.

**Control of soil pollution**

Indiscriminate disposal of solid waste should be avoided. To control soil pollution, it is essential to stop the use of plastic bags and instead use bags of degradable materials like paper and cloth. Sewage should be treated properly before using as fertiliser and as landfills. The organic matter from domestic, agricultural and other waste should be segregated and subjected to vermicomposting, which generates useful manure as a by product. The industrial wastes prior to disposal should be properly treated for removing hazardous materials. Biomedical waste should be separately collected and incinerated in proper incinerators.

**Q21. Briefly define the following terms:**

**(i) Ground Water pollution**

**Ans.** Groundwater pollution is a type of pollution, which occurs when groundwater becomes contaminated. Around the world, groundwater pollution is a very serious and costly problem, and many governments have started to take aggressive action to address it. Once contaminated, groundwater is very expensive to clean up and make usable again, and in some cases, an aquifer may be so contaminated that it has to be abandoned, which can put tremendous pressure on a community as it attempts to find a new supply of water.

There are several different types of groundwater, ranging from water, which flows freely through the ground and interacts with surface water to closed aquifers, which are theoretically very hard to contaminate. Groundwater becomes polluted when materials seep through the soil and reach the water, which can happen when rainfall washes contaminants into the ground, when polluted surface water connects with groundwater, and when buried tanks or waste disposal sites start to leach.

**(ii) Marine pollution**

**Ans.** Marine pollution can be defined as the introduction of substances to the marine environment directly or indirectly by man resulting in adverse effects such as hazards to human health, obstruction of marine activities and lowering the quality of sea water. While the causes of marine pollution may be similar to that of general water pollution, there are some very specific causes that pollute marine waters.

- The most obvious inputs of waste is through pipes directly discharging wastes into the sea. Very often municipal waste and sewage from residences and hotels in coastal towns are directly discharged into the sea.
- Pesticides and fertilisers from agriculture which are washed off the land by rain, enter water courses and eventually reach the sea.
- Petroleum and oils washed off from the roads normally enter the sewage system but stormwater overflows carry these materials into rivers and eventually into the seas.

**Q22. What do you understand by the radiation pollution? Discuss its source, hazardous effects, measures to control.**

*Or*

**Discuss the hazards of radiation pollution. [June-2011, Q.No.-3(d)]**

**Ans.** Radiation pollution is caused by radioactive substances, either natural or man-made. We are exposed to various kinds of radiation in our day-to-day life. Radiation causes an increase in the occurrence of cancers and other disorders. Apart from direct effects, it can cause genetic defects in living organisms.

Sources of Radiation Pollution: Human beings receive natural radiation from cosmic rays. Other sources are exposure to X-rays, radium-dial wrist watches, television, etc. All these are sources of ionising radiation, which, from these sources is usually not high enough to cause serious damage to health. The main source of radiation pollution is the nuclear waste from nuclear power plants and other installations related to them. The other potential source is the fall out of a nuclear bomb explosion.

Radiation pollution can be reduced by improving the safety measures taken for storage and to prevent accidents in reactors and storage facilities, and by minimising nuclear-weapons' testing.

**Effects of Radioactive pollution**

Various effects of radioactive pollution are as follows:

- Radiations have power of penetrating the tissues of body and in doing so they leave electrically charged ions in their paths. These ions are mainly responsible for the damage done by the radiation.
- The extent of damage depends on various factors such as amount of radiation exposed, its duration, age of the person exposed, the part of body affected, etc.
- The hazards of radiation on human beings may be acute, chronic or genetic damage. The acute radiation damage occurs from relatively large dose of radiation over a short period of time. It includes sudden death, death after some weeks, loss of hairs, widespread ulcers, bleeding from the mouth and gums, etc. The chronic radiation damage occurs from relatively small continuous dose of radiation over a long period of time. The genetic radiation damage represents long-term effect of radiation and it indicates changes among future generations. The genetic effects of radiation are very complex and serious and very little information is available at present for this effect.
- Higher organisms have been found to be more sensitive to radiation exposures. The consumption of such animals or plants as food by human beings may cause serious disasters.
- The various important sources of radiation are nuclear reactor, nuclear explosions, soils and rocks, use of radioactive substances in laboratories for research work and waste of radioactive substances.
- Radioactivity has detrimental effects on the active tissues of the organisms. In nutrient poor environment, a large proportion of fallout enters the food chain. In a nutrient rich environment the fall out is diluted because of high exchange capacities of soils. Hence, uptake of fall out by plants is little.

- In the areas subjected to radiation, diversity of species of plants reduces. For example, a place having a mixture of many species of shrubs and grasses, if subjected to radiation, may develop into almost pure stands or crabgrass.

**Controls of Radioactive Pollution**

The following preventive measures should be followed to control radioactive pollution:

- Leakage of radioactive materials from nuclear reactors, industries and laboratories using them should be totally stopped.
- Radioactive wastes disposal must be safe or stored in safe places so that they can decay in a harmless manner. Radioactive wastes only with very low radiation should be discharged into sewerage.
- Preventive measures should be taken so that natural radiation level does not rise above the permissible limits.
- Safety measures should be taken against accidents in nuclear power plants.
- Workers using radioactive materials should wear protective garments.

# Why Name Gullybaba?

® Gullybaba is a combination of two significant words **'Gully'** & **'Baba'**. The word 'Gully' comes from the ancient game played in Rural India–**Tip cat**. In Hindi, we call it **Gully Danda** **(गुल्ली डंडा)** which is a great **symbol of Focus & Force**. The word 'Baba' stands for **Respect & Honour**. And these are the fundamental parameters for achieving success. **Focus & Force** are required to help one go a long way in life. This is all about achieving excellence in education and giving respect & honour to everyone, and thus, the name 'Gullybaba'.

To know more about why name GullyBaba visit: **GullyBaba.com/why-name-gullybaba.html**

# Question Papers

# LSE-02: ECOLOGY
## December, 2010

*Note: Question No.1 is compulsory. Attempt any four questions from Q.Nos. 2 to 6.*

**Q1. (a) Define the following terms:-**

**(i) Cation - exchange capacity.**

**Ans.** Cation-exchange capacity is defined as the degree to which a soil can adsorb and exchange cations with a solution.

**(ii) Net primary production.**

**Ans.** Refer to Chapter No.-2, Q.No.-7

**(iii) Fidelity.**

**Ans.** Refer to Chapter No.-3, Q.No.-4

**(iv) Endangered species.**

**Ans.** Refer to Chapter No.-4, Q.No.-11

**(v) Synecology.**

**Ans.** Refer to Chapter No.-1, Q.No.-3

**(b) State whether the given statements are true or false:-**

**(i) Bright - light loving plants are called sciophytes.**

**Ans.** False

**(ii) Nitrogen is available to producers in the form of nitrate ions.**

**Ans.** True

**(iii) Keystone species commonly determine the structure of a community.**

**Ans.** True

**(iv) The first hominid species to have lived like humans was Homo sapiens.**

**Ans.** True

**(c) Fill in the blanks:-**

**(i) Biomass represents the total dry weight of living beings of different species at each ____________ level at a particular time.**

**Ans.** Trophic

**(ii) Those species that seem to be in danger, but there is not enough information about them to make a reliable estimate of their status are called _____________ species.**

**Ans.** Indeterminate

**(iii) Competition for resources between individuals of different species is called _____________ competition.**

**Ans.** Interspecific

**Q2. Differentiate between the following:-**

**(a) Exotherms and Endotherms.**

**Ans.** Refer to Chapter No.-1, Q.No.-13

**(b) Pyramid of numbers and biomass.**

**Ans.** Refer to Chapter No.-2, Q.No.-4

**(c) Parasitism and Cannibalism.**

**Ans. Cannibalism:** Cannibalism is the act of one individual of a species consuming all or part of another individual of the same species as food. Cannibalism is a common ecological interaction in the animal kingdom and has been recorded for more than 1500 species. It does not, as once believed, occur only as a result of extreme food shortages or artificial conditions, but commonly occurs under natural conditions in a variety of species. Cannibalism seems to be especially prevalent in aquatic communities, in which up to approximately 90 per cent of the organisms engage in cannibalism at some point of the life cycle. Cannibalism is also not restricted to carnivorous species, but is commonly found in herbivores and detritivores.

**Parasitism:** In parasitism, an individual organism, the parasite, consumes nutrients from another organism, its host, resulting in a decrease in fitness to the host. In extreme cases, parasites can cause disease in the host organism; in these situations, we refer to them as pathogens. We divide parasites into two categories: endoparasites, which live inside the body of their hosts, and ectoparasites, which live and feed on the outside of the body of their host. Examples of endoparasites include flukes, tapeworms, fungi, bacteria, and protozoa. Ectoparasites include ticks and lice, plants, protozoa, bacteria, and fungi. Plants and animals typically act as hosts.

**(d) Residual and Transported soils.**

**Ans.** Refer to Chapter No.-1, Q.No.-24

**Q3. Answer the following:-**

**(a) Explain the reason for decrease in temperature with increasing altitude in Troposphere.**

**Ans.** Refer to Chapter No.-1, Q.No.-12

**(b) How does overgrazing affect the ecology of an area?**

**Ans.** Refer to Chapter No.-4, Q.No.-8

**(c) Enumerate the successive changes during hydrosere and Xerosere.**

**Ans.** Refer to Chapter No.-3, Q.No.-7

**(d) Why are carnivorous fish generally more susceptible to low levels of pesticides in water than the herbivorous fish?**

**Ans.** Many pesticides are complex organic molecules, which are very persistent in the environment, and are passed on through the food chain. Thus, carnivorous fish can accumulate high levels of pesticides from their prey. Prey of carnivorous fish are usually seized and swallowed whole, because spending time chewing food would block the flow of water past their gills. Carnivorous fishes tend to have short intestines; herbivorous fish intestines are typically longer and coiled. So, carnivorous fish generally more susceptibility to low levels of pesticides in water than the herbivorous fish.

**Q4. (a) What is meant by age pyramid? Compare the different types of age pyramids.**

**Ans.** Refer to Chapter No.-3, Q.No.-19

**(b) How does the soil biota help in maintaining the soil fertility?**

**Ans.** Refer to Chapter No.-1, Q.No.-25

**Q5. (a) With the help of suitable examples briefly discuss different types of competitions within a population.**

**Ans.** Refer to Chapter No.-3, Q.No.-14

**(b) Mention two examples each, of the organisms that occupy the first, second and third trophic levels.**

**Ans. First trophic level:** Phytoplankton, algae, higher plants

**Second trophic level:** Zooplankton, cow, grasshopper

**Third trophic level:** Birds, fish, frog, wolf

**Q6. Write short - notes on any four of the following:-**

**(a) Electromagnetic spectrum.**

**Ans.** Refer to Chapter No.-1, Q.No.-11(a)

**(b) Homoeostasis.**

**Ans.** Refer to Chapter No.-2, Q.No.-9

**(c) Ecotone**

**Ans.** An **ecotone** is a transitional area between two different ecosystems, such as a forest and a grassland. In landscape ecology, an ecotone is the border area where two patches meet that have different ecological composition. The ecotone contains elements of both bordering communities as well as organisms, which are characteristic and restricted to the ecotone. Ecotones can be a wide zone where two communities gradually change from one to another or a more abrupt boundary where the change from one association to another is sharply defined. An ecotone can occur very locally or more regionally. The appearance of an ecotone varies depending on the scale of study. Thus, an ecotone can be studied at many spatial scales, from centimeters to thousands of kilometers. Ecotones are not limited to terrestrial communities; for example, the transition from soft bottom to hard bottom marine communities is an aquatic ecotone.

**(d) Air pollution.**

**Ans.** Refer to Chapter No.-4, Q.No.-19

**(e) Thermal stratification of lake.**

**Ans.** Refer to Chapter No.-2, Q.No.-35

✍ ✍ ✍

"Your vision of hope can steer a wrong turn into the right direction."

# LSE-02: ECOLOGY
## June, 2011

*Note: Question No.1 is compulsory. Attempt any four questions from Q.Nos. 2 to 6.*

**Q1. (a) Define the following terms:**

**(i) Water - logging**
**Ans.** Refer to Chapter No.-1, Q.No.-26 (xi)

**(ii) Gross - primary production**
**Ans.** Refer to Chapter No.-2, Q.No.-7

**(iii) Frequency**
**Ans.** Refer to Chapter No.-3, Q.No.-3

**(iv) Domestication**
**Ans.** Refer to Chapter No.-4, Q.No.-9 (ii)

**(v) Autecology**
**Ans.** Refer to Chapter No.-1, Q.No.-3

**(b) State whether the given statements are true or false:**

**(i) Shade loving plants are called heterophytes.**
**Ans.** False

**(ii) Denitrifying bacteria give back free nitrogen to the atmosphere.**
**Ans.** True

**(iii) The niche of an organism refers to the role it plays in the ecosystem.**
**Ans.** True

**(iv) Homo Sapiens belong to mammalian order Primates.**
**Ans.** True

**(c) Fill in the blanks:**

**(i) Excessive phosphates and nitrogenous compounds in water lead to ____________ of a water body.**
**Ans.** Eutrophication

**(ii) The increase in concentration of a toxin in a food chain at its higher trophic levels is called_____________.**

**Ans.** Biomagnification

**(iii) _____________ is the sum total of the genes of all the individuals in a population.**

**Ans.** Gene pool

**Q2. Differentiate between the following:**

**(a) Brackish water and Marine water**

**Ans.** Refer to Chapter No.-1, Q.No.-26, (iii) & (ix)

**(b) Temperate forest and Tropical forest**

**Ans.** Refer to Chapter No.-2, Q.No.-20

**(c) Commensalism and Amensalism**

**Ans.** Refer to Chapter No.-3, Q.No.-11

**(d) Indeterminate species and Vulnerable species**

**Ans.** Refer to Chapter No.-4, Q.No.-11

Vulnerable species that are declining but still have sufficient number of individuals in their natural habitat. However, in near future they might represent the category of endangered species, in case the casual factors for their decline are not removed. Musk deer, sambhar, spotted deer and black buck are a few examples of vulnerable species.

**Q3. Answer the following:**

**(a) What is atmospheric stratification? Explain with the help of diagram.**

**Ans.** Refer to Chapter No.-1, Q.No.-15

**(b) What is desertification? Explain with any Indian example.**

**Ans.** Refer to Chapter No.-2, Q.No.-27 & 41

**(c) What determines the rate of succession in fresh-water bodies?**

**Ans.** The availability of nutrients

**(d) Discuss the hazards of radiation pollution.**

**Ans.** Refer to Chapter No.-4, Q.No.-22

**Q4. (a) Draw the S - and J - shaped growth curves and explain them in terms of population ecology.**

**Ans.** Refer to Chapter No.-1, Q.No.-6

**(b) Briefly discuss the characteristics of water that are favourable to biological systems.**

**Ans.** Refer to Chapter No.-1, Q.No.-16

**Q5. (a) Explain the Survivorship Curves.**

**Ans.** A survivorship curve shows the fraction of a cohort of newborn (or newly hatched) alive individuals in subsequent year. Natural population have a great range of survivorship curves. There basis types are recognised.

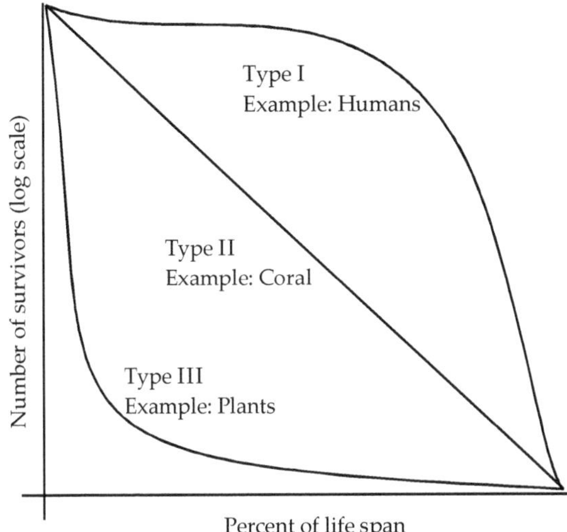


*Type 1* survivorship curves are 'rectangular' or convex on semi-logarithmic plots. They show low mortality initially that lasts for more than half the life-span, after which time mortality increases steeply. This survivorship pattern is common amongst mammals, including the Dall mountain sheep and humans. It is also displayed by such reptiles as the desert night lizard.

*Type II* survivorship curves are 'diagonal' or straight on semi-logarithmic plots. They show a reasonably constant mortality with age. This survivorship pattern is common in most birds, including the American robin and reptiles.

*Type III* survivorship curves are concave on semi-logarithmic plots. They show extremely high juvenile morality and relatively low morality thereafter. This survivorship pattern is common in many fish, marine invertebrates, most insects, and plants. It is also characteristic of the British robin.

**(b) Differentiate between atmospheric nitrogen fixation and biological nitrogen fixation.**

**Ans.** Refer to Chapter No.-2, Q.No.-18

**Q6. Write short notes on any four of the following:**

**(a) Biosphere**

**Ans.** Refer to Chapter No.-1, Q.No.-10

**(b) Characteristics of lentic ecosystem**

**Ans.** Refer to Chapter No.-2, Q.No.-33

**(c) Herbivory**

**Ans.** Refer to Chapter No.-3, Q.No.-13

**(d) Biological oxygen demand**

**Ans.** Biochemical Oxygen Demand (BOD) refers to the amount of oxygen that would be consumed if all the organics in one litre of water were oxidised by bacteria and protozoa.

The first step in measuring BOD is to obtain equal volumes of water from the area to be tested and dilute each specimen with a known volume of distilled water which has been thoroughly shaken to insure oxygen saturation.

After this, an oxygen metre is used to determine the concentration of oxygen within one of the vials. The remaining vial is than sealed and placed in darkness and tested five days later. BOD is then determined by subtracting the second metre reading from the first.

The range of possible readings can vary considerably: water from an exceptionally clear lake might show a BOD of less than 2 ml/L of water. Raw sewage may give readings in the hundreds and food processing wastes may be in the thousands.

**(e) Sedimentary cycle**

**Ans.** Refer to Chapter No.-2, Q.No.-17

✍✍✍

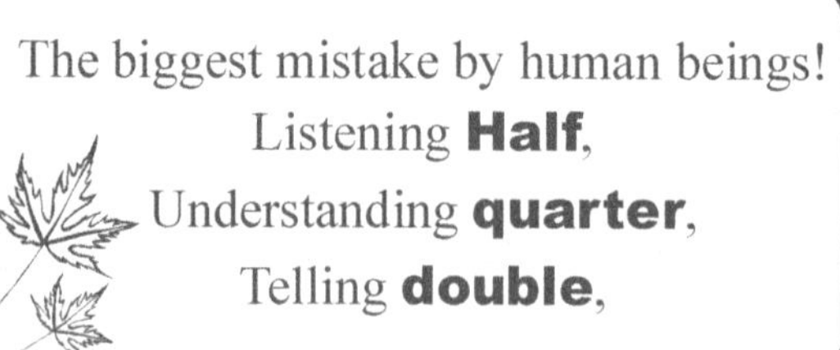

# LSE-02: ECOLOGY
## December, 2011

*Note: All sections are compulsory.*

## SECTION - A

*Note: All questions of this section are compulsory.*

**Q1. State whether the following statements are True (T) or False (F):**

**(a) Ecology is the study of plants and animals.**
**Ans.** False

**(b) Ecotone is the transitional zone between two adjacent communities.**
**Ans.** True

**(c) Heterotrophic succession begins with green plants.**
**Ans.** False

**(d) Climax community is a stable and long lasting community.**
**Ans.** True

**(e) Age pyramid is always vertical.**
**Ans.** True

**(f) Endangered species are the wild species that are not useful.**
**Ans.** False

**Q2. Give the technical term (in one word) for each of the following:**

**(a) 'Slash and burn method' of cultivation**
**Ans.** Jhum cultivation

**(b) Group of organisms of the same species**
**Ans.** Population

**Q3. Fill in the blanks:**

**(a) Activities of ____________ species determine community structure.**
**Ans.** Keystone

**(b) ____________food chain begins with dead organic matter.**
**Ans.** Detritus

**(c) Stratification is a ____________ character of a plant community.**
**Ans.** Qualitative

**(d) ____________ is the process in which solid water changes directly into vapour phase.**
**Ans.** Sublimation

**Q4. Define the following:**

**(a) Estuary**
**Ans.** Refer to Chapter No.-2, Q.No.-41

**(b) Immigration**
**Ans.** Refer to Chapter No.-3, Q.No.-21

**(c) Productivity**
**Ans.** Refer to Chapter No.-2, Q.No.-7

## SECTION - B

*Note: (i) Attempt any four questions.*

*(ii) All questions carry equal marks.*

**Q5. Describe the thermal and light stratification of lakes.**
**Ans.** Refer to Chapter No.-2, Q.No.-36

**Q6. (a) What are the types of soil water? Describe each in one or two lines.**
**Ans.** Refer to Chapter No.-1, Q.No.-24

**(b) Which of them is available to the plants?**
**Ans.** Capillary water is the main water that is available to plants as it is trapped in the soil solution right to the roots of the plants.

**Q7. With the help of a diagram briefly explain the Survivorship Curve.**
**Ans.** Refer to June-2011, Q.No.-5 (a)

**Q8. (a) Justify the statement "Organisms occupying the same habitat can belong to different nitches".**
**Ans.** Refer to Chapter No.-3, Q.No.-10

**(b) What are guilds? Give one example of a guild.**
**Ans.** Refer to Chapter No.-1, Q.No.-6

**Q9. Describe any two qualitative characters of a plant community.**
**Ans.** Refer to Chapter No.-3, Q.No.-3

**Q10. Describe the differences between natural and artificial environment with appropriate examples.**
**Ans.** Refer to Chapter No.-1, Q.No.-5(ii)

## SECTION - C

*Note: (i) Attempt any two questions.*

*(ii) All questions carry equal marks.*

**Q11. (a) What is desertification? Explain its causes.**
**Ans.** Refer to Chapter No.-2, Q.No.-28 & 29

**(b) Describe the salient features of a desert.**
**Ans.** Refer to Chapter No.-2, Q.No.-21

**Q12. (a) What are the various threats to wildlife?**
**Ans.** Refer to Chapter No.-4, Q.No.-9

**(b) Describe five important measures for the conservation of a wildlife species.**
**Ans.** Refer to Chapter No.-4, Q.No.-10

**Q13. (a) Describe the various changes in the characteristics of ecosystems during the process of succession.**
**Ans.** Refer to Chapter No.-3, Q.No.-7

**(b) Describe the three models of succession with the help of diagrams.**
**Ans.** Refer to Chapter No.-3, Q.No.-8

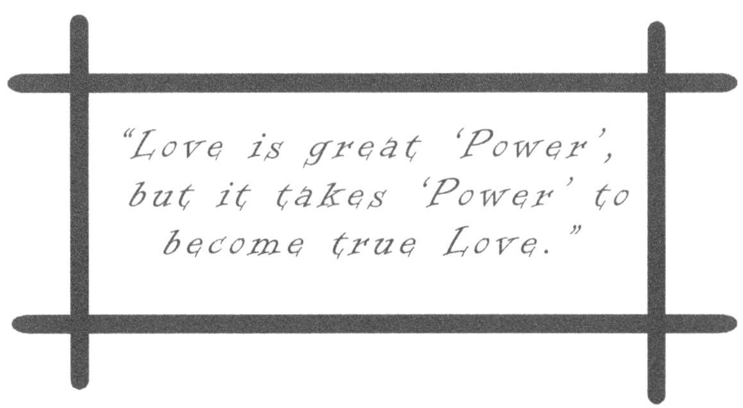

# LSE-02: ECOLOGY
## June, 2012

**Note:** *All sections are compulsory.*

### SECTION - A

*Note: All questions of this section are compulsory.*

**Q1. State whether the following statements are true (T) or false (F):**

**(a) Plant community is a biotic component of an ecosystem.**
**Ans.** True

**(b) 'Slash and burn method' of cultivation is also known as Jhum cultivation.**
**Ans.** True

**(c) Clay particles attract and hold negatively charged particles.**
**Ans.** True

**(d) Benthic zone of lakes is formed by autotrophs.**
**Ans.** False

**(e) In tropical forests a large part of organic carbon is in the plant biomass.**
**Ans.** True

**(f) Energy flow is always in multidirections.**
**Ans.** False

**Q2. Give the technical term (in one or two words) for each of the following:**

**(a) Dark amorphous colloidal material derived from partial decay of organic debris.**
**Ans.** Soil organic matter

**(b) Transitional zone between two adjacent communities.**
**Ans.** Ecotone

**Q3. Fill in the blanks:**

**(a) Light intensity is measured in the unit ________**
**Ans.** Candela

**(b) ____________ is the calendar of events in the life history of a plant.**

**Ans.** Phenology

**(c) Forests can be evergreen or ____________**

**Ans.** Semi evergreen/deciduous

**(d) Weathered materials transported by running water form ____________ soil.**

**Ans.** Alluvial

**Q4. Define the following:**

**(a) Standing crop**

**Ans.** Refer to Chapter No.-2, Q.No.-6

**(b) Profound zone**

**Ans.** It is an aphotic open water zone, which has no green plans as it is dark and so cannot support photosynthesis.

**(c) Detritus food chain**

**Ans.** Refer to Chapter No.-2, Q.No.-11

## SECTION - B

*Note: (i) Attempt any four questions.*

*(ii) All questions carry equal marks.*

**Q5. Describe the differences and similarities between impoundments and lakes.**

**Ans. Impoundments:** Lakes that are artificially created by men called reservoirs or impoundments. These have been built to fulfil specific requirements hydroelectric power generation, fisheries, water supply, irrigation industries, recreation, control of floods,, etc.

Impoundments may be called off-stem or on-stem depending on how they have been created. On-stem reservoirs-these are located in upland areas and are formed by damming a stretch of river or stream in a suitable river valley. In India, only these types of impoundments are found. Off-stem reservoirs are built in low land areas by pumping water some distance from a river or from an underground source.

**Lakes:** Most lakes occur in regions, which have recently been subjected to geological changes; say within the past 20,000 years.

Lakes arise in several ways. Some, like the tectonic lakes, are formed in basins created by geological activities such as warping and faulting of the earth's crust. Most of the Himalayan lakes are tectonic in origin. Some are formed in crater depressions of extinct volcanoes and are called crater lakes, for example lake Kounsaranag in Kashmir. Others may be a result of glacial activity. For examples most lakes of North America originated due to glacial erosions and deposition, whereby glacial abrasions of slopes in high mountain engraved basin which later became filled with melting snow and rain. Still others have been formed by deposition of silt, drift-wood and other debris in beds of slow moving streams. Lakes may also arise by landslides blocking off streams and valley.

**Q6. Describe the role of pH in nutrient availability in soil.**
**Ans.** pH plays a significant role in the nutrient availability in soil, which affects the plant growth to large extent. An increase in pH indicates the increase in the amount of calcium and magnesium in the soil solution, which enhances the plant growth. At low pH, molybdenum forms, insoluble compounds with iron and becomes unavailable. Under these conditions, plants like cauliflower, clover and citrus will suffer from molybdenum deficiency but will show better performance when soil pH is increased. Potassium availability is usually good in alkaline soils. The availability of solubility of some plant nutrients like iron and manganese decreases at higher pH. Similarly, in soil having high pH, the nutrients phosphorus and boron also tend to be unavailable. While copper and zinc have reduced availability in both highly acidic and alkaline soils. Thus, the nutrient availability is generally good at close to pH 6.5.

**Q7. What are age pyramids? Describe the three types of age pyramids.**
**Ans.** Refer to Chapter No.-3, Q.No.-19

**Q8. (a) Describe with appropriate examples the role of Keystone species.**
**Ans.** Refer to Chapter No.-3, Q.No.-10

**(b) How are Keystone species different from that of dominant species?**
**Ans.** Refer to Chapter No.-3, Q.No.-10

**Q9. Describe any two synthetic characters of a plant community.**
**Ans.** Refer to Chapter No.-3, Q.No.-4

**Q10. (a) Why does pyramid of biomass in some aquatic ecosystems acquire on inverted shape?**
**Ans.** Refer to Chapter No.-2, Q.No.-4

**(b) Explain the limitations of ecological pyramids.**
**Ans.** Refer to Chapter No.-2, Q.No.-5

## SECTION - C

*Note: (i) Attempt any two questions.*

*(ii) All questions carry equal marks.*

**Q11. (a) Describe the significance of forests.**
**Ans.** Refer to Chapter No.-2, Q.No.-25

**(b) Discuss the various causes and consequences of deforestation.**

**Ans.** Refer to Chapter No.-2, Q.No.-24

**Q12. (a) What are the various categories of threatened species? Write one or two lines about each.**

**Ans.** Refer to Chapter No.-4, Q.No.-11

**(b) Describe briefly the 'Red Data book' and 'Project tiger'.**

**Ans.** Refer to Chapter No.-4, Q.No.-12 (i)

The Government of India launched Project Tiger, a centrally sponsored scheme, in April 1973 to protect tigers and to ensure a viable population of tigers in India. The Management Plans were to form the bases for the implementation of the project. These were not approved by the State Governments and the Central Government in many cases. The Annual Plans of Operation also did not always have correlation with the management plans. The activities on the ground were very often dictated by the immediate needs of the project and the funds released by the Government. The State Governments did not, in many cases, release their share of funds. Cases of diversion of central funds for other purposes were also noticed during a adult.

The norms decided in 1972 to create Tiger Reserves stipulated an average area of 1500 sqkms. The actual areas of the Tiger Reserves were mostly less than the prescribed area. 15 out of the 28 Tiger Reserves created had area less than half the prescribed area which was definitely not conducive for conservation, protection and sustenance of a viable tiger population. Besides, the boundaries of many of the Tiger Reserves had not been demarcated nor the areas falling within the Tiger Reserves notified legally.

**Q13. (a) Briefly describe the different kinds of succession.**

**Ans.** Refer to Chapter No.-3, Q.No.-5

**(b) Describe the various steps involved in the process of succession.**

**Ans.** Refer to Chapter No.-3, Q.No.-6

✍✍✍

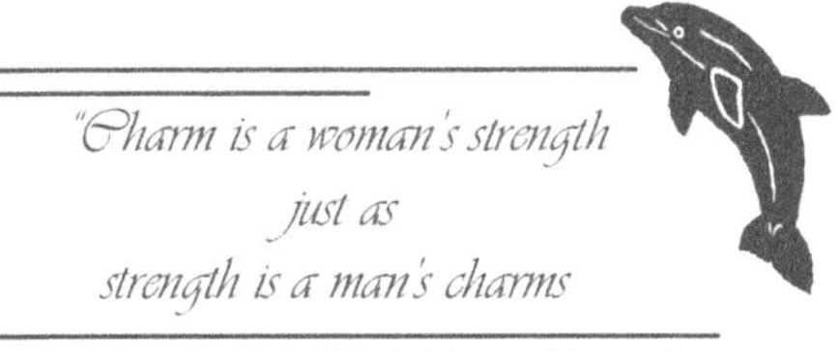

# LSE-02: ECOLOGY
## December, 2012

*Note: Question No.1 is compulsory. Attempt any four questions from Q.Nos. 2 to 6.*

**Q1. (a) Define the following terms:**

**(i) Aggregation**

**Ans.** Refer to Chapter No. 3, Q.No.-6

**(ii) Benthos**

**Ans.** Refer to Chapter No. 2, Q.No.-31

**(iii) Niche**

**Ans.** Refer to Chapter No. 3, Q.No.-10

**(iv) Homeostasis**

**Ans.** Refer to Chapter No. 2, Q.No.-9,

**(v) Littoral zone**

**Ans.** The littoral zone is operationally defined as the fraction of the ocean that supports benthic plants, whether macro-or microscopic.

**(b) Fill in the blanks:**

**(i) ____________ is the study of relationship of living organisms to one another and to their environment.**

**Ans.** Ecology

**(ii) ____________ is a special form of predation in which the predator and prey belong to the same species.**

**Ans.** Cannibalism

**(iii) The forests may be evergreen or ____________.**

**Ans.** Semi evergreen/deciuous

**(c) State whether the given statements are true or false:**

**(i) Sunlight is a major limiting factor in an aquatic ecosystem.**

**Ans.** True

**(ii) The main reservoir of nitrogen in the biosphere is ocean.**

**Ans.** False

**(iii) The estuaries do not support large organisms.**

**Ans.** True

**(iv) A dominant species can be eliminated if environmental conditions change.**

**Ans.** True

**Q2. Differentiate between any four of the following:**

**(a) Natural and artificial ecosystem**

**Ans.** Refer to Chapter No. 1, Q.No.-5 (ii)

**(b) Autogenic and allogeneic succession**

**Ans.** Refer to Chapter No. 3, Q.No.-5

**(c) Tropical rain forest and temperate rain forest**

**Ans.** Refer to Chapter No. 2, Q.No.-24 (i)

Temperate rain forests are found on the western edge of North and South America, where moist air from the Pacific Ocean drops between 60 and 200 inches of rain a year. Unlike the tropical rain forest, the temporate rain forest has seasonal variation, with summer temperatures rising to about 80 degrees Fahrenheit and winter temperatures dropping to near freezing. In the northernmost regions, winter may be cold enough for some ice and snow.

**(d) Bioaccumulation and Biomagnification**

**Ans. Bioaccumulation** is the accumulation of a substance in a biological tissue. Organisms at any trophic level may be capable of bioaccumulation.

The rate at which pollutants are accumulated in the tissues of an organism may be influenced by the following:

- The concentration of pollution in the water.
- The water temperature - if the metabolism of the organism increases, so too may its rate of uptake.
- The age and sex of the organism.

**Biomagnification** is the increasing concentration of a substance up a food chain - i.e. from one trophic level to the next

Conservative pollutants are not metabolised and therefore when an organism containing a pollutant is eaten, the pollutants are simply passed on to the predator and accumulate in its tissues. By consuming many prey an organism may build up very high concentrations of the pollutant in its tissues. This process may continue up the foodchain, leaving the top predator with very high and sometimes lethal concentrations of the pollutant. Pollutants will enter organisms via different routes eg. though the mouth and digestive tract or across gill surfaces. Small aquatic organisms absorb most toxins directly from the water whereas carnivores at the top of the food chain - e.g. birds and mammals - receive most of their pollutant uptake from their food.

**(e) Food chain and food web**

**Ans.** Refer to Chapter No. 2, Q.No.-11 & 12

**Q3. Answer the following:**

**(a) What do you understand by cation exchange capacity of soil?**

**Ans.** Soils can be thought of as storehouses for plant nutrients. Many nutrients, such as calcium and magnesium, may be supplied to plants solely from reserves held in the soil. Others like potassium are added regularly to soils as fertiliser for the purpose of being withdrawn as needed by crops. The relative ability of soils to store one particular group of nutrients, the cations, is referred to as *cation exchange capacity* or CEC.

Cations held on the clay and organic matter particles in soils can be replaced by other cations; thus, they are *exchangeable*. For instance, potassium can be replaced by cations such as calcium or hydrogen, and vice versa.

The total number of cations a soil can hold—or its total negative charge—is the soil's cation exchange capacity. The higher the CEC, the higher the negative charge and the more cations that can be held.

CEC is measured in millequivalents per 100 grams of soil (meq/100g). A millequivalent is the number of ions which total a specific quantity of electrical charges.

**(b) Describe briefly how carbon and sulphur cycles are affected by human activities.**

**Ans.** Refer to Chapter No. 2, Q.No.-13 & 15

**Q4. (a) List the three patterns of population distribution.**

**Ans.** Dispersion or distribution refers to the pattern of distribution of individuals of a population. As shown in figure, individuals in a population may be distributed in three broad patterns; a) uniform, b) random and c) clumped. Uniform distribution is more regular than random and may occur where competition between individuals is severe or where there is antagonism, which promotes even spacing. Random distribution occurs where environment is very uniform and there is no tendency to aggregate. This type of distribution is relatively rare in nature. Clumping of individuals in groups is the most common pattern. In this case, the groups could be of same or of varying size.

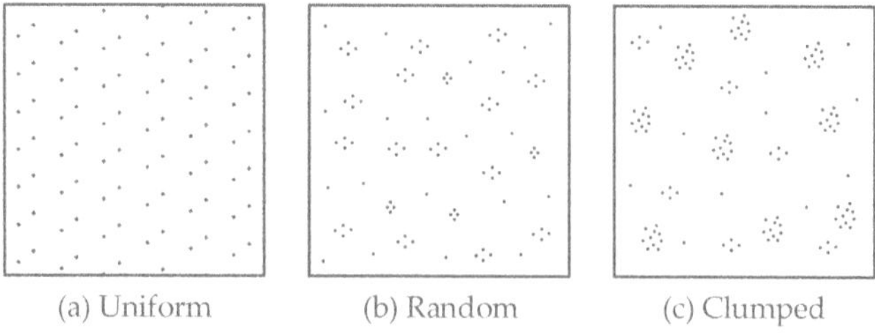


**Fig. 12.4: Distribution patterns of individuals in a population**

Again these groups could be randomly distributed, uniformly distributed or further clumped with each other. All these ways of dispersions are found in nature. It is obvious from the figure that if we examine small samples of dispersion from each population, the result will be very different. For example, a sample from a population with clumped distribution will give either too low or too high a density, when the number in the sample is multiplied to obtain the total population. So we can say that clumped populations require larger and more careful techniques for study of populations than non-clumped ones.

**(b) Discuss why infant mortality rate is an important demographic indicator.**

**Ans.** Mortality plays a vital role of determining the size of the population as it has influence on the age structure of the population. Mortality has important utility encompassing demographic analysis, population projections, health administration, developing plans for housing and educational facilities, social security programmes, and life insurance policies and services. The quality of data on deaths obtained from vital registration is usually incomplete and inaccurate. Age and sex are the two most important characteristics, which form the basis of the detailed analysis of mortality.

**(c) Explain why pyramid of energy can never assume an inverted shape.**

**Ans.** Refer to Chapter No. 2, Q.No.-4

**Q.5. Write short notes on any four of the following:**

**(a) Nudation**

**Ans.** Refer to Chapter No. 3, Q.No.-6

**(b) Defence mechanism in plants**

**Ans.** Refer to Chapter No. 3, Q.No.-13

**(c) Biogeochemical cycle**

**Ans.** Refer to Chapter No. 2, Q.No.-17

**(d) Water logging**

**Ans.** Refer to Chapter No. 1, Q.No.-26 (xi)

**(e) Keystone species**

**Ans.** Refer to Chapter No. 3, Q.No.-10

**Q.6. (a)Write the economic importance of grassland biomes.**

**Ans.** Refer to Chapter No. 2, Q.No.-22

**(b) Describe the physical properties of soil.**

**Ans.** Refer to Chapter No. 1, Q.No.-24

# LSE-02: ECOLOGY
## June, 2013

*Note: Question No. 1 is compulsory. Attempt any four questions from Q. No. 2 to 6.*

Q1. (a) Define the following terms:

(i) Ecesis

(ii) Sciophytes

(iii) Guilds

(iv) Endemics

(v) Eutrophication

(b) Fill in the blanks:

(i) A dark soil is usually rich in ____________.

(ii) The capacity of an ecosystem to self regulate or self maintain is called ____________.

(iii) In ____________ plants, to minimise water loss their leaf size is either reduced or they are modified into thorns.

(c) State whether the given statements are TRUE or FALSE:

(i) Habitat is synonymous with the niche of an organism.

(ii) Keystone species commonly determine the structure of aquatic communities.

(iii) Ecological natality is always constant for a population.

(iv) The amount of solar energy reaching the top of atmosphere is called solar constant.

Q2. Differentiate between any four of the following:

(a) Primary and secondary production.

(b) Steppes and savannas.

(c) Pyramids of biomass and energy

(d) Physical and chemical weathering of soil.

(e) Natality and mortality.

Q3. Answer the following:

(a) Discuss the role of nitrogen cycle in the ecosystem.

(b) Briefly describe any five measures for wild life conservation.

Q4. (a) What are the ecological adaptations in animals to aquatic environment?

(b) Write the pollutants and sources of ground water pollution in any two Indian cities.

Q5. Write short notes on any four of the following:

(a) Components of ecosystem

(b) Estuaries

(c) Appiko movement

(d) Biosphere

(e) Predation

Q6. (a) Explain the ways in which social forestry benefits rural masses.

(b) In what ways food web relationships promote ecosystem stability? Discuss with a suitable example.

# LSE-02: ECOLOGY
## December, 2013

**Note:** *Question No. 1 is compulsory. Attempt any four questions from Q. No. 2 to 6.*

**Q1.** **(a) Define the following terms:**

**(i)** **Mortality**

**(ii)** **Plankton**

**(iii)** **Keystone species**

**(iv)** **Primary pollutants**

**(v)** **Hydrophyte**

**(b)** **State whether the given statements are true or false:**

**(i)** **Pollen grains of pinus are specially adapted to float in air.**

**(ii)** **A food chain that begins with dead organic matter is called detritus food chain.**

**(iii)** **Lichens are pioneers of xerarch succession.**

**(iv)** **A low level of BOD indicates the high activity of aerobic decomposers in a water body.**

**(c)** **Fill in the Blanks:**

**(i)** **The specific heat of water is ____________ joule.**

**(ii)** **During nitrification ____________ is converted to nitrates.**

**(iii)** **A species is considered ____________ when its numbers are reduced to a few that it may become extinct if not given special protection.**

**Q2.** **Differentiate between the following:**

**(a)** **Colluvial soil and Alluvial soil**

**(b)** **Phanerophytes and chamaephytes**

(c) Quantitative and Qualitative defence mechanisms in plants

(d) Random and clumped population distribution

Q3. Answer the following:

(a) Discuss the importance of forests.

(b) Categorise the components of ecosystem.

(c) Describe a simplified carbon-cycle in nature.

(d) Explain the major events during a hydrosere.

Q4. (a) How do animals adapt to extreme temperatures?

(b) Write a note on the biota of on estuary

Q5. (a) Discuss the causes of water pollution.

(b) "Elimination or disturbance of habitats threatens existence of wildlife." Comment.

Q6. Write short notes on any four of the following:

(a) Photoperiodism

(b) Fidelity

(c) Extinct species

(d) Major sub-divisions of ecology

(e) Symbiotic nitrogen fixers.

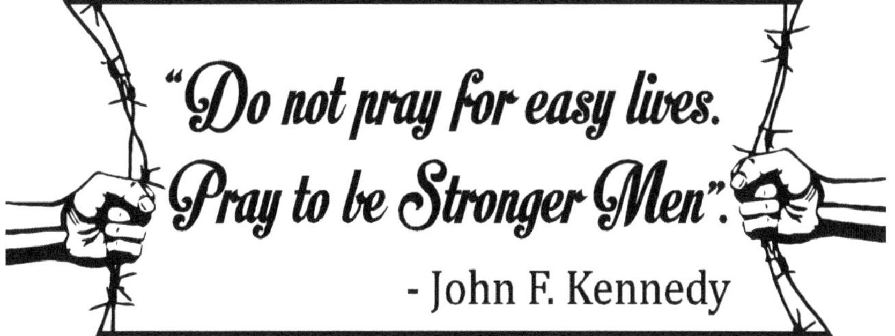

# LSE-02: ECOLOGY
## June, 2014

*Note: Question No. 1 is compulsory. Attempt any four questions from Q. No. 2 to 6.*

Q1. (a) Define the following terms:

(i) Natality

(ii) Nekton

(iii) Habitat

(iv) Secondary pollutants

(v) Succulents

(b) State whether the given statements are true or false:

(i) Silky hairs on seeds help them to float in air.

(ii) A detritus food chain operates through parasites.

(iii) Succession initiated on a bare rock is termed xerarch.

(iv) Addition of biodegradable matter relaxes the demand of oxygen in the water body.

(c) Fill in the blanks:

(i) It takes _____________ joules of energy to heat one gram of water from 4°C to 5°C.

(ii) During a nitrogen cycle the process of conversion of ammonia to nitrate is called _____________.

(iii) _____________ ultimately leads to problems like soil erosion, loss of nutrients and desertification.

Q2. Differentiate between the following:

(a) Hygroscopic water and Capillary water of soil.

(b) Hemicryptophytes and Cryptophytes

(c) Parasitoidism and Cannibalism

(d) People overpopulation and Consumption overpopulation

Q3. Answer the following:

(a) Discuss the causes of deforestation.

(b) Describe the structure of a community.

(c) Explain the concept of energy flow in an ecosystem.

(d) "Air pollution is harmful to all living systems." Comment.

Q4. (a) How do plants adapt to extreme temperatures?

(b) Write a note on biota of an ocean.

Q5. (a) Describe various kinds of interspecific interactions within a community.

(b) Comment on the human impact on sulphur cycle.

Q6. Write short notes on any four of the following:

(a) Adaptations in animals to aquatic environment

(b) Soil texture

(c) Ecotone

(d) Carrying capacity

(e) Age structure

*"It doesn't matter who you are, where you come from. The ability to triumph begins with you – always".*

-Oprah Winfrey

# LSE-02: ECOLOGY
## December, 2014

***Note:*** *All sections are compulsory.*

### SECTION - A

*Note: All questions of this section are compulsory.*

**Q1. State whether the following statements are True (T) or False (F):**

**(a) Synecology is the study of the ecology of groups.**

**(b) Light is the major limiting factor in aquatic ecosystems.**

**(c) The biomass is measured in kcal/m2/yr.**

**(d) Primary production depends on solar energy.**

**(e) Rivers are a type of lotic ecosystem.**

**(f) Carrying capacity is not the saturation level beyond which a population does not grow.**

**Q2. Give the technical term (one word) for each of the following:**

**(a) Organism interactions in which one organism benefits and the other remains unaffected.**

**(b) Zone of vegetation separating two different types of communities.**

**Q3. Fill in the blanks:**

**(a) An animal whose body temperature tends to vary with surroundings is called ____________.**

**(b) A species in imminent danger of extinction is termed as ____________ species.**

**(c) A dark soil is usually rich in ____________.**

**(d) The content of dissolved salts in brackish water is ____________ than fresh water.**

**Q4. Define the following:**

**(a) Niche**

**(b) Succession**

**(c) Stratosphere**

## SECTION - B

*Note: (i) Attempt any four questions.*

*(ii) All questions carry equal marks.*

**Q5. What is an age pyramid? Describe the types of age pyramids with suitable examples.**

**Q6. (a) What is cation exchange capacity of the soil?**

**(b) Comment upon cation saturation and nutrient absorption by plants.**

**Q7. Describe briefly the various stages of xerarch succession.**

**Q8. What are Life Forms? Describe the various types of Raunkiaer's Life Forms.**

**Q9. Compare the characteristics of an Oligotrophic Lake with a Eutrophic Lake.**

**Q10. With the help of a well labelled diagram explain the Nitrogen cycle.**

## SECTION - C

*Note: (i) Attempt any two questions.*

*(ii) All questions carry equal marks.*

**Q11. Describe the various consequences of water pollution.**

**Q12. Critically comment on the following statements:**

**(a) Primary succession proceeds slowly compared to secondary succession.**

**(b) A Grasing Food Chain in a forest ecosystem consists of a few trophic levels.**

**Q13. List the major causes of degradation of ecosystem. Discuss any two causes in detail with the help of relevant examples.**

✍ ✍ ✍

# LSE-02: ECOLOGY
## June, 2015

*Note:* *All sections are compulsory.*

## SECTION - A

*Note: All questions of this section are compulsory.*

**Q1. State whether the following statements are True (T) or False (F):**

**(a) Autecology is the study of ecology of an individual.**

**(b) Pyramid of biomass is always vertical.**

**(c) Net primary production is always higher than gross primary production.**

**(d) Wetlands are lentic ecosystems.**

**(e) Immigration is periodic departure and return of individuals.**

**(f) Succulents are found in hot and dry areas.**

**Q2. Give the technical term (one word) for each of the following:**

**(a) Diagrammatic representation of phenology.**

**(b) The group of plants and animals which are found on the bottom of an aquatic ecosystem.**

**Q3. Fill in the blanks:**

**(a) Animals which can tolerate limited range of temperature are known as ____________.**

**(b) Tropical rainforests occur near the ____________.**

**(c) The major constituent of the atmosphere is ____________ gas.**

**(d) Natality is the ability of a population to ____________ in number.**

**Q4. Define the following:**

**(a) Keystone Species**

(b) Ecesis

(c) Ecological Pyramid

## SECTION - B

*Note: (i) Attempt any four questions.*

*(ii) All questions carry equal marks.*

**Q5. With the help of diagrams, explain the two types of Growth Curves.**

**Q6. What is a soil profile? Describe the various horizons of soil.**

**Q7. Describe briefly the various stages of Hydrarch succession.**

**Q8. (a) What is Importance Value Index (IVI) of a plant community?**

**(b) Briefly describe Raunkiaer's Life Forms.**

**Q9. Describe any five salient features of a Marine Ecosystem.**

**Q10. Explain the carbon cycle with the help of a well-labelled diagram.**

## SECTION - C

*Note: (i) Attempt any two questions.*

*(ii) All questions carry equal marks.*

**Q11. Discuss the various consequences of Air Pollution.**

**Q12. Critically comment on the following statements:**

**(a) Flow of Energy is always unidirectional.**

**(b) Earth's temperature varies at different latitudes and altitudes.**

**Q13. (a) Discuss the need to conserve Wildlife.**

**(b) What is a Red Data Book?**

**As i grow older, I pay less attention to what men say. I just watch what they do.**

**- Andrew Carnegie**

## LSE-02: ECOLOGY

## December, 2015

*Note: Question no. 1 is compulsory. Attempt any four questions from no. 2 to 6.*

Q1. (a) Define the following terms:

(i) Eutrophication

(ii) Ecoclines

(iii) Plankton

(iv) Predation

(v) Residual soil

(b) Fill in the blanks:

(i) Bright light loving plants are called ________.

(ii) ______ is a free floating plant.

(iii) _______ is a large community unit that is characterised by the kind of plants and animals present in it.

(c) State whether the given statements are True or False:

(i) Most of the world's deserts are situated at 60° latitude.

(ii) All ecosystems have well defined boundaries.

(iii) The composition of the atmosphere is constant upto 80 km of height.

(iv) Ecological natality is not constant for a population.

Q2. Differentiate between any four of the following:

(a) Internal and External nutrient budgets

(b) Stationary and Stable populations

(c) Nitrification and Denitrification

(d) Colluvial and Alluvial soils

(e) Temperate evergreen forests and Temperate rain forests

Q3. (a) How does social forestry help in forest conservation? Explain.

(b) Explain with the help of illustrations the cation exchange capacity of soil.

Q4. (a) What is meant by demographic transition? Explain its different phases.

(b) Write the major adaptations in primates that ultimately led to the origin of first Homo species.

Q5. Write short notes on any four of the following. Give illustrations wherever necessary.

(a) Kinds of succession

(b) Pelagic zone

(c) Gregariousness of plants

(d) Soil profile

(e) A case of selective destruction of wildlife

Q6. (a) Briefly explain the biota of lakes.

(b) Differentiate between the two basic types of biogeochemical cycles. Diagrammatically represent any one biogeochemical cycle.

✦✦✦

## LSE-02: ECOLOGY

**June, 2016**

---

***Note:*** *Question no. 1 is compulsory. Attempt any four questions from no. 2 to 6.*

---

**Q1. (a) Define the following terms:**

**(i) Synecology**

**(ii) Ecotone**

**(iii) Red Data Book**

**(iv) Keystone Species**

**(v) Demographer**

**(b) Fill in the blanks:**

**(i) The process of vapourisation of ice without melting is called _____.**

**(ii) The pyramid of _______ can never assume an inverted shape.**

**(iii) The increase in concentration of a toxin in a food chain at higher levels is called______.**

**(c) State whether the following statements are True or False:**

**(i) Natality rate measurement is not dependent on the type of organism being studied.**

**(ii) Shorter the food chain, lesser is the availability of usable energy.**

**(iii) The estuaries are the most productive ecosystems of the biosphere.**

**(iv) The group Neuston contains animals that are swimmers.**

**Q2. (a) With the help of suitable diagrams, explain succession in fresh water body.**

**(b) Explain why removal of tropical forests often reveals poor quality of agriculture land.**

**Q3. Differentiate between any four of the following:**

**(a) Primary and Secondary production**

**(b) Lentic and Lotic ecosystem**

**(c) Natality and Mortality**

**(d) Nektons and Benthos**

**(e) Physical and Chemical weathering of soil**

**Q4. (a) Explain the concept of carrying capacity with the help of an example.**

**(b) 'Maintenance of grassland biome is essential in our country.' Explain.**

Q5. Write short notes on any four of the following:

(a) Desertification

(b) Biota of Estuaries

(c) Wilting Coefficient

(d) Ammonification

(e) Food Web

Q6. (a) Explain briefly why conservation of wildlife is essential.

(b) Discuss the consequences of water pollution.

# LSE-02: ECOLOGY

## December, 2016

*Note: Question no. 1 is compulsory. Attempt any four questions from no. 2 to 6.*

**Q1. (a) Define the following terms:**

**(i) Secondary consumer**

**Ans.** Refer to Chapter-2, Q.No.-6

**(ii) Field capacity of soil**

**Ans.** Refer to Chapter-1, Q.No.-24

**(iii) Mortality**

**Ans.** Refer to Chapter-3, Q.No.-15

**(iv) Sludge**

**Ans.** Sludge is the accumulated solids produced by a waste water treatment plant and solids left from septage, the liquid pumped from septic tanks.

**(v) Wind**

**Ans.** Strong current of air is known as wind, it is an important ecological factor as it affects plant life mainly on flat plains, along sea coasts and at high altitudes in mountains. It directly affects transpiration, causes mechanical damage and is an important agent of dispersal of pollens, seeds and fruits.

**(b) Fill in the blanks:**

**(i) On cooling, water molecules come______ which makes the water dense.**

**Ans.** Closer

**(ii) Oxygen content of hypolimnion zone of a water body is low due to its utilisation by _____ processes.**

**Ans.** Decomposition

**(iii) Fidelity refers to the degree to which a_____ is restricted in its occurrence to a particular kind of community.**

**Ans.** Species

**(c) State whether the given statements are True or False:**

**(i) If a population is growing at 2 percent growth rate, then it will double in 35 years.**

**Ans.** True

**(ii) Thiobacillus reduces $H_2S$ to $So_4$.**

**Ans.** False

**(iii) Sum of all genes of an individual is called gene pool.**

**Ans.** True

**(iv) Vegetations or ecotones are highly specialised.**

**Ans.** True

**Q2. Differentiate between any four of the following:**

**(a) Phanerophytes and Chamaephytes**

**Ans.** Refer to Chapter-3, Q.No.-3

**(b) Autecology and Synecology**

**Ans.** Refer to Chapter-1, Q.No.-3

**(c) Summer stratification and Winter stratification**

**Ans.** Refer to Chapter-2, Q.No.-35

**(d) Detritus food chain and Auxiliary food chain**

**Ans.** In addition to grazing and detritus food chains there are other auxiliary food chains operated through parasites and scavengers. Some parasitic food chains may be quite complex and may involve unrelated organisms. A deer fed upon by internal roundworms and external ticks or a man with malarial parasites in his blood are examples of parasitic food chains. Often parasitic relations are quite involved as parasites are transmitted through a variety of vectors or through unrelated intermediary host organisms. Like the other food chains, the ultimate source of energy for all auxiliary food chains is solar energy orginally harvested by plants.

**(e) Mesophytes and Xerophytes**

**Ans.** Refer to Chapter-1, Q.No.-20

**Q3. Answer the following:**

**(a) Briefly discuss the causes of air pollution.**

**Ans.** The major causes of air pollution include the following human activities:

**(1) Fossil fuel composition:** As we know, coal on combustion produces $CO_2$. Incomplete combustion yields CO and a variety of hydrocarbons including methane and soot (carbon particles of various sizes, the large ones make up dust and small ones make smoke). Most other fuels except gas contain sulphur and unburnable contaminants. Therefore, burning of coal produces $SO_2$ and ash also. About 60% of $SO_2$ emission is due to burning of coal.

**(2) Motor transport:** We often see trucks, buses, cars, two wheelers and three wheelers belch black smoke from their exhaust. Transport vehicles contribute to $NO_x$, CO and hydrocarbon emission. They also emit lead because tetramethyl lead is added to petrol as antiknock substance to increase engine efficiency.

**(3) Modern agriculture:** Agricultural activities too are a major cause of air pollution. About 60 to 65% of carbon dioxide is produced from burning of forests and savannah grassland to clear areas for pastures and cropland and 40% of methane is produced from paddy fields, guts of' livestocks and also from burning of biomass.

**(4) Industry:** Industrial activity mainly smelting of some metal ores produces large quantities of $SO_2$. Chemical manufacturing units produce thousands of hazardous chemicals. Among these chlorofluorocarbons top the list. These are non-biodegradable with a long life ranging from 7 to 10 years. Before being washed out of the atmosphere each 10 chlorine atoms destroy many as one million molecules of ozone. Chemical plants are a large source of industrial emission of toxic air pollutants responsible for about 35% of the total emission. Other major sources are paper, plastic, rubber, automobile industry.

**(b) How do organisms adapt to extreme temperatures?**

**Ans.** The deep-sea hydrothermal vents are located along the volcanic ridges and are characterized by extreme conditions such as unique physical properties (temperature, pression), chemical toxicity, and absence of photosynthesis. However, life exists in these particular environments. The organisms of these ecosystems have developed different adaptive strategies. In these environments many microorganisms are adapted to high temperatures. Moreover, to survive in these environments, living organisms have developed various strategies to protect themselves against toxic molecules such as $H_2S$ and heavy metals.

**Q4. (a) Write a brief account of defence mechanisms in plants.**

**Ans.** Refer to Chapter-3, Q.No.-13

**(b) "Domestication is a potential threat to Wildlife." Comment.**

**Ans.** Refer to Chapter-4, Q.No.-9

**Q5. (a) Briefly discuss the chemical properties of soil.**

**Ans.** Refer to Chapter-1, Q.No.-24

**(b) Discuss the various types of grasslands. Write their economic importance.**

**Ans.** Refer to Chapter-2, Q.No.-22

**Q6. Write short notes on any four of the following:**

**(a) Population Growth Curve**

**Ans.** Refer to Chapter-3, Q.No.-15

**(b) Denitrification**

**Ans.** Nitrates are readily leached from the soil and also lost through denitrification the process by which molecular or gaseous nitrogen (N2) as well as nitrous oxide (NO) and nitric oxide (N2O) and nitrogen dioxide (NO2) are formed from NO3 by bacteria (such as Pseudomonas) and fungi. They use the nitrate as a source of oxygen in the presence of glucose and phosphate. Denitrifing bacteria prefer anaerobic or partially aerobic habitats such as estuaries, bogs, lake bottoms and water-logged soils. The bacteria reduce the nitrates to nitrites which are finally converted to free nitrogen.

**(c) Carrying Capacity**

**Ans.** Refer to Chapter-3, Q.No.-16

**(d) Role of urbanisation on degradation of ecosystem**

**Ans.** Refer to Chapter-4, Q.No.-8

**(e) Phosphorus Cycle**

**Ans.** Refer to Chapter-2, Q.No.-14

# LSE-02: ECOLOGY
## June, 2017

*Note: Question No. 1 is compulsory. Attempt any four questions from Q. No. 2 to 6.*

**Q1. (a) Define the following terms:**

**(i) Primary Consumer**
**Ans.** Refer to Chapter-2, Q.No.-6

**(ii) Stratosphere**
**Ans.** Refer to Chapter-1, Q.No.-15

**(iii) Natality**
**Ans.** Refer to Chapter-3, Q.No.-15

**(iv) Bio-magnification**
**Ans.** Refer to Chapter-4, Q.No.-18

**(v) Littoral zone**
**Ans.** Littoral zone is a part of sea, lake or river that is close to the shore.

**(b) Fill in the blanks:**

**(i) Water is most dense at_____ °C.**
**Ans.** 4

**(ii) _______ is the zone that lies below epilimnion and above hypolimnion.**
**Ans.** Metalimnion

**(iii) Physiognomy is the general appearance of vegetation as determined by the growth form of______ species.**
**Ans.** dominant

**(c) State whether the following statements are true or false:**

**(i) Crude rates give the number of live births and deaths per 100 persons.**
**Ans.** false.

**(ii) Anaerobic heterotrophs reduce organic sulphur to $H_2S$.**

**Ans.** true.

**(iii) Sum of all the genes of all the individuals in a population is termed as gene pool.**

**Ans.** true.

**(iv) Floristic composition of community represents its quantitative characteristics.**

**Ans.** false.

**Q2. Differentiate between any four of the following:**

**(a) Density and Frequency**

**Ans.** Refer to Chapter-3, Q.No.-3

**(b) Fresh Water and Brackish Water**

**Ans.** Refer to Chapter-1, Q.No.-26 (iii),(vii)

**(c) Rare species and Vulnerable species**

**Ans.** Refer to Chapter-4, Q.No.-11 (Rare and Depleted species)

**(d) Photic and Aphotic zones of an ocean**

**Ans.** The zone upto which light rays penetrate in a water body is called photic zone and below this lies a zone of complete darkness called aphotic zone. The zone above compensation depth is photic zone, whereas the zone below compensation depth is aphotic zone.

**(e) Sublimation and Evaporation**

**Ans.** Refer to Chapter-1, Q.No.-19

**Sublimation** is the process by which solid water changes directly to vapour phase without passing through the intervening liquid phase. The gradual disappearance offlakes of ice during periods when the temperature remains well below freezing is a example of sublimation.

**Q3. (a) Mention the effects of air pollution on human health.**

**Ans.** Refer to Chapter-4, Q.No.-14

**(b) Describe the various forms of mutual relationship among individuals of a community.**

**Ans.** Refer to Chapter-1, Q.No.-7

**Q4. (a) With the help of suitable examples, explain resource partitioning among organisms.**

**Ans.** Refer to Chapter-3, Q.No.-14 (Results of competition).

**(b) "Introduction of a new species can be harmful to wild life." Comment.**

**Ans.** Long as human beings have travelled around the world, they have carried with them (accidentally or intentionally) many species of plants and animals, which they have introduced to new geographical areas. In some instances an opening has existed in the new environment and the foreign or alien species has been able to establish itself without seriously affecting the population size of the native species. But in other instances, the alien has been a superior predater, parasite or competitor, and has brought about extinction or near extinction of native species. It can also cause a population explosion of the existing species by killing off their natural predators. Island species are particularly vulnerable because have evolved in ecosystems with few if any natural herbivores, carnivore predators.

In 1859 a farmer in southern Australia imported a dozen pairs of wild European rabbits as a game animal. Within six years these 24 rabbits had mushroomed to 22 million so that by 1907 they had reached every corner of the country. By the 1930s, their population had reached an estimated 750 million. They competed with sheep for grass and this cut the sheep population to half. They also devoured food crops, gnawed young trees, fouled water holes and accelerated soil erosion in many places. In the early 1950s, about 90% of the rabbit population was killed by the deliberate human introduction of a virus disease. There is a concern, however, that members of the remaining population may eventually develop immunity to this viral disease through natural selection and again become the scourge of Australian farmers.

**Q5. (a) Describe the various steps of soil formation.**

**Ans.** Refer to Chapter-1, Q.No.-22

**(b) Discuss Ecological Hydrarch Succession.**

**Ans.** Hydrarch is a kind of succession that takes place in areas where the water content is very high as a result the plants grow in availability of too much of water. Thus, the plants have a tendency to develop so as to minimize the water usage. We can therefore say that the plants change from hydric conditions to mesic condition. This can be subdivided as:

(i) hydrosere - when succession starts in fresh water ecosystems like ponds, pools, lakes and marshes;

(ii) halosere - when succession starts in saline water ecosystems, e.g., mangroves, coral reefs, estuaries.

**Q6. Write short notes on any four of the following:**

**(a) Cation Exchange Capacity of a soil**

**Ans.** The adsorption of a cation by a colloid nucleus or micelle and the accompanying release of one or more ions held by the micelle is termed as 'cation exchange'. the major cations are $Ca^{2+}$, $Mg^{2+}$, $K^{+}$, $Na^{+}$, and $NH^{4+}$. Trace amounts of other cations such as $Cu^{2+}$, $Mn^{2+}$, and $Zn^{2+}$, are also present in the soil.

**(b) Ammonification**

**Ans.** Many heterotrophic bacteria, actinomycetes and fungi in soil and water, metabolise the organic nitrogen and release it in an inorganic from as ammonia. This process is known as ammonification or mineralisation. This an energy releasing reaction. For example, glycine-based protein releases 176 Kcal/mole. This energy is used to maintain the life process of the organisms that accomplish the transformation.

**(c) Keystone Species**

**Ans.** Refer to Chapter-3, Q.No.-10

**(d) Historical Overview of Human Population**

**Ans.** Refer to Chapter-4, Q.No.-2

**(e) Carbon Cycle**

**Ans.** Refer to Chapter-2, Q.No.-13

*"It doesn't matter who you are, where you come from. The ability to triumph begins with you – always".*

-Oprah Winfrey

# LSE-02: ECOLOGY
## December, 2017

*Note: Question No. 1 is compulsory. Attempt any four questions from Q. No. 2 to 6.*

Q1. (a) Define the following terms:

(i) Autoecology

(ii) Periphyton

(iii) Primary Production

(iv) Keystone Species

(v) Albedo

(b) State whether the following statements are true or false:

(i) Ecosystem ecology deals with the study of community of living organisms and their environment as an integrated unit of nature.

(ii) Glacial soils are found in Dehradun and parts of Kashmir.

(iii) Most of the gaseous cycles are imperfect.

(iv) Oligotrophic lakes are shallow and their surface to volume ratio is high.

(c) Fill in the blanks:

(i) _______ are the plants which complete their life cycle in a few months and are found in deserts and grasslands.

(ii) Organisms which cannot withstand salinity fluctuations are called ________.

(iii) In tropical forests a large portion of the nutrients are held in _______.

Q2. Differentiate between the following:

(a) Natural and Artificial ecosystem

(b) Succulent and Non-succulent xerophytes

(c) Benthic zone and Pelagic zone

(d) Habitat and Niche

Q3. (a) Discuss any five threats to wildlife which lead to its extinction.

(b) Draw a well labelled diagram of Sulphur cycle. Describe the human impact on Sulphur cycle.

Q4. (a) List the different types of ecological pyramids and describe any one of them.

(b) Discuss how social forestry can help in forest conservation.

Q5. (a) Make a clear and labelled diagram of soil profile.

(b) Elaborate the effects of water pollution on human health.

Q6. Write notes on any four of the following:

(a) Herbivore Countermeasures to Defence Mechanisms in Plants

(b) Overgrazing

(c) Ozone Depletion

(d) Shifting Cultivation

(e) Natality

✍ ✍ ✍

# LSE-02: ECOLOGY
## June, 2018

*Note: Question No. 1 is compulsory. Attempt any four questions from Q. No. 2 to 6.*

**Q1. (a) Define the following terms:**

**(i) Community**

**Ans.** Refer to Chapter-1, Q.No.-7 (Pg. No.-10)

**(ii) Estuary**

**Ans.** Refer to Chapter-2, Q.No.-40 (Pg. No.-99)

**(iii) Immigration**

**Ans.** Refer to Chapter-3, Q.No.-20 (Pg. No.-144)

**(iv) Prairie**

**Ans.** Refer to Chapter-2, Q.No.-22 (Pg. No.-71)

**(v) Standing crop**

**Ans.** Refer to Chapter-2, Q.No.-6 (Pg. No.-53)

**(b) State whether the following statements are true or false:**

**(i) Ecotone is the zone of vegetation which separates two different types of communities.**

**Ans.** True

**(ii) Competitive exclusion principle states that two species in an ecosystem can occupy the same niche.**

**Ans.** False

**(iii) The capacity of an ecosystem to self-regulate or self-maintain is called homeostatis.**

**Ans.** True

**(iv) Benthic zone forms the floor of the lake and underlies the littoral**

**and limnetic zones.**

**Ans.** True

**(c) Fill in the blanks:**

**(i) The interaction in which one species adversely affects the population of another species but remains unaffected itself is called.............. .**

**Ans.** amensalism

**(ii) In eutrophic lakes, primary productivity is ............... .**

**Ans.** high

**(iii) The succession in a wet area is known as ............. .**

**Ans.** Hydrarch succession

**Q2. Differentiate between the following:**

**(a) People overpopulation and Consumption overpopulation**

**Ans.** Refer to Chapter-4, Q.No.-6 (Pg. No.-154)

**(b) Natality and Mortality**

**Ans.** Refer to Chapter-1, Q.No.-6 (Pg. No.-10)

**(c) Qualitative and Quantitative defence mechanisms in plants**

**Ans.** Refer to Chapter-3, Q.No.-13 (Pg. No.-131)

**(d) Plankton and Nekton**

**Ans.** Refer to Chapter-2, Q.No.-31 (Pg. No.-87)

**Q3. (a) Discuss how variation in amount of light affects global and local distribution of plants and animals.**

**Ans.** Refer to Chapter-1, Q.No.-11 (Pg. No.-17)

**(b) Discuss competition in natural populations with an example and highlight the results of the competition.**

**Ans.** Refer to Chapter-3, Q.No.-14 (Pg. No.-132)

**Q4. (a) Describe the various types of food chains in an ecosystem, with examples.**

**Ans.** Refer to Chapter-2, Q.No.-11 (Pg. No.-59)

**(b) Discuss human impact on nitrogen cycle.**

**Ans.** Human impacts on the nitrogen cycle are diverse. Agricultural and industrial nitrogen (N) inputs to the environment currently exceed inputs from natural N fixation. As a consequence of anthropogenic inputs, the global nitrogen cycle has been significantly altered over the past century. Global atmospheric nitrous oxide ($N_2O$) mole fractions have increased from a pre-industrial value of ~270 nmol/mol to ~319 nmol/mol in 2005. Human activities account for over one-third of $N_2O$ emissions, most of which are due to the agricultural sector. This article is intended to give a brief review of the history of anthropogenic N inputs, and reported impacts of nitrogen inputs on selected terrestrial and aquatic ecosystems.

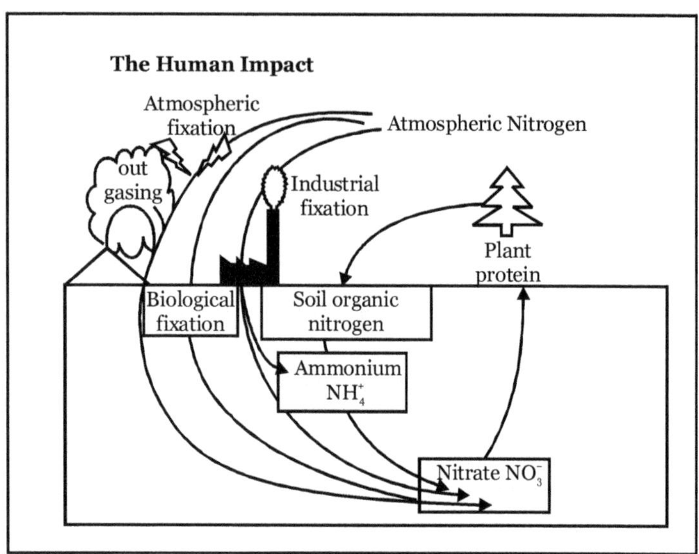


Approximately 78% of earth's atmosphere is N gas ($N_2$), which is an inert compound and biologically unavailable to most organisms. In order to be utilized in most biological processes, $N_2$ must be converted to reactive N (Nr), which includes inorganic reduced forms ($NH_3$ and $NH_4^+$), inorganic oxidized forms (NO, $NO_2$, $HNO_3$, $N_2O$, and $NO_3^-$), and organic compounds (urea, amines, and proteins). $N_2$ has a strong triple bond, and so a significant amount of energy (226 kcal $mol^{-1}$) is required to convert $N_2$ to Nr. Prior to industrial processes, the only sources of such energy were solar radiation and electrical discharges. Utilizing a large amount of metabolic energy and the enzyme nitrogenase, some bacteria and cyanobacteria convert atmospheric $N_2$ to $NH_3$, a process known as biological nitrogen fixation (BNF). The anthropogenic analogue to BNF is the Haber-Bosch process, in which $H_2$ is reacted with atmospheric $N_2$ at high temperatures and pressures to produce $NH_3$. Lastly, $N_2$ is converted to NO by energy from lightning, which is negligible in current temperate ecosystems, or by fossil fuel combustion.

Since the industrial revolution, an additional source of anthropogenic N input has been fossil fuel combustion, which is used to generate energy (e.g., to power automobiles). During combustion of fossil fuels, high temperatures and pressures provide energy to produce NO from $N_2$ oxidation. Additionally, when fossil fuel is extracted and burned, fossil

N may become reactive (i.e., $NO_x$ emissions). During the 1970s, scientists began to recognize that N inputs were accumulating in the environment and affecting ecosystems.

**Impacts of anthropogenic inputs on the nitrogen cycle**

**(1) Atmosphere**

Atmospheric N inputs mainly include oxides of N ($NO_x$), ammonia ($NH_3$), and nitrous oxide ($N_2O$) from aquatic and terrestrial ecosystems, and $NO_x$ from fossil fuel and biomass combustion. In agroecosystems, fertilizer application has increased microbial nitrification (aerobic process in which microorganisms oxidize ammonium [$NH_4^+$] to nitrate [$NO_3^-$]) and denitrification (anaerobic process in which microorganisms reduce $NO_3^-$ to atmospheric nitrogen gas [$N_2$]). Both processes naturally leak nitric oxide (NO) and nitrous oxide ($N_2O$) to the atmosphere. Of particular concern is $N_2O$, which has an average atmospheric lifetime of 114 –120 years, and is 300 times more effective than $CO_2$ as a greenhouse gas. $NO_x$ produced by industrial processes, automobiles and agricultural fertilization and $NH_3$ emitted from soils (i.e., as an additional byproduct of nitrification) and livestock operations are transported to downwind ecosystems, influencing N cycling and nutrient losses.

Six major effects of $NO_x$ and $NH_3$ emissions have been cited:

(1) decreased atmospheric visibility due to ammonium aerosols (fine particulate matter [PM]);

(2) elevated ozone concentrations;

(3) ozone and PM affects human health (e.g. respiratory diseases, cancer);

(4) increases in radiative forcing and global climate change;

(5) decreased agricultural productivity due to ozone deposition; and

(6) ecosystem acidification and eutrophication.

**(2) Biosphere**

Terrestrial and aquatic ecosystems receive Nr inputs from the atmosphere through wet and dry deposition. Atmospheric Nr species can be deposited to ecosystems in precipitation (e.g., $NO_3^-$, $NH_4^+$, organic N compounds), as gases (e.g., $NH_3$ and gaseous nitric acid [$HNO_3$]), or as aerosols (e.g., ammonium nitrate [$NH_4NO_3$]). Aquatic ecosystems receive additional nitrogen from surface runoff and riverine inputs.

Increased N deposition can acidify soils, streams, and lakes and alter forest and grassland productivity. In grassland ecosystems, N inputs have produced initial increases in productivity followed by declines as critical thresholds are exceeded. Nitrogen effects on biodiversity, carbon cycling, and changes in species composition have also been demonstrated. In highly developed areas of near shore coastal ocean and estuarine systems, rivers deliver direct (e.g., surface runoff) and indirect (e.g., groundwater contamination) N inputs from agroecosystems. Increased N inputs can result in freshwater acidification and eutrophication of marine waters.

**Q5. (a) Explain the 'biotic potential' of a species. Discuss factors affecting 'biotic potential'.**

**Ans.** Refer to Chapter-3, Q.No.-16 and Q.No.-17 (Pg. No.-139, 141)

**(b) Describe energy flow in an ecosystem with a well labelled diagram.**

**Ans.** Refer to Chapter-2, Q.No.-6 (Pg. No.-53)

**Q6. Write notes on any four of the following:**

**(a) Herbivore interactions with plants**

**Ans.** Refer to Chapter-3, Q.No.-13 (Pg. No.-130)

**(b) Global warming and Greenhouse effect**

**Ans.** Refer to Chapter-4, Q.No.-14 (Pg. No.-166)

**(c) 'Selective destruction' as a threat to wildlife**

**Ans.** Refer to Chapter-4, Q.No.-9 (Pg. No.-158)

**(d) Adaptations in hydrophilic plants**

**Ans.** Refer to Chapter-1, Q.No.-20 (Pg. No.-32)

**(e) Cation exchange capacity of soil**

**Ans.** Cation exchange capacity (CEC) is the total capacity of a soil to hold exchangeable cations. CEC is an inherent soil characteristic and is difficult to alter significantly. It influences the soil's ability to hold onto essential nutrients and provides a buffer against soil acidification. Soils with a higher clay fraction tend to have a higher CEC. Organic matter has a very high CEC. Sandy soils rely heavily on the high CEC of organic matter for the retention of nutrients in the topsoil.

Therefore, Cation exchange capacity (CEC) is a measure of the soil's ability to hold positively charged ions. It is a very important soil property influencing soil structure stability, nutrient availability, soil pH and the soil's reaction to fertilisers and other ameliorants.

# LSE-02: ECOLOGY
## December, 2018

*Note: Question no. 1 is compulsory. Attempt questions from all sections as per instructions given.*

Q1. (a) Fill in the blanks with the alternatives given in the parentheses.

(i) (Hippocrates/Theophrastus) was the first person to introduce ecological approach before the term ecology was coined.

(ii) (Troposphere/Thermosphere) is the part of the atmosphere where life can exist.

(iii) (Precipitation/Condensation) is the process by which water changes from vapour phase to a liquid state.

(iv) (Ephemeral annuals/Succulents) are plants adapted to hot and dry areas.

(b) Match the items given in column A with those given in column B :

| | Column A | | Column B |
|---|---|---|---|
| (i) | Phagotrophs | (I) | Role played in ecosystem |
| (ii) | Nudation | (II) | Herbivorous |
| (iii) | Niche | (III) | Seasonal changes |
| (iv) | Primary consumer | (IV) | 1st step for primary succession |
| | | (V) | Cannot manufacture their food |

(c) Define the following terms:

(i) Autecology

(ii) Population

SECTION B

Attempt any four questions from this section.

Q2. Explain the ecological adaptation that has taken place in animals to aquatic environment.

Q3. Explain the importance of social forestry in forest conservation.

Q4. Describe the biotic components of an ecosystem.

**Q5. Compare and contrast keystone and dominant species in a community.**

**Q6. Explain how urbanisation has led to environmental degradation.**

## SECTION C

**Attempt any two questions from this section.**

**Q7. Explain the process of xerarch succession taking place in an ecosystem.**

**Q8. Describe the characteristic of human population growth with a reference to age-sex distribution.**

**Q9. Discuss the processes involved in the formation of soil.**

✍ ✍ ✍

Whatever you do, do with determination. You have one life to live; do your work with passion and give your best. Whether you want to be a chef, doctor, actor, or a mother, be passionate to get the best result.

# LSE-02: ECOLOGY
## June, 2019

---

*Note: Question no. 1 is compulsory. Attempt any four questions from question No. 2 to 7.*

---

**Q1.** **(a) Fill in the blanks with the appropriate words given in the parentheses :**

**(i)** **Study of the ecology of groups or communities in relation to their environment is called__________**

**(Autecology/Synecology)**

**(ii)** **The __________ zone includes areas too deep to be penetrated by light useful for photosynthesis.**

**(profundal/limnetic)**

**(iii)** **Shade loving plants are called__________**

**(heliophytes/sciophytes)**

**(iv)** **__________ grow in moist habitat and well aerated soils.**

**(Xerophytes/Mesophytes)**

**(v)** **__________ is defined as the process by which water changes from vapour phase to liquid state.**

**(Condensation/Sublimation)**

**(b)** **State whether the given statements are True (T) or False (F) :**

**(i)** **The processes involved in the formation of soil are rapid and discontinuous.**

**(ii)** **Plants absorb water from the soil and this reduces quantity of moisture in the soil.**

**(iii)** **Exponentially growing animal populations can overshoot the carrying capacity of their habitat.**

(iv) Dodo was the first animal species whose extermination is not fully documented.

(v) IUCN has established two categories of threatened species.

(vi) Traces of ozone (Os) in the air are harmful to plants, animal and human beings.

(c) Define the following :

(i) Habitat Ecology

(ii) Transpiration

Q2. (a) Describe the ecological adaptations in animals to aquatic environment.

(b) Discuss the process of soil formation.

Q3. (a) Explain the concept of tolerance range and limiting factors.

(b) Describe the various types of food chains by giving suitable examples.

Q4. What is biogeochemical cycle? Explain its importance. Explain nitrogen cycle in nature.

Q5. (a) What is Succession ? Describe the various processes involved in succession.

(b) What is Herbivory ? Discuss the mechanisms evolved in plants to discourage predation.

Q6. (a) What is Wildlife ? Describe the various threats for the survival of wildlife.

(b) What is Pollution ? Explain the various causes of water pollution.

Q7. Write short notes on any two of the following:

(a) Natural and Artificial Ecosystem

(b) Species Diversity

(c) Genetic diversity of the population

(d) Estuaries

# LSE-02: ECOLOGY
## December, 2019

*Note: (i) Question no. 1 is compulsory.*
*(ii) Attempt any four questions from question No. 2 to 7.*

**Q1. (a) Fill in the blanks with the appropriate words given in the parentheses.**

**(i) __________ is study of ecology of an individual in relation to the environment.**

**(Habitat Ecology/Autecology)**

**(ii) __________ is the rate at which individuals of a population emigrate or migrate from an area.**

**(Diversity/Dispersal)**

**(iii) __________ measures the intensity of light.**

**(Radiometer/Photometer)**

**(iv) The temperature decreases with increasing __________.**

**(latitude/altitude)**

**(v) __________ control body temperature to a considerable range by behavioural means.**

**(Exotherms/Endotherms)**

**(b) State whether the following statements are True (T) or False (F).**

**(i) Troposphere is the upper most layer extending upto an altitude of 15km at the equator.**

**(ii) Condensation is the process by which solid water changes directly to vapour phase without passing through liquid phase.**

(iii) Mesophytes grow in moist habitats and well aerated soils.

(iv) Most aquatic animals excrete the extra amount of water from the body by osmoregulation.

(v) Chemical forces acting upon the rocks cause physical weathering.

(vi) The rural environment is a product of man's own design.

(c) Define the following.

(i) Sublimation

(ii) Food web

Q 2. (a) Describe the various aquatic adaptations in plants.

(b) Explain the adaptations in animals to different light conditions and extremes of temperature.

Q 3. What are Ecological Pyramids? Describe different kinds of ecological pyramids and their limitations.

Q 4. (a) Discuss thermal stratification of lake ecosystem.

(b) Differentiate between oligotrophic and eutrophic lake.

Q 5. Describe the different synthetic characters used to study a biotic community.

Q 6. (a) Explain the various meteorological factors responsible for causing air pollution.

(b) Discuss the various devices used to control air pollution.

Q 7. Write short notes on any two of the following.

(a) Importance of conserving wildlife

(b) Carrying capacity

(c) Hydrarch

(d) Deserts

www.ingramcontent.com/pod-product-compliance
Ingram Content Group UK Ltd.
Pitfield, Milton Keynes, MK11 3LW, UK
UKHW021705190726
13853UKWH00001B/421

9 789382 688167